RISK IN THE MODERN AGE

ANGLO-GERMAN FOUNDATION FOR THE STUDY OF INDUSTRIAL
SOCIETY

The Anglo-German Foundation for the Study of Industrial Society was
established by an agreement between the British and German governments after a
state visit to Britain by the late President Heinemann, and incorporated by Royal
Charter in 1973. Funds were initially provided by the German government; since
1979 both governments have been contributing.

The Foundation aims to contribute to the knowledge and understanding of
industrial society in the two countries and to promote contacts between them. It
funds selected research projects and conferences in the industrial, economic and
social policy areas designed to be of practical use to policymakers.

Titles include:

Bernhard Blanke and Randall Smith (*editors*)
CITIES IN TRANSITION
New Challenges, New Responsibilities

John Bynner and Rainer K. Silbereisen (*editors*)
ADVERSITY AND CHALLENGE IN LIFE IN THE NEW
GERMANY AND IN ENGLAND

Maurie J. Cohen (*editor*)
RISK IN THE MODERN AGE
Social Theory, Science and Environmental Decision-Making

Stephen Frowen and Jens Hölscher (*editors*)
THE GERMAN CURRENCY UNION OF 1990
A Critical Assessment

Eva Kolinsky (*editor*)
SOCIAL TRANSFORMATION AND THE FAMILY IN
POST-COMMUNIST GERMANY

Howard Williams, Colin Wight and Norbert Kapferer (*editors*)
POLITICAL THOUGHT AND GERMAN REUNIFICATION
The New German Ideology?

Anglo-German Foundation
Series Standing Order ISBN 0–333–71459–8
(*outside North America only*)

You can receive future titles in this series as they are published by placing a standing order.
Please contact your bookseller or, in case of difficulty, write to us at the address below with
your name and address, the title of the series and the ISBN quoted above.

Customer Services Department, Macmillan Distribution Ltd
Houndmills, Basingstoke, Hampshire RG21 6XS, England

Risk in the Modern Age

Social Theory, Science and Environmental Decision-Making

Edited by

Maurie J. Cohen
Oxford Centre for the Environment, Ethics and Society
Mansfield College, Oxford University, UK
and
Environmental Studies Program
Binghamton University, USA

Published by
PALGRAVE
Houndmills, Basingstoke, Hampshire RG21 6XS and
175 Fifth Avenue, New York, N. Y. 10010
Companies and representatives throughout the world

PALGRAVE is the new global academic imprint of
St. Martin's Press LLC Scholarly and Reference Division and
Palgrave Publishers Ltd (formerly Macmillan Press Ltd).

ISBN 0-312-22216-5

This book is printed on paper suitable for recycling and
made from fully managed and sustained forest sources.

A catalogue record for this book is available
from the British Library.

Transferred to digital printing 2001

Printed and bound in Great Britain by
Antony Rowe Ltd, Chippenham, Wiltshire

For Jeremy

Contents

List of Figures and Tables

Figures

Tables

List of Contributors

Lee Clarke is Associate Professor, Department of Sociology, Rutgers University, New Brunswick, NJ 08903, USA.

Maurie J. Cohen is Visiting Assistant Professor of Geography and Environmental Studies, Binghamton University, Binghamton, NY 13902, USA, and Associate Fellow at the Oxford Centre for the Environment, Ethics, and Society, Mansfield College, Oxford University, Oxford OX1 3TF, United Kingdom.

Stephen R. Couch is Professor, Department of Sociology, The Pennsylvania State University, Schuylkill Haven, PA 17972, USA.

Michael R. Edelstein is Professor of Environmental Psychology, School of Social Science and Human Services at Ramapo College of New Jersey, Mahwah, NJ 07430, USA.

Klaus Eder is Professor, Institute for the Social Sciences, Humboldt University, D-10099 Berlin, Germany.

William R. Freudenburg is Professor, Department of Rural Sociology and Environmental Studies, University of Wisconsin, Madison, WI 53706, USA.

Duane A. Gill is Professor, Social Science Research Center and Department of Sociology, Anthropology, and Social Work, Mississippi State University, Mississippi State, MS 39762, USA.

Joris Hogenboom is a PhD researcher, Environmental Sociology and Social Methodology Group, Wageningen Agricultural University, NL-6706 KN Wageningen, The Netherlands.

Carlo C. Jaeger is Professor, Department of Sociology, Darmstadt University, Residenzschloss, D-64283 Darmstadt, Germany, and Research Director of the Human Ecology Division, Swiss Federal Institute for Environmental Science and Technology, CH-8600 Duebendorf, Switzerland.

Jeffrey D. Kindler is a psychologist and a partner in Duncan, Kindler and Associates, 682 North Brookside Road, Wescosville, PA 18106, USA.

Steve Kroll-Smith, is Professor, Department of Sociology, University of New Orleans, New Orleans, LA 70148, USA.

Rolf Lidskog is Associate Professor of Sociology, Department of Social Sciences, University of Örebro, SE-701 82 Örebro, Sweden.

David Lowenthal is Professor Emeritus, Department of Geography, University College London, London WC1E 6BT, United Kingdom.

Arthur P. J. Mol is Lecturer, Environmental Sociology and Social Methodology Group, Wageningen Agricultural University, NL-6706 KN Wageningen, The Netherlands.

J. Steven Picou is Professor and Chair, Department of Sociology and Anthropology, University of South Alabama, Mobile, AL 36688, USA.

Kristen Purcell is a graduate student, Department of Sociology, Rutgers University, New Brunswick, NJ 08903, USA.

Ortwin Renn is Professor of Environmental Sociology, University of Stuttgart and a member of the Board of Directors of the Center of Technology Assessment in Baden-Württemberg, Industriestrasse 5, D-70565 Stuttgart, Germany.

Linda Renzulli is a graduate student, Department of Sociology, University of North Carolina, Chapel Hill, NC 27599, USA.

Eugene A. Rosa is Professor and Chair, Department of Sociology, Washington State University, Pullman, WA 99164, USA.

Gert Spaargaren is Lecturer, Environmental Sociology and Social Methodology Group, Wageningen Agricultural University, NL-6706 KN Wageningen, The Netherlands.

Thomas Webler is Core Faculty, Doctoral Program in Environmental Studies, Department of Environmental Studies, Antioch New England Graduate School, Antioch University, 40 Avon Street, Keene NH, 03431, USA.

Preface

This volume was prepared with a couple of different objectives in mind. First, environmental sociology, as a constituent specialization within the overarching discipline of which it is part, has during the past decade come to consist of two disjointed schools of thought. On one hand, there is a largely American tradition with roots stretching back to the 1970s. The birth of this school coincided with the rise of contemporary ecological concerns and has had a mixed history during the course of its maturation over the past two decades. The success of this branch of the subdiscipline has roughly paralleled the changeable fortunes of the modern environmental movement. Phases of sanguine enthusiasm calling for paradigmatic transformations have been followed by more melancholy intervals characterized by pragmatic empiricism. On the other hand, a more recent European expression of environmental sociology has developed around a social theoretical framework. Drawing on the work of a small number of prominent theorists, this vigorous new wing of environmental sociology raises both threats and opportunities to the older, more established variant. This book takes up the tricky challenge of trying to bring together these two currents into a single stream. The intent, obviously, is not to pursue a vague merger for the sake of enhanced organizational coherence, but rather to achieve a mutually beneficial combination.

Though the perils of this initial task are striking, the book's second objective is perhaps still more ambitious. Environmental sociology, whether the American empirical type or the more theoretical European variety, has had a relatively minor impact on public policy. Sociology's meager success in this regard becomes particularly prominent when it is compared with other branches of the social sciences, especially economics. This volume places center stage the unique perspective that environmental sociology can bring to our understanding of ecological risks. In approaching this project it must be stated unequivocally at the outset that environmental sociology is unlikely to provide the same sorts of ready-made solutions that policy-makers have come to expect from the other disciplinary approaches. Environmental sociology's comparative advantage is its ability to provide interpretations that are informed by the social and cultural context of actual experience.

It is surely no accident that environmental sociologists should be making a bid to develop their public role just when institutional decision-making seems to be in such desperate need of assistance. Disputes ranging from the serialized saga that has been playing out in Britain throughout much of the 1990s over the human health effects of bovine spongiform encephalopathy (BSE), or Mad Cow Disease, to the marketing practices of industrial firms to distribute genetically modified foodstuffs speak to a crisis of faith on the part of sizeable segments of civil society. While such controversies invariably raise numerous issues requiring the careful application of certain technical skills, they also suggest that the props supporting our modern lifestyles, most centrally science and the idea of continual progress, may not be as secure as we commonly believe.

An increasing number of commentators contend that the antagonism between experts and the lay public seems to be reaching critical levels as policy-making bodies cling to prescriptive interventions that become less convincing with each passing day. Government officials claim to be acting on the basis of unassailable scientific evidence only to find it necessary to reverse themselves with the next contradictory disclosure. In the meantime, major media figures work with little appreciation of the esoterica that these crises throw up. Journalists are forced to translate imprecise and uncertain research findings to a public that is continually pulled from pillar to post. Perhaps more menacing is the situation in those communities that live with the ambiguity that arises from more acute breakdowns of our technological infrastructure. These victims frequently face a gray wall of bureaucratic intransigence and indifference as they struggle to cope with the health impacts that stem from ruptured chemical-storage tanks, radioactive leaks, and plumes of industrial pollutants.

This volume derives from a workshop entitled 'Risk in the Modern Age' organized by the Oxford Centre for the Environment, Ethics, and Society at Mansfield College, Oxford on 30 June–1 July 1997. Contributors subjected their original papers to lively critique during the conclave and subsequently revised them for inclusion in this collection. In addition to the authors represented here I would like to express my thanks to Barbara Adam, John Adams, Michael Bell, Sonja Boehmer-Christiansen, Robert Gramling, Robin Grove-White, Maarten Hajer, Jost Halfmann, Alan Irwin, Andrew Jamison, Klaus Japp, Wolfgang Krohn, Brent Marshall, Jerry Ravetz, Peter Simmons, Bronislaw Szerszynski, and Brian Wynne. The success of this workshop was entirely the result of the enthusiastic participation of this distinguished group of scholars.

An enterprise of this magnitude could not have taken place without assistance of a supportive institution and I convey my appreciation to the fellows of Mansfield College, and in particular to Dennis Trevelyan, David Marquand, and Neil Summerton. I also extend my sincere gratitude to Anne Maclachlan for her Herculean effort helping to organize the workshop and to coordinate thousands of other details issuing from this event. Anne Rafique expertly and cheerfully shepherded the manuscript through the final stages of production. Finally, I would like to thank the Ove Arup Foundation for its generous support of my work during the past three years. Further financial support for this workshop was provided by the Alfried Krupp von Bohlen und Halbach Foundation, the Friedrich Ebert Foundation, the Anglo-German Foundation for the Study of Industrial Society, and the British Academy.

Oxford, September 1998   MJC

Part I
Introduction

1 Environmental Sociology, Social Theory, and Risk: an Introductory Discussion
Maurie J. Cohen

INTRODUCTION

Ranging from food security to nuclear safety to biodiversity conservation, governments have created vast bureaucracies to alleviate risk in the modern age. These organizations are in the perilous business of managing uncertainty and they typically define risk in narrow, ostensibly objective terms – for instance the number of expected deaths per 1000 people or cases of cancer in a delimited geographic area. Due to the seeming pervasiveness of public concern, contemporary societies spend tremendous sums of money and mobilize vast armies of professional personnel to reduce hazard exposure. Especially prominent in this battle are experts in arcane fields such as toxicology, environmental chemistry, epidemiology, and nuclear physics. In particularly thorny cases, social scientists – most commonly economists – are enlisted to handle the human dimensions of risk. Unsurprisingly, most large industrial corporations have on staff specialists with similar qualifications, for example to keep firms in compliance with their pollution permits. Despite its tremendous diversity and scope, nearly all of the work within this domain can be defined as constituting the determination of 'acceptable risk.'

Our penchant to express anxiety about the future in terms of risk is a relatively new preoccupation that replaces age-old tendencies to view uncertainty in fatalistic terms.[1] We no longer attribute evil to the indiscriminate forces of nature, to spirits from the netherworld, or to our own hapless misfortune. Instead, we convene public hearings to ascertain the ramifications of minute mathematical approximations and exchange information with one another from the latest scientific research reports so as not to fall victim to some hitherto unknown threat.

Given the apparent novelty of risk as a key notion of our age it is instructive to reflect on its origins. Until quite recently, risk was confined principally to insurance and financial transactions. As such, actuaries and traders of various kinds spoke in the language of risk. With respect to the environment, an area in which discussions of risk now loom especially large, problems were conventionally cast in relatively straightforward terms, say cleaning up a contaminated river or ridding the air of visible pollutants. Even a cursory review of most any day's newspaper speaks to the fact that this is no longer the case.

To find the root of this transformation – from the environment as the focus for a largely moral and aesthetic crusade to the environment as a backdrop for scientific hairsplitting – we must go back to the 1970s. From the earliest days of the modern environmental era industrial corporations, environmentalist organizations, and regulatory agencies were complicit in initiating roughly similar changes in all advanced nations.

First, passage of the initial wave of landmark legislation to control unhealthful chemical emissions during the so-called first environmental decade imposed appreciable costs on industry. Despite this burden, more ominous for managers was what the future might hold and whether they would be able to continue to shift these expenses onto consumers. To defend themselves against the prospect of declining profitability due to racheting environmental controls the largest firms mobilized their own technical staffs and instructed them to refute the flow of bad news. This proved to be a prudent strategy because it used the skepticism that underlies science to positive effect. As long as administrative procedures required claimants to substantiate scientifically the adverse effects of specific industrial practices, the circumspection inherent in this form of knowledge could be used to thwart calls for environmental improvement. In other words, as long as the prevailing credo was 'safe until proved otherwise' science would be an indispensable ally of defenders of the status quo.[2]

Second, it would be incorrect to conclude that unsuspecting environmentalists were caught dozing by an industrial conspiracy to move to a more favorable venue the emerging contest over public controls of industrial activity. In many instances, large advocacy groups (e.g. Sierra Club, Friends of the Earth) were more than eager to shift the fight for stronger legal provisions to protect the environment into the scientific arena. After all, key figures in the modern environmental movement – Rachel Carson, Barry Commoner, Paul Ehrlich and Garrett Hardin – were themselves scientists and it was the authority of their voices that had first raised the ecological alarm. During an era in which science was held in high esteem it seemed shrewd to hitch the campaign for more rigorous environmental standards to the reliable engine provided by scientific knowledge. Once launched, the momentum to continue in this direction became self-generating. The new emphasis on science gave rise to a large professional contingent of environmental lawyers, economists, and scientists who took control of the major advocacy organizations, gradually displacing the prior generation of outdoor enthusiasts.[3]

Finally, governments during the 1970s embarked on environmental reform under the impression that problems were clearly delineated and could be addressed without the appropriation of sizeable resources. Chief on many policy-makers' minds was that environmental protection should not in any significant way interfere with mechanisms for generating economic growth. Accordingly, they delegated responsibility for these new mandates to poorly equipped administrative agencies optimistically thinking that quick-fix solutions would prove sufficient. Once engaged, the state came to see that the correction of deteriorating ecological conditions was far more complicated than previously believed and significant headway would require a substantive commitment. This reappraisal led to heated disputes over the stringency of environmental controls and it became clear that environmental decision-making would need to be grounded in an unambigious epistemology. A close collaborative relationship between science and the state had been gradually building for more than a century and this association intensified during World War II. After the war it became increasingly difficult for governments to continue to disregard the ill effects of unfettered industrial production. The state needed a source of authority that would prevent their new regulatory undertaking from spinning out of control and science filled this breach.

With this tripartite confederation pressing to elevate science into the role of chief environmental arbiter the language of this recondite body of knowledge invariably came to serve, albeit in a transmogrified form, as a public discourse. Maarten Hajer has evocatively described this process of scientization as part of an effort to 'take the sting out of the tail of radical environmentalism.'[4] The use of science to decipher the environment has over the past two decades become widespread and this means of defining environmental problems now constitutes the dominant view in all advanced nations. The framing of environmental risks within the paradigm of the natural sciences invariably prefigures the sorts of questions that we can reasonably pose. Such a conceptualization keeps discussion carefully circumscribed and makes it very difficult, say, to ascribe responsibility for malfeasance or to grapple with concerns regarding the fairness with which particular hazards are distributed across a population. These political issues are simply judged to be out of bounds. More problematic still are attempts to engage meaningfully with the provocative question James Short asked more than a decade ago: 'What happens to networks of personal relationships, to the possibilities of a culturally pluralist society, as a result of *fears* associated with risks?'[5] Because they truncate reality so severely, natural science definitions of risk offer no traction to explore how certain threats might jeopardize the social fabric.

Social scientists like Short who have the temerity to advance such impertinent questions are typically scorned as chronic malcontents irrationally opposed to scientific progress and the technological bounty it promises. However, if we scratch the surface of this caricature we are liable to find scholars – as well as a growing number of lay persons – who situate their understanding of risk within a wider social context. Adherents of this less conventional view are likely to reject declarations that reduce the potential of adversity to probability estimates derived from mathematical models. Furthermore, such individuals are prone to look askance at theories that conceptualize people as autonomous risk-takers ceaselessly adjusting their behavior in accordance with an endless stream of expert information. Holders of this alternative view are more inclined to acknowledge that risk decisions are embedded in the structure of society and efforts to manipulate it exceed the capabilities of individual agency.

This volume mobilizes the distinctive capabilities of environmental sociology to take up Short's challenge. To avoid confusion it is important to point out that in pursuing this question of how contemporary sources of uncertainty might rend the social fabric the intent is not to disavow unconditionally the relevance of natural science. Rather, we take the position that the conventional view affords an unduly tapered lens through which to glimpse the ways that risk insinuates itself into modern societies. Sociology, especially in comparison to some of the other social science disciplines, has in past years been conspicuously absent from key environmental policy-making circles, largely because of some peculiarities related to the constitution of the discipline. In an effort to explain this situation, this chapter provides a brief historical account of the field of environmental sociology, first as it developed in the United States and later in Europe. These two schools have yet to fuse into a single entity and this chapter describes the different, though complementary, perspectives on risk that they provide. It is useful to bear in mind that neat prescriptive propositions are unlikely to flow from these perspectives as their comparative advantage resides primarily in an ability to offer explanations for the environmental policy debacles that seem so prominent these days. The chapter then explores how it might be possible to use the study of risk to forge a mutually beneficial collaboration between American and European environmental sociologists before concluding with a summary of the volume's contributions.

SOCIOLOGY AND THE ENVIRONMENT

Environmental sociology coalesced in the United States as a distinct field within the wider discipline of which it is a part during the late 1970s, largely as a result of the work of Catton and Dunlap.[6] These authors charged that sociology, due to its need to delineate itself during the nineteenth century from biological and geographical determinism, was seriously handicapped from its earliest days by an anti-materialist bias. Three centuries of scientific and industrial progress had imposed a distinctively human stamp on the modern world and it appeared, in the eyes of the discipline's founders, that the biophysical environment was becoming increasingly irrelevant to social life. This situation encouraged early sociologists to downplay – indeed to ignore – non-social facts in devising explanations for social phenomena.[7] Early sociologists who endeavored to couch their explanations in terms of environmental variables, say climate or soil type, were severely rebuked by their colleagues.

Under these circumstances, the discipline assumed an anthropocentrism that has made it difficult for contemporary sociologists to engage substantively with environmental issues. Giddens summarizes the situation as, 'Ecological concerns do not brook large in the traditions of thought incorporated into sociology, and it is not surprising that sociologists today find it hard to develop a systematic appraisal of them.'[8] Perhaps most problematic has been sociology's inability to acknowledge the existence of biophysical constraints on social activity and humanity's ultimate embeddedness in ecological systems. Catton and Dunlap referred to this mode of thinking – which incidentally was not to their minds exclusively confined to sociology – as the Human Exemptionalist Paradigm (HEP). In its place they called for the adoption of an alternative worldview termed the New Ecological Paradigm (NEP).[9]

This new sociological outlook would be concerned with the broad context of human–environment interactions: the ways in which human actions were shaped by the environment (both artificial and natural) and vice versa. This was no doubt an ambitious aim. As Buttel noted in a review of the field during the late 1980s: 'Environmental sociologists sought nothing less than the reorientation of sociology toward a more holistic perspective that would conceptualize social processes within the context of the biosphere.'[10]

Despite sociology's predisposition to dismiss biophysical facts, a small group of incipient environmental sociologists was not completely without a foundation on which to build a more ecologically aware epistemology.[11] Certain of the discipline's specializations that had emerged during the preceding decades, most importantly rural sociology and the sociology of disasters, had long been forced to address the interaction of human societies with ecological systems.[12] Given their strong interest in communities dependent on natural resources and agriculture, rural sociologists were routinely accustomed to dealing with the materiality of social life.[13] Similarly, natural disasters, because they can press the survivability of social organization to its limits, have been a traditional focus of sociological attention. Hurricanes, tornadoes, and earthquakes, tied as they are to ineluctable natural processes, place in bold relief the dialectic relationship between human beings and their environments.[14]

Environmental sociology in the United States continued to develop during the 1980s under these dual influences, although enthusiasm was dampened during the early portion of the decade. The fortunes of the field over the past two decades have (for both good and ill) been tied to the ebb and flow of the environmental movement. The blatant anti-environmentalism in Washington during the first years of Ronald Reagan's presidency placed both academics and activists with an interest in the environment on the defensive.[15] It was not until mid-decade that environmental proponents were able to find their feet. During this period the field was split essentially into two groups: sociologists of environmental issues and environmental sociologists.[16] Though individual researchers occasionally crossed over from one side of the divide to the other, this differentiation, as we will see, has remained conspicuous.

On one hand, intellectual progress within the so-called sociology of environmental issues moved forward apace with scholars looking at the social bases of environmental attitudes and values, the socio-demographic composition of the environmental movement, and the social impact of extractive practices such as mining and oil extraction. An especially prominent research area, discussed in further detail in the following section, has been the study of the social and social-psychological dynamics of communities affected by undesirable land uses (e.g. nuclear power plants, waste incinerators), as well as various overt forms of environmental contamination. Regardless of its specific focus, the sociology of environmental issues has been characterized by a strong empirical orientation and researchers have proceeded without feeling a need to anchor themselves within a well-articulated theoretical framework.[17] To the extent that this wing of the field has attempted to develop beyond the purely micro-level, scholars have geared their contributions toward middle-range theories with the result being that their work has to date been relatively inconsequential for the discipline of sociology and the social sciences more generally.[18]

On the other hand, advances during this period to formulate a theoretical core for environmental sociology took place, largely due to the discipline's epistemological confines, much more slowly. Catton and Dunlap's initial presentation of the HEP–NEP distinction proved difficult to translate into testable hypotheses and the strong pragmatism undergirding the social sciences in the United States stigmatized metatheoretical pursuits. Accordingly, there was little progress toward the formulation of a comprehensive paradigm capable of challenging dominant sociological conventions. As we will see below, European sociologists have over the past few years begun to adjust the empirical orientation that has been a characteristic feature of environmental sociology.

ENVIRONMENTAL SOCIOLOGY AND RISK

During the 1980s several American environmental sociologists, some with expertise in either the study of social problems or natural disasters, were drawn to communities around the country that appeared to be confronting a novel class of environmental threats.[19] Particularly notable was the discovery of buried chemicals at Love Canal, a neighborhood in Niagara Falls, New York. In the earlier part of the century industrial firms had used a partially constructed canal to dispose of their chemical wastes. Once the site had lost its economic utility it was filled in and eventually forgotten. During the intervening years the original owners sold the property to the municipal government for the construction of a school, and a residential community gradually developed in the vicinity surrounding the disused canal. It was not until the late 1970s that residents began to realize that the odorous substances oozing down the walls of their basements, the strange burns on their pets, and the ill-health of their children were portents of a dilemma of the modern age. After a protracted battle with state and federal authorities local homeowners were able to secure compensation for their valueless homes and to relocate away from the area.[20] The situation at Love Canal, which was widely reported in the media, initiated wild prognostications on the extent of the country's buried industrial legacy and sparked the passage of ambitious legislation in the form of the Comprehensive Environmental Response, Compensation, and Liability Act of 1980, better known as Superfund.[21]

A major accident at the Three Mile Island nuclear power station near Harrisburg, Pennsylvania in 1979 provided further evidence that the country's technological infrastructure could pose serious problems for human health and the environment.[22] This incident was quickly followed by disclosure that the local government in Times Beach, Missouri had mixed hazardous dioxins into the asphalt used to pave local streets.[23] Then in 1984 the notorious accident at the Union Carbide chemical plant in Bhopal, India, provoked still further popular indignation toward multinational chemical corporations and sparked allegations in the United States that installations at home threatened similar dangers.[24] Numerous other revelations, in part prompted by Superfund's requirement to create a national inventory of contaminated sites, gave rise to a sense that the country had crossed the technological equivalent of the Rubicon.

The environmental sociologists attracted to these sites tried to get to grips with the diverse understandings that the lay public came to impart upon these hazards and the emergent strategies people used to cope with the profound uncertainty. In some respects, local reactions to these events resembled the social responses witnessed during the aftermath of natural disasters, but it was the dissimilarities that were most compelling. In particular, sociological research has long suggested that disasters have a strong tendency to encourage solidarity among victims and this bonding process facilitates individual and collective recovery.[25] However, initial fieldwork in the growing number of contaminated communities suggested that these situations were substantially different from more customary catastrophes and the conventional model was not adequate.[26] Instead of promoting a therapeutic response, it appeared that technological disasters, because they provoked such scientific puzzlement, fomented social dissension and fragmentation. The absence of unambiguous carnage and destruction caused by the power of nature did not catalyze altruism, but instead provoked baser strategies for self-preservation.[27]

The path-breaking work of Kai Erikson was especially helpful in giving these researchers a handle on how technological mishaps can impose unique forms of harm on individuals and communities.[28] During the 1970s, Erikson studied the effects of a flood on the residents of Buffalo Creek, West Virginia. The roaring cascade of water that flowed through this narrow mountain hollow was not, however, due simply to a heavy downpour of rain. Rather, the disaster was caused by the failure of an impoundment dam located at higher ground above the hamlets strung along the valley. This artificial embankment was owned by a coal-mining company and used as part of its operations. Following the flood, which took the lives of 125 people, Red Cross and government-aid workers shepherded survivors into makeshift settlements where they descended over the subsequent weeks and months into a spiral of despondency, grief, and internecine conflict. Eventually, the residents of Buffalo Creek initiated a class-action law suit against the mining company and Erikson was able to gather data on the victims' experiences while serving as an expert sociological witness for the plaintiffs' attorneys. This research offered important initial insight into the social reverberations of technological accidents and described how these events, in part because human agency is culpable for the harm, can place the social fabric at risk.

More recently, Erikson, as part of an effort to advance the contention that disasters can effect a collective form of trauma, has noted that there is 'a profound difference between those disasters that can be understood as the work of nature and those that need to be understood as the work of humankind.'[29] This assessment is supported by a growing body of empirical evidence – both qualitative and quantitative – from a broad range of contaminated communities across the United States.[30] Additionally, due to Americans' propensity for litigation, sociological research is now becoming a frequent feature of legal proceedings throughout the country to apportion responsibility for technological-risk events.[31]

Certain other strands of sociology, most prominently the sociology of organizations, have also been influential in shaping the research agenda on risk within environmental sociology.[32] As Clarke and Short remark succinctly in a recent review of this topic, 'It is organizations, mostly, that set the terms of debate concerning risk acceptability. And it is organizations, and their putative masters, that make choices about risk that often have implications well beyond their immediate environs.'[33] This observation reminds us that public reactions to hazards are deeply embedded in social structure and are powerfully shaped by notions of equity and legitimacy with respect to the organizations that are in place to ensure safety and reliability.

In summary, within American environmental sociology the study of risk has typically been shaped by an empirical emphasis that largely treats the technological hazards of contemporary society as social problems involving contested knowledge.[34] The ambiguity, uncertainty, and lack of boundedness associated with the aberrant performance of complex industrial systems create conditions that encourage antagonism and give rise to community discord. On occasion, aggrieved individuals will initiate litigation against potentially responsible parties in an effort to assign blame and to recover monetary compensation. This protracted process is, however, not benign and can compound personal distress and collective dissension. Freudenburg and Jones have described these local dynamics as the 'corrosive' effects of contamination.[35]

These untoward events touch on one of the most perplexing paradoxes of modern life, namely why has our increasing prowess to control nature not made us more secure? What are the social causes and political implications of an ever more pervasive sense of anxiety? While this particular stream of scholarship has made important inroads toward the formulation of answers to these questions it has not attempted to link its findings to larger processes of societal change. Fortunately, a new cadre of European social scientists has begun to address such issues, reinvigorating environmental sociology and leading to stimulating insights into these seminal concerns.

ENVIRONMENTAL SOCIOLOGY IN EUROPE: THE RISE
OF ENVIRONMENTAL SOCIAL THEORY

Environmental sociology beyond the borders of the United States
developed much more slowly and there is little evidence of a de-
finable field prior to the second half of the 1980s.[36] With the
emergence of Green Parties in many European countries, most
particularly *Die Grünen* in Germany, and further prompted by wider
sociological interest in 'new social movements,' a growing international group of scholars has begun to create a new wing of
environmental sociology.[37] While some of these authors exhibit familiarity with the pre-existing American body of literature, most of
this work sets itself the challenging task of recreating an environmental sociology from whole cloth. Grounded in a much stronger
social theoretical tradition, this largely European environmental
sociology was catalyzed by the publication of the German sociologist Ulrich Beck's prominent book *Risikogesellschaft* in 1986 (published
in English in 1992 as *Risk Society*).[38] Subsequently, there has been
explosive interest in the environment both as a focus of specific
study in its own right and as a point of entrée for theorizing central social scientific concerns regarding industrialism, capitalism, and
modernity.[39] Especially vibrant national contexts for this work have
been -- in addition to Germany -- Britain, the Netherlands, and the
Nordic countries.[40]

A further key influence driving the development of European
environmental sociology has been the recent writings of Anthony
Giddens whose work parallels Beck's in many ways.[41] These authors
integrate, essentially for the first time, issues of the environment
into mainstream social theory. Especially important themes in these
treatments are the expanding role of expertise in contemporary
societies, the increasing process of individualization, the social pre-
occupation with certain low probability/high consequence events,
the declining levels of institutional trust among the lay public, and
the emergence of enhanced individual and institutional reflexivity.[42]

Much of this new wave of environmental social theory draws heavily
on the sociology of science and the sociology of scientific knowledge. In keeping with the commitments of these particular fields
this recent work is characterized by a strong social constructivist
perspective.[43] Inherent in this view is an emphasis on social interpretation and the dismissal of biophysical facts. Adherents contend
that the accumulation of all knowledge is a social activity and thus

invariably guided, both implicitly and explicitly, by political predispositions and cultural filters. We should be very careful, social constructivists contend, about conferring upon science a mantle for objective truth-finding as its practitioners are unlikely to generate accounts that are any more genuine than those produced by other societal spheres. In other words, science offers manufactured explanations of the world that should have no privileged claim on authenticity. Due to the sanctioning functions of science, especially for political institutions, we need to exercise profound skepticism in accepting its declarations.

The constructivist perspective obviously has serious implications for policy-making because to advance an environmental claim (e.g. global warming, acid rain, ozone depletion) normally requires doing so in the context of data from the natural sciences. If the validity of scientific knowledge is open to question, the legitimacy of many administrative actions with respect to the environment is undermined. Furthermore, both industrial operators and environmental campaigning organizations are forced to seek out alternative justifications grounded in say, ethics, to support their objectives. For this reason, social constructivism has met stiff resistance among policy-makers.

Needless to say, critics have strenuously attacked the social constructivist perspective as misguided, if not dangerous.[44] Science, they argue, is governed by rigorous rules for validating evidence and it is fallacious to impute that this form of knowledge is on a par with more mundane epistemologies. Despite hostility in many quarters to sociological insights pertaining to the environment, this theoretical work opens up new intellectual terrain. Importantly, this scholarship holds the prospect for invigorating a new generation of environmental research capable of dislodging the increasingly jaded positivist concepts that continue to shape policy prescriptions. These developments also hold the prospect for the dissemination of more nuanced ecological thinking regarding risk, sustainability, and environmental decision-making into academic realms that have to date resisted serious consideration of such topics.

Tempering this enthusiasm, however, is the lack of a clear and unified vision among environmental sociologists on how to resolve their desire for wider public policy and social scientific relevance with the discipline's exclusive commitment to cultural symbolism. As Dunlap and Catton recently observed, '[a] staunchly constructivist program [leads] to a very restricted form of environmental sociology, one that analyzes knowledge claims about environmental conditions and avoids analyses of societal–environmental interactions.'[45] Nonetheless, there are indications that within the field so-called strong constructivism is giving way to a more modest skepticism of dominant forms of knowledge and is less antagonistic to science.[46] Champions of these revised perspectives speak about the need for critical or ontological realism that combines sociological and scientific epistemologies. These approaches move away from cynical relativism and in a direction that, ironically, is quite consistent with long-standing scientific methodologies to confront dogmatic contentions with circumspection.

RISK AND THE FORMULATION OF AN INTERNATIONAL ENVIRONMENTAL SOCIOLOGY

The study of risk within environmental sociology is thus presently divided between two principal schools – an American school of approximately two decades' standing grounded largely in a social problems perspective and a European school of more recent vintage that operates within a more social theoretical framework.[47] Tempering their respective attributes are certain emblematic handicaps. On the one hand, American scholarship in the field suffers from an overemphasis on empirical investigation and an insufficiently robust theoretical core that could link research to broader sociological and social scientific currents.[48] On the other hand, European environmental sociology has been criticized for its abstruseness and for devoting insufficient attention to validating its insights. Further, there are concerns that this school's strident commitment to social constructivism leaves its practitioners open to ridicule (particularly from environmental scientists) because of their inability to address seriously the materiality of the biophysical environment.

To a certain degree, these inadequacies stem from the distinct ways in which the two schools have evolved and the various means through which the social sciences have become institutionalized in different national contexts. For instance, American empiricism is in many respects an artifact of political demands for social control and a cultural tendency to stress pragmatism over ideology. This particular style is attributable, at least in part, to the relative weakness of the American state and its need to ground policy initiatives in a source of extra-governmental legitimacy.[49] The situation in Europe is obviously more complicated because of greater political and cultural diversity. To take but a single example, the distinct qualities of contemporary German social science can be explained as arising from a deliberate desire to restrict the reach of this expertise for fear of how such knowledge could be used for nefarious purposes.[50]

Such a situation invariably begs the question of whether there should be closer ties among environmental sociologists grounded in the field's different intellectual traditions. Would movement toward greater international synthesis be advantageous? Does greater coherence hold the potential for innovative insights or will it create an unimaginative *mélange*? This volume endorses the position that greater interaction is likely to prove mutually beneficial, particularly in terms of the study of risk. This view appears to be garnering support across the field. For instance, Dunlap and Catton recently wrote, 'The eventual merging of these theoretical and empirical efforts promises to yield important advances in understanding the nature of societal–environmental relations.'[51] Despite cautious endorsement for this project, we should not underestimate the difficulties of overcoming divisions – and indeed chauvinism – in both technique and emphasis.

While the current volume is designed as an initial contribution for fostering greater international collaboration among environmental sociologists, it would be disingenuous to assert that this effort is underpinned by a grand architecture. This kind of coordinating scheme might have helped to promote some degree of efficiency, but it is highly unlikely that meaningful integration between American and European perspectives could be achieved in accordance with a prefigured plan. Furthermore, the formulation of a previously construed guiding vision, however flexible, would imply the existence of far greater internal cohesion within the two schools than is actually the case. In a related vein it would be fanciful to claim that the resultant product of this venture is meant to serve as the final word on this matter. It is probable that the following chapters will raise as many questions as they retire. Ironically, such a response would signify the success of this incipient effort as it would evince the desirability of continued dialogue. It is with this objective in mind that this volume was conceived and it is to a brief overview of its constituent parts that we now turn our attention.

OVERVIEW OF THE CONTENTS

Across nearly the full breadth of the social sciences theories of rational action have become enormously influential during the past two decades. A seemingly endless flow of books informed by this perspective regularly hit the shelves of bookstores and proponents of the 'rational actor paradigm,' or RAP, compete vigorously with one another to influence policy-makers with seductive recommendations. RAP posits a world in which individuals are discriminating, calculative decision-makers who are able to assemble and evaluate assiduously a large number of alternative scenarios. So pervasive has this approach become, complete with its cost–benefit analyses and other quasi-rational appraisals, that it has acquired an axiomatic quality and its assumptions have typically been placed beyond scrutiny. Critics are regularly denounced as apostates and placed beyond the bounds of polite society. The chapters that comprise Part II of this volume critique this conventional view and in the end find it severely deficient.

Ortwin Renn, Carlo Jaeger, Eugene Rosa, and Thomas Webler describe the tensions that have persisted during the past twenty years between technical risk management and certain social science understandings of risk. On the one hand, the scientific evaluation of hazards – perhaps best exemplified by engineering, toxicology, and epidemiology – interprets threats to human health and the environment as the probability of the occurrence of an adverse outcome. Specially trained experts make claims to unique and powerful knowledge that is capable of ascertaining the likelihood of untoward effects and formulating strategies to minimize their consequences. On the other hand, a diverse group of social scientists – comprising principally sociologists, anthropologists, and psychologists – has advanced a variety of theoretical perspectives that suggest human responses to risk must be understood in more expansive terms that include such considerations as social structure, power relations, and individual perception. Though these two overarching views have coexisted with varying degrees of unease, Renn and his colleagues point to some key markers to suggest that this period of relative accommodation is coming to end.

The authors argue that due to the inability of the social science perspectives to cohere into a unified paradigm and to produce adequate predictability, a singular preference is now emerging among policy-makers for technical assessments of risk based on economistic models of human behavior. The authors concede that RAP approaches may provide useful insights into decision-making processes that are narrowly goal-oriented and satisfy the models' underlying assumptions of perfect information, independence of actors, and so forth. They are, however, heavily critical of efforts to explicate the more variegated aspects of social life – for instance the formulation of trust or the building of social solidarity – using such a reductionist framework. The diverse range of human experience is inevitably infused with the need to seek meaning, to achieve emotional satisfaction, and to pursue social bonds. Such activities cannot be realistically interpreted within the constricted confines of purposeful, strategic action.

Renn and his colleagues advance the provocative notion that RAP proponents are motivated more by an ideological desire to craft a world subject to social control through rational decision-making than they are by the pursuit of meaningful theoretical analysis of human behavior. Policy-makers' reliance on such simplistic renditions is highly problematic, especially for the management of high-risk technologies. The authors contrast RAP with alternative approaches, specifically the systems theory of Luhmann and the structuration theory of Giddens, and conclude that these perspectives are also, when viewed in isolation, less than satisfactory. Nonetheless, they provide useful complements to the RAP models. Social scientists, it is urged, should be less concerned with providing policy-makers with ambitious unified theories of risk that override the complexity of modern life. Instead, they should acknowledge this inherent condition and adopt a posture that applies theories with greater discrimination.

The inadequacy of rational approaches for understanding the diversity of human responses to risk is further elaborated upon in the second chapter of this part by Kristen Purcell, Lee Clarke, and Linda Renzulli who examine the familiar conceptual distinction between 'voluntary' and 'involuntary' risks. Originally introduced into the academic literature nearly thirty years ago, this classificatory scheme has long been an implicit element of most social theories of risk. It has, in particular, exerted a powerful, covert influence on models predicated upon rational understandings of human behavior. On one level it would appear to be self-evident that individuals have considerable freedom and flexibility over the risks to which they subject themselves. Cigarette smoking and driving without a seatbelt perhaps provide the most obvious examples.

Purcell and her colleagues contend that this intuitively sensible means of apportioning responsibility according to degrees of apparent voluntariness is long overdue for critical appraisal. They argue that this demarcation, influenced by fanciful and unrealistic assumptions, is largely motivated by proponents' ideological commitments. Moreover, this perspective is not especially illuminating because it fails to recognize the centrality of institutional constraints on contemporary lifestyles. All members of society – even the wealthy, educated men who are the archetype for most RAP models – have far less discretion than such theoretical approaches impute. In particular, the authors highlight the cultural and social buffers through which we invariably filter risk. By this they do not mean to align themselves with proponents of strong social constructivism. Rather, their argument is more nuanced, contending that culture and social structure frame our perceptions of safety and, importantly, the range of acceptable alternatives. These constraints on decision-making are embedded in the social fabric and they become part of everyday routine, hence are invisible most of the time. It is only during the immediate aftermath of a catastrophic accident that we question our unconscious risk evaluations and become momentarily mindful of the artificial narrowness of our menus of choice. The chapter encourages risk theorists to abandon the false distinctions associated with 'voluntariness' and to refocus their conceptual lens on the institutional constraints that limit individual choice.

As noted above, theories of reflexive modernization have been quite influential among environmental social theorists. This general approach suggests that advanced societies are currently experiencing a process of transformation in which the central pillars of modernity, such as the centrality of scientific knowledge and the beneficence of continual technological progress, are becoming the focus of critical examination. The contributors to Part III take different views of the utility of reflexive modernization for pressing forward our understanding of the social significance of environmental risks in contemporary society.

Joris Hogenboom, Arthur Mol, and Gert Spaargaren describe how reflexive modernization can be effectively applied to prevailing concerns in environmental sociology. Integrating aspects of Beck's theory of risk society with the theory of ecological modernization, the chapter describes a shift in the conceptualization of environmental problems.[52] Most environmental critiques produced over the past two decades have tended to favor processes of demodernization and to place science and technology in a disapproving light. Rather than admonish expert knowledge and its artefacts as sources of environmental harm, the authors contend that today's political discourses on the environment hope science will produce – albeit with differing degrees of enthusiasm and not without contradiction – the solutions to contemporary ecological problems. They further argue that this transformation reflects a new role for rational knowledge in society and is central to efforts to grasp the dynamics of current controversies involving environmental risk.

Hogenboom and his colleagues maintain that the public no longer views science in celebratory terms but takes this knowledge as contingent and examines its relevance in specific situated contexts. The forces responsible for these dynamic processes of change do not necessarily originate in the sphere of environmental policy-making. In fact, these developments are heavily grounded in wider social and economic concerns raised by such phenomena as the 'crisis' of the welfare state, the eroding authority of nation-states, and other political processes with global dimensions. Drawing on examples from the Netherlands, Hogenboom and his colleagues elaborate upon the way in which powerful social forces are reshaping customary politics as well as contributing to the emergence of new forms of subpolitical activity. For instance, the role of the state in environmental affairs is being modified by pressure to reform regulatory frameworks to favor more flexible and responsive policy tools. Furthermore, outside mainstream politics novel forms of environmental expression that bypass the usual channels are gaining ground.

The authors identify the vigorous public protests following Shell's 1995 announcement to scuttle its *Brent Spar* offshore oil drilling platform in the North Sea as an example of the new subpolitics. On a more local level, decisions by Dutch households to buy bottled water rather than use central sources are political statements that can have profound consequences for environmental management. We should not, however, interpret these developments as public disaffection with science and technology, as the new commitments retain a strong dependence on expert systems. Instead, the chapter suggests we are witnessing the reflexive reinvention and modification of these forms of knowledge.

In this part's second contribution William Freudenburg takes a more critical tack in evaluating several of the central aspects of reflexive modernization. While commending Beck and Giddens for

their efforts to give the environment theoretical credence in contemporary sociology, he takes issue with their narrow emphasis on
dramatic forms of risk. Both of these theorists consider 'truly formidable' threats, as manifest most prominently in the potential of
nuclear conflagration or global ecological collapse, to be the most
salient types of risk. In contrast, Freudenburg argues that low prob-
ability/high consequence events, especially as experienced before
the dissolution of the Soviet Union, tend to be socially unifying, at
least within individual nations. He contends that the focus on catastrophic risks overlooks the ordinary threats of everyday life. More
socially divisive are the less consequential risks that emanate from
everyday technologies such as hazardous chemicals and civilian
nuclear-power facilities.

Nonetheless, we must view the public sense of vulnerability to
the adverse effects of applied science and technology as a curious
development given the tremendous improvements over the past
century in the most straightforward measure of risk, namely life
expectancy. Freudenburg attributes the accomplishments of modernity
to an ever-increasing societal division of labor, but considers these
achievements to be one side of a double-edged sword. While intensifying specialization has made possible extraordinary feats, it
has also led to greater complexity. Inherent in this Janus-faced process
of development is the difficulty – indeed the virtual impossibility –
of ensuring that all members of society will perform their jobs properly. He postulates that the very capabilities that have enabled modern
societies to reduce the risks of death also lead to a loss of social
control over a vast and interdependent socio-technological system.
When components fail, as they invariably will, it is virtually impossible to identify the specialist individuals responsible for the lapse.
Freudenburg invokes the term 'recreancy' to describe the failure
of experts to execute diligently the tasks entrusted to them and
identifies the reorientation of future theoretical development in this
direction as a major challenge.

Part IV takes up the ambitious task of trying to substantiate
empirically some of the insights emerging from environmental social
theory. In particular, the contributors to this section draw on their
own extensive fieldwork in hazardous communities to examine the
assertion that modern societies are being transformed into risk
societies. Such approaches provide a potentially useful way of span-
ning the theoretical–empirical divide in environmental sociology. While

the two chapters isolate different facets of the risk society thesis, it is instructive that both sets of authors have only partial success corroborating their experiences with the theory's central tenets.

Michael Edelstein explores the psychosocial experience of living in a hazardous environment and describes the way in which it alters individual and collective sensibilities. This chapter introduces a model that elaborates how the idiosyncratic geographic, social, and historical characteristics of a contaminated community condition local responses to contemporary risk events involving toxic chemicals, radiation, and other similar agents. Of particular interest to Edelstein are the differential perspectives that victims and casual observers develop to interpret the local manifestations of certain features of a purported risk society. In Giddens' terminology, 'ontological security' is shattered as the surrounding environment, previously taken for granted as safe, becomes a potential source of severe threat to residents' personal health and safety. Among other effects, this process of redefinition undermines relational networks and community solidarity. A pattern of dependency emerges in which victims necessarily reach out to public institutions (e.g. health departments, aid agencies) that are frequently ill-equipped to handle the novel demands placed on them. Such a situation galvanizes affected individuals to come together to form new social movement organizations that are roughly consistent with the ideational forms that Beck describes as arising out of risk society.

Importantly, an enormous chasm exists between the victims of contamination and those individuals living at a distance and for whom it remains an abstract problem. Edelstein describes, in language available only to someone who has immersed himself in contaminated communities, the way in which victims become stigmatized by wider society. The empirical evidence from the United States confirms at the micro-level the manifestation of certain aspects of the risk society thesis. However, the chapter argues that modern societies' more general tendency to retain their prevailing worldview poses serious questions about the theory's more general propositions, specifically those concerning the diffusion of a more reflexive consciousness. Furthermore, Edelstein finds that while risk as a conceptual rubric has become fashionable in current academic discourses surrounding environmental uncertainty, it has little relevance for members of the lay public.

Steven Picou and Duane Gill pursue some of the same issues as Edelstein but take a decidedly different tact. Their chapter extracts from Beck's global theoretical reflections certain key concepts which they then subject to empirical consideration. The authors relate several speculative claims regarding reflexive modernization, such as the 'anxiety community' and political mobilization in the face of an encroaching risk society, to the body of fieldwork on the social and social psychological impacts of contamination on affected communities. They explore the connections between macro-level theorizing and micro-level analysis by relating their own experiences studying the social dimensions of the 1989 *Exxon Valdez* oil spill off the coast of Alaska. Though Picou and Gill identify some important correlates, their overall assessment is that the risk society provides a rather poor description of the social responses of localities subjected to extreme events.

In particular, Picou and Gill argue that the social circumstances surrounding contamination do not auger well with Beck's claims concerning the emergence of a 'solidarity of anxiety' and the advent of purposeful political action to address the resultant problems of risk society. Rather, they suggest that the obverse is more likely to be the case. Affected individuals often become caught in a dangerous downward spiral in which their resilience is compromised and their interpersonal support networks splinter causing disabling processes of community fragmentation. More encouragingly, the authors' analysis offers robust empirical support for other elements of risk society theory. This more positive assessment is perhaps most clearly exemplified in their description of the contested use of science in the *Exxon Valdez* case and the way in which the various actors in the controversy manipulated scientific practice to generate data that accorded with their individual prerogatives.

The chapters comprising Part V initiate a discussion on how perspectives from environmental sociology might be usefully employed to inform processes of environmental decision-making. The authors of these contributions agree that much of the success of science derives from its ability to generalize across spatial and temporal distances. A consequence, however, of this universalizing tendency is the disregard of data derived through more contextual ways of knowing, a feature that is especially prominent in expert systems pertaining to the environment. This section's contributions advance suggestions on how different forms of knowledge might be integrated so as to compensate for their respective deficiencies.

In the part's first contribution, Stephen Couch, Steve Kroll-Smith, and Jeffrey Kindler examine the dialectical process that can take place between communities and sociological experts. Their research suggests that the lay public has a tendency to appropriate abstract knowledge and to use it creatively to help define what may be anomalous or exceptional situations. This observation stands in stark contrast to the oft-made assertion that the public is irrational or is prone to summarily reject learned advice. The authors specifically focus their attention upon so-called hazardous environments, or locales that have been subjected to environmental risks with a high degree of uncertainty and danger. They are interested in ascertaining the ways in which local, situated knowledge is shaped and conditioned by interaction with professional sociologists and how, in turn, this experience informs social scientific inquiry.

The authors develop their discussion from two case studies. The first example describes the researchers' personal experiences studying the social dynamics set in motion by an underground mine fire in the small town of Centralia, Pennsylvania. Their second illustration is a provocative interpretation of Picou and Gill's interventions to ameliorate the social upheaval caused by the *Exxon Valdez* oil spill. Through their theoretical description and analytic discussion of these unconventional research settings Couch and his colleagues explore hermeneutical processes of institutional reflexivity. They also subject to empirical investigation Giddens' observation that in late modernity 'there is a continuous filter-back of expert theories, concepts, and findings to the lay population.'[53] This type of knowledge production invariably requires researchers to devise methodological innovations that deviate from customary approaches that claim to provide scientific objectivity and strive to keep expert and subject distinct. In the course of developing structures through which lay and expert knowledges can mutually inform one another, the authors identify possible access points for resolving long-standing epistemological controversies surrounding the ways in which social scientists conceptualize the physical world.

Rolf Lidskog, in this part's following chapter, takes up this theme concerning lay knowledge and its relationship to universal science in controversies surrounding environmental risks. He describes a transformation that appears to characterize late modernity, one in which hazards are no longer visible and readily bounded, but are instead diffuse and transcend conventional space-time demarcations. Without any direct means to ascertain these new problems, the environment becomes a battleground over cultural symbols. In choosing sides, ordinary people must judge the credibility of expert institutions and contrast these interpretations with their own experiences. The question Lidskog raises is whether we should see the formulation of strategies to address environmental risk as the province of special expertise or lay perspectives grounded in situated knowledge.

Lidskog's chapter proceeds to respond to this dilemma by sketching out in ideal-typical terms the difference between scientific and social rationality. The author contends that it is not especially instructive to distinguish rigorously between the two epistemologies because they frequently co-determine one another. It is thus not a question of which form of knowledge is superior, but how best to devise social mechanisms that facilitate their interaction and complementarity. In embracing this challenge Lidskog describes a communicative approach to risk that goes beyond customary calls for more democratic science and technology policies. He neither disparages science for undermining traditional patterns of knowing nor elevates lay knowledge to privileged status. Rather, Lidskog contends that it is through communication that we can encourage all relevant perspectives to contribute to environmental decision-making under conditions of profound uncertainty.

In this part's final chapter Klaus Eder pursues further this discussion regarding the role of communication in environmental decision-making. He pursues the question of whether it is in fact rational and functional to devise institutions that facilitate dialogue. Furthermore, he asks if such approaches can be useful in resolving contemporary dilemmas associated with risk society. In fact, Eder contends that it is associativeness predicated upon communication that has been the principal force of modernity, giving rise to contemporary social forms ranging from parliamentary democracy to science. He argues that we must not turn our backs on this tradition. Rather, we need to enhance its reach by opening up to dialogue a wider range of societal processes of producing knowledge and making decisions.

This challenge, Eder argues, is particularly critical during the present period when modern society is subjected to powerful forces of increasing functional differentiation. Contemporary lifestyles are becoming more complex and existing institutions are struggling to manage the numerous contingencies for action thrown up by these changes. As these inadequacies become more pronounced it becomes necessary to dissolve pre-existing hierarchical and corporatist structures and to invent new discursive arrangements to encourage consensus in a more pluralistic world. Expanding on the assessments of this section's earlier contributions, Eder adopts a neo-institutionalist perspective and draws on examples from Germany to argue that improved decision-making – for the environment as well as for other domains – is more than a process of generating contextual knowledge. Efforts to make tractable the complexity of modern society require the design and implementation of discursive mechanisms that are capable of legitimating decisions and disseminating responsibility across a diverse constituency.

In the volume's final part David Lowenthal brings to bear the keen eye of a historian and offers a few reflections on the social study of risk and the project to create an international environmental sociology. He notes that while national differences in intellectual style may persist, environmental problems do not respect these artificial divides. Contemporary ecological dilemmas are becoming increasingly global in scale. Furthermore, we are moving from an era in which environmental threats were readily observable to a new period that presents us with dangers that are largely invisible and difficult to ascertain.

Efforts to get a handle on such challenging circumstances require us to supersede the limitations imposed by present-day forms of knowledge production. Lowenthal argues that institutions engaged in environmental decision-making must overcome their zealous campaign to wrestle certainty from uncertainty. This obsession has contributed to the impression that all problems can be successfully subdued once they are reduced to a handful of mathematical formulae. It is this same drive for control that has led to the widespread dissemination of conceptual typologies that segregate nature and culture. It is only by recognizing the inseparability of nature and culture that we can begin to understand contemporary anxieties. In the modern age, risk has become a master frame for expressing a medley of societal preoccupations, foremost of which are increasing societal complexity, deepening dependence on recondite expertise, and conflicting attitudes about the consequences of human avarice.

NOTES

1. A. Giddens, *The Consequences of Modernity* (Cambridge: Polity Press, 1990).

2. More recent calls to shift the burden of proof onto the perpetuators of environmental harm has been termed the 'precautionary principle.' See T. O'Riordan and J. Cameron, *Interpreting the Precautionary Principle* (London: Earthscan, 1994).
3. This transition of environmental organizations was particularly profound in the United States. See M. Dowie, *Losing Ground: American Environmentalism at the Close of the Twentieth Century* (Cambridge: MIT Press, 1996).
4. M. Hajer, *The Politics of Environmental Discourse: Ecological Modernization and the Policy Process* (Oxford: Clarendon Press, 1995).
5. J. Short, 'The Social Fabric at Risk: Toward the Social Transformation of Risk Analysis,' *American Sociological Review*, 49(6) (1984): 711–25.
6. See, in particular, W. Catton and R. Dunlap, 'Environmental Sociology: A New Paradigm,' *American Sociologist*, 13(1) (1978): 41–9; W. Catton and R. Dunlap, 'A New Ecological Paradigm for Post-Exuberant Sociology,' *American Behavioral Scientist*, 24(1) (1980): 14–47; R. Dunlap and W. Catton, 'Environmental Sociology: A Framework for Analysis,' pp. 57–85 in T. O'Riordan and R. C. d'Arge, eds, *Progress in Resource Management and Environmental Planning*, vol. 1 (Chichester: John Wiley, 1979); and R. Dunlap and W. Catton, 'Environmental Sociology,' *Annual Review of Sociology*, 5 (1979): 243–73. An analysis of the contributions of these two authors is provided by R. Gramling and W. Freudenburg, 'The Emergence of Environmental Sociology: Contributions of Riley E. Dunlap and William R. Catton, Jr.,' *Sociological Inquiry*, 59(4) (1989): 439–52. The term 'environmental sociology' appears to have first been used by Samuel Klausner in his landmark book, *On Man in His Environment* (San Francisco: Jossey-Bass, 1971).
7. More recent contributions have stressed that the early indifference of the nineteenth-century theorists toward the natural environment was not as striking as conventionally considered. See, for example, F. Buttel, 'Sociology and the Environment: The Winding Road Toward Human Ecology,' *International Social Science Journal*, 38(3) (1986): 337–56 and T. Benton, ed., *The Greening of Marxism* (New York: Guilford Press, 1996).
8. Giddens, *The Consequences of Modernity*.
9. In their initial formulations Catton and Dunlap referred to the Human *Exemptionalist* Paradigm as the Human *Excemptionalism* Paradigm. Similarly, they originally designated the New Ecological Paradigm to be the New Environmental Paradigm. The history of this terminological change is discussed in Freudenburg and Gramling, 'The Emergence of Environmental Sociology.'
10. F. Buttel, 'New Directions in Environmental Sociology,' *Annual Review of Sociology*, 13 (1987): 465–88.
11. The institutional and organizational history of environmental sociology in the United States has been recounted elsewhere. For recent reviews refer to R. Dunlap and W. Catton, 'Toward an Ecological Sociology: The Development, Current Status, and Probable Future of Environmental Sociology,' pp. 11–31 in W. D'Antonio, M. Sasaki, and Y. Yanegayashi, eds, *Ecology, Society, and the Quality of Social Life*

(New Brunswick, NJ: Transaction Books, 1994) and R. Dunlap, 'The Evolution of Environmental Sociology: A Brief History and Assessment of the American Experience,' pp. 21–39 in M. Redclift and G. Woodgate, *The International Handbook of Environmental Sociology* (Cheltenham: Edward Elgar, 1997).

12. Sociological human ecology also played a central role in the formulation of environmental sociology, especially for Dunlap and Catton. Allan Schnaiberg's work provides an important alternative view drawing primarily on neo-Marxist and neo-Weberian perspectives. See A. Schnaiberg, *The Environment: From Surplus to Scarcity* (Oxford: Oxford University Press, 1980).

13. On the role of rural sociology in shaping environmental sociology see D. Field and W. Burch, *Rural Sociology and the Environment* (Westport, CT: Greenwood Publishers, 1988) and F. Buttel, 'Environmental and Resource Sociology: Theoretical Issues and Opportunities for Synthesis,' *Rural Sociology* 61(1) (1996): 56–76.

14. See, for example, S. Prince, *Catastrophe and Social Change* (New York: Columbia University Press, 1920) and P. Sorokin, *Man and Society in Calamity* (New York: Dutton, 1942). For explicit discussion of the influence of disasters on environmental sociology refer to Dunlap and Catton, 'Environmental Sociology'; J. S. Picou, D. Gill, and M. Cohen, eds, *The* Exxon Valdez *Disaster: Readings on a Modern Social Problem* (Dubuque, IA: Kendall-Hunt, 1997); J. S. Kroll-Smith and S. Couch, *The Real Disaster is Above Ground: A Mine Fire and Social Conflict* (Lexington: University Press of Kentucky, 1990).

15. Buttel, 'New Directions in Environmental Sociology.'

16. This distinction has become firmly established in the field. See Dunlap and Catton, 'Environmental Sociology' and Buttel, 'New Directions in Environmental Sociology.'

17. Certain exceptions to this characterization do of course exist. See, for example, Short, 'The Social Fabric at Risk'; Kroll-Smith and Couch, *The Real Disaster is Above Ground*, especially chapter 9; and K. Erikson, *A New Species of Trouble: Explorations in Disaster, Trauma, and Community* (New York: W. W. Norton, 1994).

18. For the tentative endorsement of this argument see Gramling and Freudenburg, 'Environmental Sociology.'

19. Risk, broadly defined, is also of interest to environmental sociologists other than those described in the following section, namely those working on siting conflicts (e.g. industrial installations, waste incinerators, landfills) and environmental justice. These two areas are excluded from the current essay because they leave to the side many of the issues that occupy the attention of European theorists such as the problematization of science and scientific knowledge. Furthermore, these two strands of research do not engage with concerns pertaining to the social versus material construction of the natural environment. Accordingly, they do not provide much fertile ground on which to promote the sort of integration described in this chapter.

20. The case is described in detail in A. Levine, *Love Canal: Science, Politics, and People* (Lexington, MA: Lexington Books, 1982).

21. For a comprehensive account of the history and implementation of Superfund refer to J. Hird, *Superfund: The Political Economy of Environmental Risk* (Baltimore, MD: Johns Hopkins University Press, 1994).
22. C. Perrow, *Normal Accidents: Living with High-Risk Technologies* (New York: Basic Books, 1984).
23. H. Reko, *Not an Act of God: The Story of Times Beach* (St Louis, MO: Ecumenical Dioxin Response Task Force, 1984).
24. P. Shrivastava, *Bhopal: Anatomy of a Crisis* (Cambridge MA: Ballinger, 1987).
25. A. Barton, *Communities in Disaster: A Sociological Analysis of Collective Stress Situations* (Garden City, NY: Doubleday, 1969).
26. S. Couch and J. S. Kroll-Smith, 'The Chronic Technical Disaster: Towards a Social Scientific Perspective, *Social Science Quarterly*, 66(3) (1985): 564–75.
27. M. Cohen, 'Economic Dimensions of Environmental and Technological Risk Events; Toward a Tenable Taxonomy,' *Industrial and Environmental Crisis Quarterly*, 9(4) (1996): 448–81.
28. K. Erikson, *Everything in its Path: Destruction of Community in the Buffalo Creek Flood* (New York: Simon & Schuster, 1976).
29. Erikson, *A New Species of Trouble*.
30. See, for example, Kroll-Smith and Couch, *The Real Disaster is Above Ground*; Picou, et al. *The* Exxon Valdez *Disaster*; M. Edelstein, *Contaminated Communities: The Social and Psychological Impacts of Residential Toxic Exposure* (Boulder, CO: Westview Press, 1988).
31. J. S. Picou, 'Toxins in the Environment, Damage to the Community: Sociology and the Toxic Court,' pp. 211–24 in P. Jenkins and J. S. Kroll-Smith, eds, *Witnessing for Sociology: Sociologists in Court* (Westport, CT: Praeger, 1996).
32. See, in particular, Perrow, *Normal Accidents: Living with High-Risk Technologies*.
33. L. Clarke and J. Short, 'Social Organization and Risk: Some Current Controversies,' *Annual Review of Sociology*, 19 (1993): 375–99.
34. See also Picou, et al., *The* Exxon Valdez *Disaster*.
35. W. Freudenburg and T. Jones, 'Does an Unpopular Facility Cause Stress? A Test of the Supreme Court Hypothesis,' *Social Forces*, 69(4) (1991): 1143–68.
36. Dunlap and Catton, 'Toward an Ecological Sociology,' p. 20. For a comprehensive review of early European work in this area see W. Rüdig and P. Lowe, 'Political Ecology and the Social Sciences: The State of the Art,' *British Journal of Political Science*, 16 (1986): 513–50.
37. See, for example, K. Eder, *The New Politics of Class: Social Movements and Cultural Dynamics in Advanced Societies* (London: Sage, 1993).
38. U. Beck, *Risk Society: Toward a New Modernity* (London: Sage, 1992).
39. Recent contributions include T. Benton, *Natural Relations: Ecology, Animal Rights, and Social Justice* (London: Verso, 1993); P. Dickens, *Reconstructing Nature: Alienation, Emancipation, and the Division of Labour* (London: Routledge, 1996); K. Eder, *The Social Construction of Nature: A Sociology of Ecological Enlightenment* (London: Sage, 1996);

and S. Lash, B. Szerszynski, and B. Wynne, eds, *Risk, Environment, and Modernity: Towards a New Ecology* (London: Sage, 1996).
40. Important British work includes, among others, M. Redclift and T. Benton, eds, *Social Theory and the Global Environment* (London: Routledge, 1994) and S. Yearley, *Sociology, Environmentalism, Globalization: Reinventing the Globe* (London: Sage, 1996). On environmental sociology in the Netherlands refer to G. Spaargaren, *The Ecological Modernization of Production and Consumption: Essays in Environmental Sociology* (Wageningen: Wageningen Agricultural University, 1997). A useful introduction to environmental sociology in the Nordic countries is a special issue of the journal *Acta Sociologica* (vol. 39, no. 1, 1996). A recent compendium, comprised largely of chapters written by European scholars, is Redclift and Woodgate, *The International Handbook of Environmental Sociology*. It must be noted that interest in environmental social theory is not exclusively limited to Europeans and important contributions have been made by Canadians and Australians, among others.
41. Giddens, *The Consequences of Modernity*. See also his *Modernity and Self-Identity: Self and Society in the Late Modern Age* (Cambridge: Polity Press, 1991) and U. Beck, A. Giddens, and S. Lash, *Reflexive Modernization: Politics, Tradition, and Aesthetics in the Modern Social Order* (Cambridge: Polity Press, 1994).
42. For a detailed survey of several of the authors most central to this area refer to D. Goldblatt, *Social Theory and the Environment* (Cambridge: Polity Press, 1996).
43. Mary Douglas and Aaron Wildavsky provide the most forceful statement of this perspective. See their classic book *Risk and Culture: An Essay on the Selection of Technical and Environmental Dangers* (Berkeley: University of California Press, 1982). Refer also to J. Hannigan, *Environmental Sociology: A Social Constructivist Perspective* (London: Routledge, 1995).
44. This is not the place for a lengthy review of the attack on social constructivism. Suffice to say, most of these critiques have emanated from outside the ranks of sociology. See, for example, P. Gross and N. Levitt, *Higher Superstition: The Academic Left and its Quarrels with Science* (Baltimore, MD: Johns Hopkins University Press, 1994) and several of the contributions in P. Gross, N. Levitt, and M. Lewis, eds, *The Flight from Science and Reason* (New York: New York Academy of Sciences, 1996).
45. R. Dunlap and W. Catton, 'Struggling with Human Exemptionalism: The Rise, Decline, and Revitalization of Environmental Sociology,' *The American Sociologist*, 25(1) (1994): 5–30.
46. Recent efforts to bridge the divide include L. Laudan, *Beyond Positivism and Relativism: Theory, Method, and Evidence* (Boulder, CO: Westview Press, 1996) and G. Delanty, *Social Science: Beyond Constructivism and Realism* (Milton Keynes: Open University Press, 1997). For contributions by environmental sociologists that attempt to promote a new consensus see R. Murphy, *Rationality and Nature: A Sociological Inquiry into a Changing Relationship* (Boulder, CO: Westview

Press, 1994); C. New, 'Sociology and the Case for Realism,' *Sociological Review*, 43(4) (1995): 808–27; E. Rosa, 'Meta-Theoretical Foundations for Post-Normal Risk,' *Journal of Risk Research*, 1(1) (1998): 15–44; G. Woodgate and M. Redclift. 'From a Sociology of Nature to Environmental Sociology: Beyond Social Construction,' *Environmental Values*, 7(1) (1998): 3–24.
47. The reasons for the cleavage between American empiricism and continental theorizing have been a frequent topic of discussions within the history of the social sciences. See, for example, W. Lepenies, *Between Literature and Science: The Rise of Sociology* (Cambridge: Cambridge University Press, 1988). The small number of notable contributions that connect the two overarching modes of thought within environmental sociology include S. Yearley, *The Green Case: A Sociology of Environmental Issues, Arguments, and Politics* (London: Routledge, 1991) and A. Irwin, *Citizen Science: A Study of People, Expertise and Sustainable Development* (London: Routledge, 1995). It is useful to observe that both of these authors are British and this presumably places them in an effective position to bridge the divide between the United States and the European continent.
48. Dunlap and Catton, 'Toward an Ecological Sociology,' p. 21. See also Buttel, 'New Directions in Environmental Sociology.'
49. On the historical factors that have shaped American sociology see T. Haskell, *The Emergence of Professional Social Science: The American Social Science Association and the Nineteenth-Century Crisis of Authority* (Urbana: University of Illinois Press, 1977).
50. D. Gasman, *The Scientific Origins of National Socialism: Social Darwinism in Ernst Haeckel and the German Monist League* (London: MacDonald, 1971).
51. Dunlap and Catton, 'Struggling with Human Exemptionalism,' p. 15.
52. On ecological modernization refer to A. Mol, *The Refinement of Production: Ecological Modernization Theory and the Chemical Industry* (The Hague: CIP-Data Koninklijke Bibliotheek, 1995).
53. A. Giddens, 'Living in a Post-Traditional Society,' pp. 56–109 in Beck et al., *Reflexive Modernization*, p. 91.

Part II
Critiques of Risk and Rationality

2 The Rational Actor Paradigm in Risk Theories: Analysis and Critique

Ortwin Renn, Carlo C. Jaeger, Eugene A. Rosa, and Thomas Webler

INTRODUCTION

Coping with risk has captured the attention of policy-makers and laypersons alike to become a pivotal topic for technological elites, as well as social thinkers. Technical experts – engineers, toxicologists, epidemiologists, and social scientists – and social theorists have been competing for public attention in the risk arena.[1] A model of coexistence juxtaposing the technical understanding of risk and the social science perspective has emerged over the last two decades. Risk in this sense can be summarized as both a potential for harm, as well as a social construction of worry.[2] Defining risk as a combination of hazard and outrage, as Peter Sandman has suggested, has been the fragile but prevailing compromise in this debate, at least in the United States.[3] Although the formula of 'risk equals hazard plus outrage' does not provide answers of how to combine scientific assessments with public perceptions, it seemed to please the professional audience and was accepted as a conceptual guideline for risk management agencies. These agencies were well-advised to base their decisions on both expert assessments and public concerns, which was a common practice in risk analysis and management.

This fragile compromise has recently come under severe attack. In his presidential address at the Annual Meeting of the Society for Risk Analysis – Europe, in Guildford, John Graham complained about the tendency of risk management institutions to base risk-reduction policies on risk perception rather than risk assessments.[4]

He claimed that most public risk perceptions are at odds with the best scientific estimates, are inconsistent with rules of formal logic, and vary considerably among populations and over time. Using perceptions as guidelines for policy would imply that more people than necessary would become victims of risks, and that industry and other risk producers would suffer from the capricious tempers of public rage. The same argument was presented at the Probabilistic Safety Assessment and Management Conference in June of 1996 by keynote speaker David Okrent.[5] He questioned the use of public perceptions as guidelines for risk management on the basis that perceptions violate principles of *intra*generational as well as *inter*generational justice and equity. Risk aversion among the affluent societies and for the present generation would lead to the imposition of risks onto less developed nations and future generations.

These attacks represent the sudden revitalization of an old debate. Early in its development the field of risk analysis argued over the role of laypersons and about the significance and function of social science research in risk management. In our view, there are three reasons for the recurrence of these debates. The main reason has been that money for risk reduction has become an even more scarce resource than ever before. As long as risk managers had rather large budgets to spend, it was relatively easy to please all camps, the experts, the public, and the social scientists who studied both. Policy-makers spent money on the top-risk priorities of experts and the public alike. In times of tighter budgets, and less public attention to environmental issues, risk managers found that they could no longer afford to please both 'clients.'[6]

The second reason stems from the fact that pleasing the public turned out to be more difficult than anticipated on first glance from the psychological studies on risk perception. In the 1970s and 1980s, social scientists collected public perception data at a highly aggregated level.[7] Risk priorities for the public were normally based on the average values of individual risk perceptions that reflected either estimates of small groups of respondents or mean values of larger samples. Most risk managers were not aware that mean values tend to obscure the large amount of variance to be found among individuals. More sophisticated research designs revealed a wide array of risk estimates among individuals and social groups and a variety of risk priorities depending on group affiliation, personal values, and social orientations.[8] The gap between experts and the public turned out to be transformed into numerous gaps among experts and among publics.[9] The resultant confusion motivated many risk managers to abandon the idea of public input altogether and to return to the safe haven of technical expertise.

The third reason has been that public opposition to technologies and other risk-inducing activities has been less pronounced than in the past. Many former opponents of technology have become professionals in risk management and adopted at least parts of the risk assessment methodology of their former foes.[10] Public concern for risky technologies, though still high on the agenda (as measured by social surveys), has not translated into widespread public protest or political action. With less public support, the concerns of environmentalists and other pressure groups are less visible in the political arena and, as a result, less important for designing risk policies.

The key question at this juncture is: will the pendulum swing back to a new era of expert domination in risk policies? The trend seems to point in this direction. In response to new developments, several social scientists have suggested that social research on risk should be based on theoretical frameworks that risk managers and natural scientists would also find attractive. In particular, they have argued that the postmodern views on risk have been counterproductive and that systems theories in contemporary sociology have only produced the less than helpful insight that risk debates cannot be resolved.[11] Their advice has therefore been to use rational actor theories as a basic framework for understanding social responses to risk and to design policies that fit the needs of risk managers.[12]

This chapter aims to analyze the potential of rational actor theories to provide an explanatory framework for understanding the social experience of risk in modern societies. Our main thesis is that these conceptual approaches may be well-suited to describe individual actions under uncertainties, but fail to provide satisfactory explanations for collective risk actions or decisions. Furthermore, we claim that rejecting rational actor theories at the collective level does not necessarily lead to the hyper-relativism of postmodernism or to the pessimism of social systems theory.[13]

THE FOUNDATION OF RATIONAL ACTOR THEORIES

The notion that rational action forms the philosophical basis for explaining risk comes in three levels of abstraction. In its broadest expression (as a worldview) it presupposes that human beings are capable of acting in a strategic fashion by linking decisions with outcomes.[14] Humans are purposive agents, are goal-oriented, have alternatives for action available, and select options considered appropriate to reach their objectives. In this expansive form, most people would take this worldview for granted. With the exception of postmodern theories, there is hardly any disagreement among the different schools in the social sciences that rational action is not only possible, but also a 'touchstone' of human action. If the postmodernists were correct, social science-based risk studies would make little sense except as socially constructed knowledge systems amenable to rhetorical criticism or deconstruction.

The second, more refined version of rational action can be called the rational actor paradigm (RAP). It is a general theory of human action that makes a whole set of further claims that are more specific. Many special theories on risk and uncertainty rely on this second-level RAP and its assumptions. These assumptions refer to human actions based on individual decisions.[15] Among the most important are:

- *Atomistic view of rationality.* All actions can be reduced to individual choices.
- *Analytical separability of means and ends.* People as well as institutions can in principle distinguish between ends and means to achieve these ends.
- *Goal-attainment motivation.* Individuals are motivated to pursue self-chosen goals when selecting decision options.
- *Maximization or optimization of individual utility.* Human actors select the course of action that promises to lead to more personal satisfaction than any other available competing course of action.
- *Existence of knowledge about potential outcomes.* People who face a decision can make judgments about the potential consequences of their choices and their likelihood.
- *Existence of human preferences.* People have preferences about decision outcomes based on values and expected benefits.
- *Predictability of human actions (if preferences and subjective knowl-*

edge are known). Rational actor theory is not only a normative model of how people should decide, but also a descriptive model of how people select options and justify their actions.

This set of fundamental assumptions linked to individual behavior is also extrapolated to situations of collective decision-making and collective impacts of individual decisions. These situations refer to three classes of phenomena: (1) to human actions that reduce or enlarge the potential for actions of others (external effects); (2) to a multitude of rational (individual) actions that create social structures, such as markets or political institutions, in which the aggregate effect of many rational actions provide predictability and consistency even in the absence of a 'self-conscious' collective will (in the language of Durkheim the so-called 'social facts'); and (3) to actions that are designed and/or implemented by more than one actor or other forms of actions that lead to or stem from interactive effects among different individual actions (structural effects such as class biases).

Specifically designed to explain collective behavior, there is a third level of interpretation of RAP. In this interpretation, humans maximize their utility by choosing among different options the one that promises maximum payoff. In its collective version, such rational behavior leads to a social and economic equilibrium within a web of rational actions as long as humans have equal access to resources and information and are allowed to compete with each other. This particular interpretation of RAP is closely linked to economic theory and its basic understanding of rationality as a process of the efficient selection of means to reach a predefined goal. The main thrust of the third level is the transference of factors that govern individual action to the realm of collective action and the implication of the transference for institutions and social structures. In addition to the above-mentioned assertions of individual actions, the realm of collective actions within this level of RAP comprises a whole set of additional claims:

- *Methodological individualism.* All aggregate social actions can be interpreted as a complex net of individual actions.
- *Treatment of organizations or social groups as 'virtual' individuals.* Organizations act like individuals and they select the most efficient means to reach pre-determined goals.
- *Possibility of extending individual preferences to aggregate preference structures.* Institutions that aggregate individual preferences

such as markets or political decision-making bodies resemble not only the sum of individual preferences, but also their combined collective interest.

- *Availability and effectiveness of organizational principles and practices.* Markets, democracy, negotiations, and so forth provide a systematic link between individual utility maximization and social welfare (in particular the so-called invisible hand of markets).
- *Reasonable knowledge of individual actors about the effect of social inferences.* Actors have knowledge of the actions of others that might interfere with their own probability to attain goals (handling of complexity).
- *Indifference to the genesis and promulgation of values and preferences.* Values are seen as pre-existent or exogenous; RAP can only make predictions on the premise that preferences are given, not created in the decision process.
- *Independence between allocation of resources and distributional effects.* It is rational for societies to assign priority to the most efficient allocation of resources regardless of distributional effects before redistributing the wealth among the members according to preconceived principles of social justice. In some *laissez-faire* versions of RAP, a Darwinist selection rule for distributing wealth is assumed as most appropriate since the most successful entrepreneur should also reap most of the benefits. Modern versions inspired economists of the neo-liberal (Hayek) school to emphasize the distinction between allocation of resources and equitable distribution. RAP models are appropriate for ensuring the most effective and efficient production and exchange of goods and services, but need auxiliary ethical norms or moral principles to distribute equitably the added value among society's members.

THE OPTIMIZATION PRINCIPLE

Underlying the individual, as well as the collective interpretation of RAP, is the basic assumption that all human actions can be described as problems of maximization or, in more contemporary versions of RAP, optimization. The social world is divided into countless decision problems each of which require the generation of options for future actions and some kind of an algorithm (decision rule) to choose one among the available options. This algorithm is meant to guide an individual or collective strategy to the optimization of its own benefits. The algorithm may be well-founded in many social arenas such as markets and political debates. It may, however, be unfounded for other social structures such as those creating mutual trust among actors, building individual and social identity, gaining ontological security, or constructing solidarity among people with similar interests. Although these latter social activities are certainly goal-oriented and thus fit the first level of rational actors (worldview), they do not lend themselves to a process of optimization. Thus, the assumptions of neither the second, nor the third level of RAP are met under circumstances where optimization is not the primary goal of action.

It makes no sense to think of trust, identity, or solidarity as resources to be maximized or optimized as is understood in the RAP tradition. These social phenomena are products of communication and mutual understanding, elements of social life itself that require pre-existing cultural meaning and constant feedback to reach stability. They are always endangered by the perceptions of strategic or disruptive social actions and need to be fueled by reciprocal actions and the exchange of symbols that emphasize shared values and convictions. Such a process of offering, sustaining, and symbolic reinforcement cannot be adequately described by an optimization process, although some of the contemporary rational actor theorists have made some attempts to phrase these phenomena in the language of RAP.[16] These attempts include many additional *ad hoc* assumptions and qualifying conditions beyond the RAP framework. As Thomas Kuhn has pointed out in his classic study of scientific paradigms, a scientific theory becomes weak when it needs too many *ad hoc* explanations to subsume phenomena that do not fit the original predictions.[17] Such was the case with the Ptolomean view of the solar system with its *ad hoc* epicycles.

Our main point here is that the realm of the monarch RAP has been extended beyond its scope to areas that cannot and should not be regarded as maximization or optimization problems.[18] RAP assumes that individuals pursue the three requisite steps of decision-making: generation of options, evaluation of consequences, and selection of the most beneficial alternative. Without a doubt there are many social situations that can be described, or at least simulated, in such a fashion. There are many other conditions, however, in which the model of decision-making as an act of optimizing outcomes appears to be a weak descriptor for what actually happens, let alone for what the actors perceive to happen. Social reality becomes impoverished if all actions have only one common goal: to maximize or optimize one's own utility. Balancing social relations, finding meaning within a culture, showing sympathy and empathy to others, as well as being accepted or even loved by other individuals, belong to a class of social phenomena that do not fit neatly into the iron rule of RAP. Individuals may conscientiously or unconscientiously behave in accordance with the means–ends optimization process of RAP some of the time, but certainly not all of the time. A major task of post-RAP theories is therefore to identify and define additional schemata of social actions that are based on intentionality, but use routes other than optimizing outcomes.

This criticism is not directed towards RAP on the first level of analysis, and only partially to its application for understanding individual action as exercised on the second level. Rather the criticism refers to the imperialistic extension of RAP to social phenomena that are not suitable for the assumptions of RAP at both the individual and the collective levels. To our knowledge no RAP theoretician or practitioner has taken up this suitability issue. Rather they continue to defend their claim that RAP offers a universal perceptive for understanding human risk (and other) social behavior. Empirically proven deviations from the assumptions of RAP are treated as anomalies or noise. The major question of whether optimizing strategies underlie all classes of human and social actions has not been adequately addressed by the defenders of the monarch.

The problem of optimization alone requires a critical discussion about the limits of RAP as a general theory of human action. But there are numerous additional targets for criticism with respect to the major assumptions. Critics of RAP have raised many of these points, which in turn have been partially addressed by the paradigm's adherents. We can categorize these criticisms into two groups: criticism of RAP as a theory of individual choice and action, and criticism of RAP as a theory for collective choice and social action.

RAP AND INDIVIDUAL CHOICE

The most prominent debate surrounding RAP stems from the empirical evidence that humans more often violate than conform to the rules of rational action. RAP seems plausible as a normative standard for judging individual action if it can be framed as a decision problem. But, as a descriptive tool for predicting people's actions it has only limited validity. This is true even if the analyst has access to the preferences and subjective knowledge of the individual decision-maker. Most psychological experiments demonstrate only modest correlations between rationally predicted and intuitively chosen options.[19] Furthermore, by asking people in 'thinking-out-loud experiments' how they arrive at their decision, all kinds of rationales are articulated of which only a few have any resemblance with the prescribed procedures of rational actors.[20]

The accumulation of observed deviations from RAP-based decisions led two leading cognitive scientists to conclude:

> . . . the logic of choice does not provide an adequate foundation for a descriptive theory of decision-making. We argue that the deviations of actual behavior from the normative model are too widespread to be ignored, too systematic to be dismissed as random error, and too fundamental to be accommodated by relaxing the normative system. We conclude from these findings that the normative and descriptive analysis cannot be reconciled.[21]

In response to this empirical challenge, proponents of RAP perspectives in psychology and economics have proposed five modifications that would bring the theory more in line with actual observations of behavior.[22]

First, they claim that the procedures prescribed by RAP theory serve only as analytical reconstructions of the intuitive choice process in humans. Whether humans follow these prescriptions consciously or not does not matter as long as the outcome of the decision process is close to what rational theories would predict.[23]

Second, people use simplified models of rationality such as the lexicographic approach (choose the option that performs best on the most important attribute), the so-called 'elimination by aspects' scheme (choose the option that meets most of the aspects deemed important), or the satisficing strategy (choose the option that reaches a satisfactory standard on most decision criteria). All of these methods represent strategies of bounded rationality with suboptimal outcomes.[24] These suboptimal outcomes are either sufficient for the person (the additional increase in utility is less than the cost of such a decision) or the time saved to come to a satisficing solution is more valuable than the additional benefits derived from an optimal decision. Recent experiments have shown that people use more complex and elaborate models of optimization when the decision stakes are high (large potential payoffs), while they prefer the simplified models when the decision stakes are low.[25] Introducing simplified models for suboptimal decision-making increases the validity for making predictions of chosen decision options substantially.

Third, most applications of RAP theory equate utility with an increase in material welfare. However, people may feel an increase in satisfaction when they act altruistically or when they enhance their reservoir of symbolic gratifications. Although experiments are usually designed to exclude these factors (or to keep them constant), it is not clear whether symbolic connotations (such as accepting money for a trivial task) may play a role in the decision-making process.[26] Some of the aforementioned 'thinking-out-loud experiments' revealed that certain subjects felt that they should opt for the most cumbersome decision option because that way they felt they deserved the promised payoff.

Fourth, people in such experiments often adopt a strategic posture. They assume that their choices will depend on the actions and reactions of others, even in experimental settings that focus on individual actions without any interference from other actors. By deliberating over how others could influence their preferred choices, they may select suboptimal options because such solutions avoid the strategic responses of the assumed others. Game-theoretical models, though normatively inappropriate for these conditions, may actually offer better predictions than those based on expected utility.

Finally, some analysts claim that the artificial situation of a laboratory as well as the 'playful nature' of the subjects (normally undergraduate students) are the main reasons for many observed deviations from RAP.[27] In real-life situations, with real stakes, people would be more inclined to use rational, or at least bounded rational, models to select their preferred decision options. Yet, comparative studies among students, laypersons, and experts show that, while there are intergroup differences, all have perceptions that deviate from expectations.[28]

This is not the place to review all these arguments in detail. However, two implications emerge from them. First, if utility encompasses all aspects that matter to people, then the model becomes tautological and is non-falsifiable. We do not challenge the contention that humans act intentionally. However, if altruism, feelings of solidarity, and struggling for meaning are all manifestations of utility, the concept of utility itself becomes meaningless and trivial.[29] Second, if closeness to real-life situations and the inclusion of bounded rationality indeed improves the predictability of decision choices, as many experiments suggest, then the conclusion is justified that many individual decisions can be explained by a modified rational actor approach. The alteration to include simplified models is not tautological (they exclude many potential options from the selection) and the utility measurements are still defined in terms of actual payoffs. Finally, even granted that rational choice occurs at the individual level in many instances, many other human actions do not follow the optimization processes of RAP.

Laboratory experiments narrowly frame the situation as a decision-making context. Left out of this framing are many of the social forces that define humanness. Many human actions are motivated by cultural imperatives, most notably habituation – for example imitation, conditional learning, emotional responses, and subconscious reactions. These responses are not perceived as decision situations and hence people do not even take rational strategies into conscious consideration. In addition, anecdotal evidence tells us that many actions are functions of both cognitive balancing and emotional attractiveness. The fragmentation of the psychological profession into communities of clinical, cognitive, and analytical psychologists has blinded researchers from testing the relative importance of these factors in motivating human actions. Nevertheless, it seems quite appropriate to conclude that rational actor theories can provide a normative algorithm for decision-making. RAP is also able to describe some important aspects of human actions that center around decisions – in particular those decisions involving measurable outcomes. The real issue seems to be what happens to other aspects of social life and to what degree actions are closely or loosely coupled to decision-making in the RAP sense.

RAP AND COLLECTIVE CHOICE: A CRITICAL VIEW FROM SYSTEMS THEORY

These problems of finding the limitations and boundaries of RAP are especially relevant for two applications that extend the paradigm's realm beyond the individual level, namely to collective decision-making and to the impacts of individual choices on other individuals. RAP encounters numerous conceptual problems when it is applied to collective decision-making. On the most fundamental level, all rational actor theories imply that individuals have sufficient knowledge about the consequences of their potential courses of action. This assumption has been strongly contested by sociologists belonging to the systems theory camp, such as Niklas Luhmann. System theorists claim that prediction of outcomes may already be too difficult to accomplish in a complex world, even if there are no other actors. But with the presence of a multitude of other actors, all of whom are likewise making strategic choices and thus able to affect the outcomes of one's own action in a myriad of different directions, it is almost impossible to predict the consequences of one's own action. The individual decision-maker is trapped in a web of contingencies and uncertainties. In such instances, RAP does not provide a very meaningful orientation. The belief that rational action is possible and normatively required turns out to be an 'ideological' element of those social systems (or subcultures) that would like its members to believe that the world is governed by rational decisions.[30]

Furthermore, there are clearly social contexts in which RAP seems out of place. It is not uncommon for someone to have no idea of what the impacts of various decision options (such as accepting one of several job offers) might be. Information-seeking strategies may turn out to be insufficient or too time-consuming to produce sufficient clarity about options and potential outcomes. In this case, RAP would suggest guessing or a conservative 'better safe than sorry' strategy. Social theory, and systems theory in particular, would suggest, however, that social systems need more coherence and predictability of individual actions than this seemingly random strategy would provide. If human actions were random occurrences – as in the case of insufficient knowledge – social integration would be jeopardized. In response to this problem, systems theorists claim that conformity and predictability are accomplished through a variety of functionally equivalent procedures of which rational choice is only one among others. In particular, orientation through reference group judgments and secondary socialization by organizations and subcultures provide selection rules for options independent of the expected outcome for the individual.[31] In addition, these selection rules include other motivational factors such as emotions or social bonds that play no or only a minor role in RAP. Again option selection does not result from an optimization process, but from social or cultural orientations. Individual choices are made on a social basis such as judging the desirability of or proximity to the aspired lifestyle of one's reference group.

The conflict between expected and experienced outcomes is likely to increase with the degree of social and cultural complexity. This leads, on the one hand, to an increased variability of human action and thus to a growing number of potential choices that are open to each individual. Increased complexity, on the other hand, necessitates an increased effort for coordinated actions. This dilemma has been resolved in modern societies with the evolution of semi-autonomous systems that provide a network of orientations within each distinct social grouping.[32] Such systems organize and coordinate the necessary transfer of information and services through specialized exchange agents. Depending on the cultural rules and images of these social groupings, rational expectations may play a larger or smaller role in shaping these orientations. That is why appealing to rational decision-making is only attractive to some groups (e.g. bankers), but repulsive to others (e.g. evangelists). Absolute rationality – the strongest form of RAP – has lost its integrative power over the diverse system rationalities that each group has accepted as binding reference points for action and legitimation.[33] Complex, modern societies are characterized by the coexistence of multiple rationalities – RAP being just one of them – that compete with each other for social attention and influence.

This trend towards multiple rationalities is reinforced by the disintegration of collectively approved and confirmed social knowledge. Each group produces its own rules for making knowledge claims. These rules determine which claims are justified as factual evidence compared to those assertions that are mere constructions, ideology, or myths. Furthermore, they govern the process of selecting those elements of an abundant reservoir of knowledge claims that seem relevant to the group members and match the body of previously acknowledged and accepted claims.

Under such circumstances it is difficult to predict the factual consequences of different decision options. How can individuals make prudent judgments about options if the relevant knowledge is not only uncertain, but also contested by the relevant stakeholder groups? The result of this growing uncertainty and indecisiveness of potential outcomes leads, on the one hand, to a larger share of non-rational incentives to ensure conformity and, on the other hand, to a concerted effort to create certainty often in the form of RAP-based strategies such as quantitative risk assessments. This polarization fuels an ongoing conflict among the subsystems, which continue to develop their own mechanisms of internal integration and development, while threatening external coherence (the well-known autopoiesis theory of Luhmann).[34]

The nation-state and its political agents have become more and more powerless in developing and allocating resources for regulating the exchange of materials and communication, as well as relations among social groups. They seem to be engaging in a losing battle. It is increasingly difficult for social and political elites to provide a commonly accepted and legitimate system of meta-rationality that encompasses the plural rationalities of each subsystem. However, it is unclear whether the battle is being lost in principle or whether the RAP approach is merely insufficient to provide such a meta-rational framework. In either case, institutional trust is eroded and political legitimacy is seriously jeopardized. Because of these ramifications (and other equally grave problems) and because RAP does not provide the requisite meta-rules demanded for ensuring coordination among competing rationalities, we later conclude the need for an alternative, or at least modified, framework.

RAP CLAIMS IN THE LIGHT OF COMPETING SOCIAL THEORIES

The struggle for a comprehensive and overarching framework of rationality has been the focus of many new social theories because of the theoretical challenge outlined above. This challenge also represents one of the most pressing problems of contemporary societies. Although one can observe a renaissance of RAP models to provide a common base for a meta-rational integration of competing subsystem claims, it is very doubtful that this rejuvenation will be effective for a variety of reasons. The growing uncertainty and complexity of modern societies obscures the relationship between rationally derived expectations and actual outcomes. Too many social system variables intervene between the rational axiom of expected utility and the experienced cause–effect relationships in everyday life. These discrepancies make the application of rational actor theories less convincing for members of the various self-governing subsystems, and thus weaken its potential power as a meaningful interpreter of and predictor for social responses. High-risk technologies are the most prominent examples of this phenomenon. The weakness of the RAP approach to offer a commonly accepted rationale for designing and legitimizing public policies for managing these risks grows in recognition. As this weakness has become clearer in the eyes of most observers, it has challenged RAP's hegemony over risk-knowledge claims. It has also undermined its legitimacy as a policy and management tool.

Thus, RAP is threatened by two key assaults to its foundations. First, individuals in a complex society are unable to foresee the consequences of their actions. Second, there is a need to devise functional equivalents that create conformity and commonly accepted selection rules without reference to expected outcomes. These problems are further aggravated by the contemporary trend toward emphasizing the personal development and self-realization of individuals. The experience of incoherence, when individuals desire to accomplish one goal but achieve another, conflicts with the expectation of self-realization. One social mechanism to cope with this conflict is to reinterpret the actual outcome as a variant of the desired outcome (Is not what I got what I really wanted or needed?). Religions frequently use this reinterpretation when they try to explain why bad things happen to good people. Either the allegedly good people had sinned after all, or the bad fate turned out to be a blessing when seen in a different light. Another mechanism is to offer a system of symbolic gratifications and incentives that compensate for the experience of conflict. However, all these *post hoc* methods of easing this friction perform poorly in creating social conformity and individual happiness at the same time.

RAP's failure to produce the requisite conformity attracts a notable theoretical alternative, namely critical theory. This body of literature suggests that, with the decline of a universal-rationality proposition, we need to generate new social norms and values that provide collective orientations but do not conflict with personal aspirations.[35] Similar suggestions have been recently proposed by the 'New Communitarians.'[36] In contrast to systems theory, in which such new norms are part of an evolutionary process, remote from any individual voluntaristic influence, critical theory believes in the integrative potential of free and open discourse. Such discourse is not only an arena for resolving conflicts about competing claims (as is practiced in conflict-resolution models based on RAP), but also as an arena for the establishment of commonly agreeable social norms or values. All participants voluntarily agree to accept the quest for common principles of evaluating validity claims and to comply with these principles via discourse because they perceive them to be intuitively valid and socially rewarding (see also the chapter in this volume by Klaus Eder).

Systems theorists are extremely skeptical of this approach. They claim that each system has developed its own language, reference system of knowledge, and norms, all of which cannot be amalgamated under the umbrella of procedural or substantive meta-norms. Normative agreements need to be based on some commonalties. If these initial points of consensus are missing, or if participants in a discourse are unable to understand, let alone accept, the arguments of other (language) camps, a discourse becomes an arena of window dressing – everyone talks but no one understands. Under these circumstances, agreements remain elusive acts of chance, strategy, or power. Regardless of whether systems theory or critical theory is correct in this debate, RAP-based theories cannot offer any solution.[37] This is because normative discourse (not aimed at optimizing utilities, but at ensuring social cohesion) is outside of its conceptual universe. Norm evolution (other than serving higher norms) and the genesis of values are explicitly excluded from the body of knowledge within RAP. For RAP – they are simply 'given' or 'out there' – exogenous to any particular context of choice. One of the major drawbacks of RAP is therefore its inability to explain two of the most eminent conflicts in modern societies: How do we accomplish normative coherence? How do we develop solutions for coping with plural claims for collectively binding moral principles?

STRUCTURAL PRESSURES ON INDIVIDUAL BEHAVIOR

RAP also faces major problems when it comes to structural influences on individual behavior. The problem is conceptualized in two ways. First, many individual actions occur in a restricted social context in which the variety and quantity of decision options are limited or are perceived as limited by individual actors. Such a limitation is not a serious challenge to RAP. The well-known RREEMM model (resourceful, restricted, evaluating, expecting, maximizing man) accounts for the restrictions and barriers that people face when making rational decisions.[38] Problems arise if the decision-maker feels guided by context variables – norms, obligations, values, habits, and so forth – and does not perceive the situation as one of individual choice. This not only applies to habitual behavior in the form of personal routines that are performed in everyday life quasi-unconsciously, but also to cultural routines that are based upon complex stimulus–response mechanisms. The enactment of culturally shaped behavior is mainly below conscious awareness and does not imply any type of internal cost–benefit-analysis – certainly not conscious calculation.

Second, the outcomes of individual actions produce external effects for other individuals – the so-called interferences. These non-intended and very often unpredictable side-effects do not only limit the ability of actors to anticipate or predict the consequences of their own actions (as discussed above), they also form the structural conditions for collective actions in the future. A major reason for the necessity of having transpersonal institutions in society is to assure predictability and social orientation even in the presence of unpredictable side-effects of individual actions. RAP-based theories do not deny the existence or the relevance of these structural elements. Rather, they regard them either as constraints on rational choice (these constraints can be traced back to individual actions of the past) or as a social learning process that teaches individuals to cope with interferences by predicting interactive effects more accurately. In addition, if collective action is rather homogeneous, RAP treats social aggregates as if they were rational individuals.[39] Organizations are seen as *persona ficta*. They are entities that have goals, evaluate options, and pursue an optimization strategy. They select the most efficient means for reaching predefined goals similar to individual decision-makers. The transfer of individual choice to collective action characterizes the RAP approach and is accomplished via the route of methodological individualism. All aggregate phenomena are interpreted as if they were reducible to the decisions of an individual actor. Methodological individualism has often been criticized on the ground that social actions cannot be reduced to individual actions alone (see also the chapter in this volume by Kristen Purcell, Lee Clarke, and Linda Renzulli). Simmel already claimed that in sociology the house is more than the sum of its stones. Accordingly, the appropriate theoretical organization is not methodological individualism, but methodological holism. However, RAP theorists eschew holism. They emphasize that complex social actions can indeed be explained by referring to the same terms of reference that have explained individual actions. The claim for the universal applicability of RAP is not justified by postulating that individual and social behaviors exhibit an identical or isomorphic internal structure. If so, the two action categories would necessitate identical or interchangeable terms and theories, which is clearly not the case. RAP does postulate, however, that complex social actions can be decomposed analytically to a variety of individual actions that in turn provide the database for explaining and predicting actions of aggregates.[40] RAP theorists would, in one sense then, agree with the statement that the house is more than the sum of its stones. Nonetheless, the additional quality can be derived from studying the sum of the stones and the mortar holding them together rather than from investigating the house as an entity *sui generis.*

EXAMPLES

We provide here two illustrations that may help to demonstrate the RAP understanding of complex social systems. The first example comes from economic behavior. In the field of economics, a rational actor must accept the rules of the market, the present price structure, and the availability of resources as external constraints, although these restrictions are a product of all the actions of other rational actors. Learning in this context is a function of (intelligent) trial and error in which individual actors strive to cope with the effect of interferences and to improve their ability to predict future outcomes more accurately.

The second illustration comes from the political arena. In politics, rational actors must accept the norms, laws, and rules of decision-making as external constraints. Again these constraints were presumably generated by rational actors in the first place. Learning takes place, for instance, through the process of elections where the individual candidates can assess how their expectations of popularity are measured in votes. After a defeat, he or she may learn to rearrange their political program or communication method to incorporate the possible effects of the message on voters' behavior. In general, observing the individual actor provides enough insights to understand the structural effects of all the collective actions relevant in the respective social or political arena.

Structural theorists in sociology do not deny the possibility of looking at structural phenomena from an individualistic perspective. However, they prefer the alternative orientation of methodological holism. Treating social structures and institutions as entities *sui generis* supposedly provides more adequate insights and more explanatory power for understanding collective actions than the atomistic view of methodological individualism.[41] Social scientists adhering to RAP theories are convinced that treating aggregate phenomena as manifestations of individual actions may indeed help to get us closer to a 'unified social theory.' Other social scientists believe that such an approach is bound to fail. It will either produce trivial results or will be applicable only to a limited range of social phenomena. Structural theories claim instead that they have found similarities and regularities in the behavior of aggregate structures that are difficult or impossible to explain by individual actions (although they clearly impact on individual actions). Seminal studies on institutions, economic or regulatory styles, class structure, and others have identified many of these structural phenomena that apparently influence individual behavior without entering into the rational calculations of each actor and were never 'invented' by actors through rational choices.

One attempt to combine the individual focus of RAP and the structural focus of many macro-sociological theories has been the structuration theory of Anthony Giddens.[42] Giddens describes this approach as one of duality – a synergy between the actor-agent and social structure. Giddens rejects the idea that individuals calculate the expected utilities of the various consequences of behavioral options. Instead, they orient themselves within a complex arrangement of traditions, individual routines, and socio-cultural expectations. Each individual actor is part of the forces that shape the future context of actions for others. At the same time each individual is bound to structural constraints that are the outcome of past actions and choices of others. Such an open system would tend to be chaotic if society did not develop consistent patterns of behavior. In other words, routinization provides invisible guidelines for individuals in choice situations. These patterns are not simply an aggregation of individual actions, but instead develop a structural logic of their own. For example, traditional norms do not promise maximum payoff or even an improvement of individual satisfaction. Rather, they assure system continuity and stability. Likewise, power structures are often cherished even by those who lack power because they provide ontological security to society. The main argument that Giddens proposes is that individuals do have agency – they have choices to orient themselves within different social frames (such as traditions, special institutions, system rationalities).[43] But the frames constitute developments of structural forces that go beyond individual actions and their effects on others.

EXTERNAL EFFECTS: DEVIATIONS FROM NORMALITY?

A final concern for RAP is the treatment of external effects.[44] Although discussed frequently in the RAP literature, their treatment points to a major weakness in the assumptions of RAP theories. RAP presumes that under certain conditions the pursuit of individual rational actions would lead almost automatically to collectively rational outcomes. But the opposite often occurs in reality, namely that individually rational actions frequently lead to socially undesirable outcomes. This has always been discussed within RAP as a deficiency of the conditions. Perhaps the most well-known example of such failures is the free-rider problem. The common RAP response to the problem of individual versus collective rationality, and hence the potential conflict between the pursuit of individual rationality and the common good, has been twofold. On the one hand, RAP theorists believe in the 'invisible hand' in the sense that under the condition that external effects can be internalized as costs to the individual actor, the outcome of individual actions would be equivalent to the overall social good. On the other hand, corrective actions are mandated if the market fails to allocate social costs to those who cause them. In such a case, market-compatible instruments are readily available to impose external costs on the guilty party. Among these mechanisms are the extension of property rights to all affected parties or the stimulation of market prices to include social costs (Pigovian taxes or Coase property rights).

The same argument can be made for the political sector. Individual rationality is sufficient to provide a framework of laws and regulations that will automatically enhance the common good under the premise that each individual has the same right to influence political outcomes. In both cases, economics and politics, collective action enhances the common good if the conditions of rationality and perfect market structure are met. But the real world is devoid of such perfections. Thus, the conditions are not ripe for collective welfare. The strategy of 'blaming' the conditions for impeding the congruence of individual and collective rationality effectively builds a wall of immunization around RAP theories. Since all conditions for a perfect market or a truly rational political system are never met, deviations from theoretically derived predictions can always be explained by imperfect conditions. Relying on perfect conditions also reduces the explanatory power of RAP since it explains neither how markets or political structures arise in the first place nor how people behave in an imperfect world.

The main defense RAP theorists make for treatment of deviations from rationality as a consequence of imperfect economic or political conditions, however, is the fiction of a hidden social tendency toward an equilibrium stage of perfect market conditions and political structure.[45] If this were true, social systems would tend to orient themselves in line with the guiding principles of rationality in their pursuit to reach the goal of perfect conditions. In reality, however, many systems and institutions profit from imperfection. Even if we assume that they behave like rational actors, their particularistic interest is, and has been, to make sure that conditions in the economic or the political market do not change. Imperfection creates losers and winners. It is not clear if and why social systems would tend to enforce a movement towards more 'perfection.' There may even be some good normative reasoning to allow for some imperfection in society if such a system could enhance social stability, solidarity, or cohesion.

Finally, many structural barriers such as market segmentation, incomplete knowledge, possibilities of manipulation, market-scale effects, and numerous others make it unlikely, if not impossible, to accomplish a situation that ever comes close to perfect market conditions. Political will, even if available, is not sufficient to assure a transition to a more perfect world. There are structural barriers that are impossible to overcome without sacrificing other highly esteemed social goods. The real world will always consist of economic and social structures that do not resemble the vision of perfection that RAP theorists share. One may even raise the question whether perfect conditions in the economy and politics would constitute a desideratum for societies. Rather than a vision for the future, the RAP equilibrium may turn out to be a nightmare. We might find a creature that looks like a utility-maximizing robot that has perfect knowledge, preprogrammed preferences, and all equal opportunities, but who knows nothing of habit, culture, commitment, and sociability.

CONCLUSIONS

The preceding discussion leads to the following conclusion. The most eminent problem for RAP is the assumption that all human behavior can be modeled as variants of optimization procedures. There is sufficient doubt that such a structure superimposed on all human actions can offer a satisfactory perspective for studying and explaining such phenomena as trust, solidarity, identity, affection, and, of course, risk.[46] Furthermore, major problems for RAP lie in the fact that more and more areas of social life demonstrate specific patterns of behavior that make sense neither in the light of the paradigm's own assumptions nor with respect to actual human choices. Outcomes have become less predictable so that orientations for future actions can be based only partially on expected consequences. Interferences between social actions have increased over time so that distributional impacts of one party's action on the resources of another party have become politically and socially more important. Under such conditions social processes for optimal allocation of resources take a back seat.

In essence, RAP presumes a world that does not exist – at least not to the extent that the paradigm's proponents would like to see it. Social development has created a complex world in which the conditions for applying RAP are seldom met and hence there is a growing discrepancy between model and reality. As a result, many RAP theorists have become ardent advocates for changing the world in the direction of the model rather than for adjusting the model in the direction of the world.

This practice is common for any good theory in the sciences. Theories must always live with anomalies. Good theories are not proven wrong over time, but proven either irrelevant in the face of new developments, or only applicable to special cases. The kingdom of the monarch RAP may not collapse because of its weaknesses, but it may be swallowed up by a new empire. Afterward, the kingdom will be one important, but only fractional, part of the entire empire.

What does this mean for the recent debate on the role of social science for risk policies? Explanations based on RAP may help risk managers to understand why individuals behave in particular ways when they face uncertain outcomes of their actions. Such an explanation, however, can only yield valid results if the individual perceives the risk problem as a problem of optimizing outcomes and if the conditions of choice meet RAP assumptions. If responses to risk are grounded in solidarity with others, or motivated by reference group judgments, RAP does not make much sense. If the focus of social research is on collective risk behavior, theories based on RAP are still less convincing. They may even serve the function of disenfranchising individual from political actions or restricting freedom since the actions are deemed 'irrational.' The main difficulty here is that RAP presupposes stable preferences and knowledge about outcomes beyond the individual aspiration level. Furthermore, there is the assumption that the sum of individual actions would tend to form an equilibrium. The evidence for all of these claims is extremely weak.

It is therefore our judgment that social science research on risk needs to include more than the RAP perspective when analyzing risk behavior. All challengers to RAP, most notably systems theory, critical theory, and postmodernism, face other theoretical and practical problems when they deal with risk. They do provide, however, the missing links in the gaps that RAP cannot bridge. Until we have a unified social theory for risk, we are forced to live with a patchwork of different concepts. This is not a plea for eclecticism, but a cautious argument for matching theories with the corresponding type of problem. In the end, social theory will be judged according to its potential to explain social responses to risk, not by its ability to please risk managers. Regardless of whether risk managers prefer to set policies according to the numerical results of risk assessment studies or not, they are, and will continue to be, faced with social reactions to their policies. Some will challenge or even counteract the basis of their policies. It is the task of the social scientist to provide meaningful explanations for these responses and to promote critical reflection on risk policies in the light of the research results. RAP-based examinations will play a role in this endeavor, but we would like to caution ardent proponents of this approach to overstress neither its explanatory nor its policy power. In particular, at a time when social research is under attack, one should not put all the eggs in the same basket.

NOTES

1. For a philosophical appraisal of risk theories see K. Shrader-Frechette, *Risk and Rationality: Philosophical Foundations for Populist Reforms* (Berkeley: University of California Press, 1991), pp. 53ff. For a sociological review see S. Krimsky and D. Golding, eds, *Social Theories of Risk* (Westport, CT: Praeger, 1992) or J. Short and L. Clarke, 'Social Organization and Risk,' pp. 309–21 in J. Short and L. Clarke, eds, *Organizations, Uncertainties, and Risk* (Boulder, CO: Westview Press, 1992).

2. Review of the implications of a constructivist versus a realist concept of risk can be found in: J. Bradbury, 'The Policy Implications of Differing Concepts of Risk,' *Science, Technology, and Human Values*, 14(4) (1989): 380–99; O. Renn, 'Concepts of Risk: A Classification,' pp. 53–79 in S. Krimsky and D. Golding, eds, *Social Theories of Risk* (Westport, CT: Praeger, 1992); and E. Rosa, 'Metatheoretical Foundations for Post-Normal Risk,' *Journal of Risk Research*, 1(1) (1998): 15–44. A pronounced constructivist approach can be found in B. Wynne, 'Institutional Mythodologies and Dual Societies in the Management of Risk,' pp. 178–204 in H. Kunreuther and E. Ley, eds, *The Risk Analysis Controversy: An Institutional Perspective* (Berlin: Springer Verlag, 1982); N. Luhmann, *Risk: A Sociological Theory* (New York: Aldine de Gruyter, 1993); J. Adams, *Risk* (London: UCL Press, 1995); and K. Japp, *Soziologische Risikotheorie* (Munich: Juventa, 1996). Realist perspectives in the social sciences can be found in W. Catton, *Overshoot: The Ecological Basis of Revolutionary Change* (Urbana: University of Illinois Press, 1980); R. Dunlap, 'Paradigmatic Change in Social Science: From Human Exemptionalism to an Ecological Paradigm,' *American Behavioral Scientist*, 24 (1) (1980): 5–14; P. Dickens, *Society and Nature: Towards a Green Social Theory* (Hemel Hempstead: Harvester Wheatsheaf, 1992).

3. P. Sandman, 'Hazard versus Outrage: A Conceptual Frame for Describing Public Perception of Risk,' pp. 163–8 in H. Jungermann, R. Kasperson, and P. Wiedemann, eds, *Risk Communication* (Jülich: Research Center, 1988).

4. J. Graham, 'The Biases of Public Perception,' *SRA-Europe Meeting*, Guildford: University of Surrey, 1996.

5. D. Okrent, 'Risk Perception Research Program and Applications: Have They Received Enough Peer Review?' pp. 1255–9 in C. Cacciabue and I. Papazoglu, eds, *Probabilistic Safety Assessment and Management ESREL '96-PSAM '96* (Berlin: Springer-Verlag, 1996). See also H. Sapolsky, 'The Politics of Risk,' *Daedalus*, 119(4) (1991): 83–96.

6. For the United States refer to R. Zeckhauser and K. Viscusi, 'The Risk Management Dilemma,' *Annals of the American Academy of Political and Social Science*, 545 (1996): 144–55.

7. See the classic article by B. Fischhoff, P. Slovic, S. Lichtenstein, S. Read, and B. Combs, 'How Safe is Safe Enough? A Psychometric Study of Attitudes Toward Technological Risks and Benefits,' *Policy Sciences*, 9 (1978): 127–152 and P. Slovic, B. Fischhoff, and S. Lichtenstein, 'Rating the Risks,' *Environment*, 21(3) (1979): 14–20, 36–9. For a critical

review written at the time refer to H. Otway and K. Thomas, 'Reflections on Risk Perception and Policy,' *Risk Analysis*, 2(11) (1982): 69–82.

8. Early sociological surveys suggested such a large variance within the public, but it was hardly acknowledged by risk management agencies. See for example: L. Gould, G. Gardner, D. DeLuca, A. Tiemann, L. Doob, and J. Stolwijk, *Perceptions of Technological Risk and Benefits* (New York: Russell Sage Foundation, 1988) and O. Renn, 'Man, Technology, and Risk,' *Jül-Spez-115* (Jülich: Research Center, 1981). More sophisticated psychological research designs revealed a variety of different risk perceptions depending on social and cultural orientations. Refer also to K. Dake, 'Orienting Dispositions in the Perceptions of Risk: An Analysis of Contemporary Worldviews and Cultural Biases,' *Journal of Cross-Cultural Psychology*, 22(1) (1991): 61–82 and B.-M. Drottz-Sjöberg, *Perception of Risk: Studies of Risk Attitudes, Perceptions, and Definitions* (Stockholm: Center for Risk Research, 1991), pp. 163ff.

9. B. Fischhoff, 'Public Values in Risk Research,' *Annals of the American Academy of Political and Social Science*, 545 (1996): 75–84.

10. T. Dietz, P. Stern, and R. Rycroft, 'Definitions of Conflict and the Legitimation of Resources: The Case of Environmental Risk,' *Sociological Forum*, 4(1) (1989): 47–69.

11. H. Margolis, *Dealing with Risk: Why the Public and the Experts Disagree on Environmental Issues* (Chicago: University of Chicago Press, 1996), in particular pp. 214ff.

12. R. Kleim and I. Ludin, *Reducing Project Risk* (Aldershot: Gower, 1997), pp. 23ff.

13. The content of this paper summarizes a recent effort by the four authors to publish a book on this subject: C. Jaeger, O. Renn, E. Rosa, and T. Webler, *Risk, Uncertainty, and Rational Action*, in preparation.

14. R. Dawes, *Rational Choice in an Uncertain World* (New York: Harcourt, Brace, Jovanovich, 1988).

15. See also D. Green and I. Shapiro, *Pathologies of Rational Choice Theory: A Critique of Applications in Political Science* (New Haven, CT: Yale University Press, 1994), pp. 14–17.

16. Cf K.-D. Opp, *The Rationality of Political Protest: A Comparative Analysis of Rational Choice Theory* (Boulder, CO: Westview Press, 1989) and K.-D. Opp, *Die Entstehung sozialer Normen: Ein Integrationsversuch soziologischer, sozialpsychologischer, und ökonomischer Erklärungen* (Tübingen: Mohr, 1983).

17. T. Kuhn, *The Structure of Scientific Revolutions* (Chicago: University of Chicago Press, 1962).

18. Cf. R. Abelson, 'The Secret Existence of Expressive Behavior,' pp. 25–36 in J. Friedman, ed., *The Rational Choice Controversy: Economic Models of Politics Reconsidered* (New Haven, CT: Yale University Press, 1996).

19. A. Tversky and D. Kahneman, 'Judgement Under Uncertainty: Heuristics and Biases,' *Science*, 185 (1974): 1124–31; D. von Winterfeldt and W. Edwards, *Decision Analysis in Behavioral Research* (Cambridge: Cambridge University Press, 1986); Dawes, *Rational Choice in an Uncertain World*.

20. H. Jungermann, 'Zur Wahrnehmung und Akzeptanz des Risikos von Grosstechnologien,' *Psychologische Rundschau*, 23 (1982): 217–38, pp. 217ff.
21. A. Tversky and D. Kahneman, 'Rational Choice and the Framing of Decisions,' pp. 67–84 in R. Hogarth and M. Reder, eds, *Rational Choice: The Contrast between Economics and Psychology* (Chicago: University of Chicago Press, 1987).
22. R. Lane, 'What Rational Choice Explains,' pp. 107–26 in Friedman, *The Rational Choice Controversy*.
23. W. Edwards, 'How to Use Multiattribute Utility Measurement for Social Decisionmaking,' *SMC-7, IEEE*, 1977.
24. H. Simon, *Administrative Behavior: A Study of Decision-Making Processes in Administrative Organizations* (New York: Basic Books, 1976) and A. Tversky, 'Elimination by Aspects: A Theory of Choice,' *Psychological Review*, 79 (1972): 281–99.
25. Dawes, *Rational Choice in an Uncertain World*.
26. J. Weimann, *Umweltökonomik: Eine theorieorientierte Einführung* (Berlin: Springer Verlag, 1991).
27. C. Heimer, 'Social Structure, Psychology, and the Estimation of Risk,' *Annual Review of Sociology*, 14 (1988): 491–519.
28. S. Lichtenstein, P. Slovic, B. Fischhoff, M. Layman, and B. Combs, 'Judged Frequency of Lethal Events,' *Journal of Experimental Psychology: Human Learning and Memory*, 4 (1978): 551–78.
29. Explaining solidarity as a mutual exchange of support misses many manifestations of identity that are driven either by expressive feelings (sense of belonging) or by the search for social orientation. For the RAP position on this point see M. Hechter, *Principles of Group Solidarity* (Berkeley: University of California Press, 1987). A critical review is N. Deuzim, 'Reading Rational Choice Theory,' *Rationality and Society*, 2 (1990): 172–89.
30. S. Rayner, 'Risk and Relativism in Science for Policy,' pp. 5–23 in B. Johnson and V. Covello, eds, *The Social and Cultural Construction of Risk* (Dordrecht: Reidel, 1987).
31. A. Giddens, 'Living in a Post-Traditional Society,' pp. 56–109 in U. Beck, A. Giddens, and S. Lash, *Reflexive Modernization: Politics, Tradition, and Aesthetics in the Modern Social Order* (Cambridge: Polity Press, 1994).
32. K. Bailey, *Sociology and the New Systems Theory* (Albany: State University of New York Press, 1994), pp. 243ff.
33. N. Luhmann, *Ökologische Kommunikation* (Opladen: Westdeutscher Verlag, 1986).
34. N. Luhmann, 'The Autopoiesis of Social Systems,' pp. 172–92 in R. Geyer and J. van der Zouven, eds, *Sociocybernetic Paradoxes: Observation, Control, and Evolution of Self-Steering Systems* (London: Sage, 1986).
35. J. Habermas, *Strukturwandel der Öffentlichkeit: Untersuchungen zu einer Kategorie der bürgerlichen Gesellschaft* (Neuwied: Luchterhand, 1969) and M. McCarthy, *The Group* (Harmondsworth: Penguin Books, 1971).
36. A. Etzioni, *A Responsive Society: Collected Essays on Guiding Deliberate Social Change* (San Francisco: Jossey-Bass, 1991).

37. J. Habermas and N. Luhmann, *Theorie der Gesellschaft oder Sozialtechnologie: Was leistet die Systemforschung?* (Franfurt am Main: Suhrkamp, 1971).
38. H. Esser, *Alltagshandeln und Verstehen: Zum Verhältnis von erklärender und verstehender Soziologie am Beispiel von Alfred Schuetz und 'rational choice'* (Tübingen: Mohr, 1991), pp. 40ff.
39. K. Dowding and D. King, 'Introduction,' pp. 1–19 in K. Dowding and D. King, eds, *Preferences, Institutions, and Rational Choice* (Oxford: Clarendon Press, 1995).
40. J. Coleman, *Foundations of Social Theory* (Cambridge: Belknap Press, 1990), pp. 138ff.
41. T. Parsons, *The Social System* (Glencoe, NY: Free Press, 1951).
42. A. Giddens, *Central Problems in Social Theory: Action, Structure, and Contradiction in Social Analysis* (Berkeley: University of California Press, 1979).
43. A. Giddens, *The Constitution of Society: Outline of the Theory of Structuration* (Cambridge: Polity Press, 1984).
44. Green and Shapiro, *Pathologies of Rational Choice Theory*, pp. 72ff.
45. Bailey, *Sociology and the New Systems Theory*, pp. 88ff and Green and Shapiro, *Pathologies of Rational Choice Theory*, pp. 23ff.
46. Similar conclusions are advanced in M. Taylor, 'When Rationality Fails,' pp. 223–34 in Friedman, *The Rational Choice Controversy*.

3 Menus of Choice: the Social Embeddedness of Decisions

Kristen Purcell, Lee Clarke, and Linda Renzulli

INTRODUCTION

How to think about constraint and choice is a basic problem in social theory.[1] Convincing explanations of behavior usually reference how power operates, why people think what they do, and how and why people relate to each other. Social life inherently involves someone constraining the options of someone else. It inherently involves some options being considered more possible than others. And it inherently involves the myriad connections that people find themselves in, connections that people use as resources to get through the day and as reference points for moral direction.

Constraint and choice also entail ideas about freedom. Certainly, ideas about freedom are woven into theories of risk, danger, environment, and disaster. In economics, which has the most developed (though not the most correct) theory of decision-making, actors enjoy nearly unconstrained choice in picking among competing goods, services, and trade-offs. Real constraints are either temporary inefficiencies, aberrations that market forces will eventually eliminate, or 'exogenous variables,' norms and values that are outside the purview of good economic theory. For most environmental sociologists people (at least rich, white people) to some degree at least are free to choose where to live, how to consume, and how many children to have. In social movement theories a key problem is why people who are free to choose nonetheless join organizations designed to promote certain political ideals (which themselves sue for some conception of freedom).

There are concomitant notions of responsibility that go along with conceptions of choice. People who are not free to choose are not responsible for their actions. Chinese peasants being persecuted for having more children than government officials say is allowed

62

are not quite as responsible for the damage those extra children inflict on the world's resources as are the arrogant elites who impose their will. Similarly, people who smoke cigarettes are somehow more responsible for the ills that befall them than the companies that profit so handsomely from their weakness. Smokers are apparently freer to choose health than companies are to choose profit loss.

In writings on risk the most explicit conceptions of choice and constraint – and of freedom and responsibility – revolve around ideas of 'voluntary' and 'involuntary' risks. Chauncey Starr explicitly juxtaposed 'voluntary' and 'involuntary' risks and in the process imported the economic conception of unbridled choice into debates about safety.[2] Starr's basically political argument has been subjected to considerable critical scrutiny, but the notion of voluntariness is easy to find.[3] The degree of discretion that people enjoy to choose their poisons, as it were, can even serve as the conceptual basis of hierarchies of acceptability.[4]

Of course, we have hardly been blind to the issue of institutional forces. Some commentators, reacting against the extreme individualism of economics and the moderate individualism of psychology, insist that organizations are the key arbiters of risk;[5] others talk about the social construction of risk technologies;[6] others theorize how accountability changes with increases in technological specialization.[7] While all these writings emphasize institutional forces, they nonetheless contain some conception of the voluntary. That conception, sensibly, is chiefly that those who are more free are subject to lesser degrees of institutional constraint.

Yet while some people are obviously freer than others, the distinction between voluntary and involuntary may be finally futile, a conceptual red herring that leads us away from creating better theories and towards sterile exercises in apportioning responsibility. In fact, the notion of solitary, unbridled freedom may have no empirical content at all, its sole function in social theory strictly ideological. For institutions are implicated in the apparent choices of even the most apparently free actor, say the rich, educated, young cigarette smoker. The very menu of things from which to choose is given by the institutional makeup of society.

This is so, moreover, independently of what actors think of the choices they face. The heroin addict feels she must inject herself, though there are plenty of former users. The smoker really needs his cigarette, but we all know he could skip it. The poor family has no choice other than to live in the house they have recently discovered was built on a toxic-waste dump, while the rich family is free to move to safer ground until their powerful lawyers can bail them out. In all these examples it is certainly easy to see the difference between what appears to be constraint and discretion, between free and non-free action. Furthermore, should we get into a debate, say with economists or policy-makers, over those differences we would certainly draw on the degree to which the victims (of heroin, tobacco, toxics, poverty) thought they were compelled to act one way rather than the other. While such an argument might not be wrong, it would not be a discussion that would advance our understanding of choices regarding risk. Even people who consider themselves full of free will are actually full of institutions. People's perceptions of their choices are effects of institutions – they are not themselves the institutional patterns. For even if the non-addict, the non-smoker, and the non-poor think they are free – and would answer as such in an interview – the menus of choices from which they pick are culturally bound and structurally given.

Unrestrained choice does not happen. The idea of choice is itself a social construction, a matter of agreement that some behaviors are more free than others. Theories of decision-making, of power-wielding, and of institutional design could benefit from more explicit consideration of what is meant by constraint and discretion. Theories that conceptualize social action in terms of relative degrees of freedom are contaminants from the legal arena, where we find highly restrictive notions of constraint and very narrow notions of free will.

This chapter first sketches some of the meanings and ambiguities in ideas about what is voluntary. We go on to discuss some ways that culture and social structure bound what is commonly called 'voluntary.' The chapter proceeds to advance an argument that framing work on risk along a voluntary–involuntary dimension is not going to help us understand why people think and behave as they do. We then discuss some of the ways that social life is embedded in webs of meaning, networks of relations, and the organization of resources. The question is not whether behavior is voluntary or involuntary, but which kinds of institutional forces are at play.

WHAT IS 'VOLUNTARY' RISK?

The concept of voluntary risk has not been subjected to sufficient critical scrutiny. Instead, we have more or less adopted a commonsensical notion of freedom, one that emanates from economic theory. It all began nearly thirty years ago with Chauncey Starr's highly prestigious article in *Science*, 'Social Benefit Versus Technological Risk,' in which he argued for two distinct, diametrically opposed categories of action. There are 'voluntary' risks, defined as activities in which people rationally choose to engage. There is little or no constraint or institutional context in this sort of action. People just decide what they want to do, and do it. They have the license and autonomy to pursue a course of action that best addresses their personal needs.

Then there are 'involuntary' risks which are risks people must take because participation is imposed by controlling groups in the larger society. Voluntary risks are chosen on grounds of personal assessment of the costs and benefits of alternatives. Involuntary risks hinge on the criteria of controlling groups such as government agencies, scientific communities, and political associations. Institutions obviously make an appearance here, but since the point is to account for the irrational beliefs of the public (they do not understand real danger, they just do not like being told what to do), the point is missed that the implicit opposition of markets (which are free) to hierarchies (which are not) may be a false one in the first place.

CONSCIOUSNESS, CHOICE, AND EVALUATION

Starr is a conspicuous target and there is little point in simply firing another salvo in his direction. Our point is a broader one of assessing the voluntary–involuntary continuum. Doing so suggests three critical elements of 'voluntary' risk: consciousness, choice, and evaluation. Arguing that an individual chooses a particular risk activity implies a fundamental state of consciousness in which people are aware they are making judgments involving danger. The image is that of a computer given the task of calculating the elements of a formula. As well, people choose among a range of options. The image is that of a shopper, standing in front of a garment rack trying to find shirts that might be acceptable. Once people have that range of options, they evaluate (if they are rational) the pros and cons of behaving one way rather than another. The image is that the computer can find the best solution, or that the shopper will pick the very best shirt on the rack.

Common examples of voluntary risks are smoking and car-driving. We are in control of the dangers from these activities, some say, so we feel unthreatened by them. 'It is not likely to happen to me' is the motto here, which must explain why people still smoke cigarettes and drive cars without using seat belts. So Mr Smoker is fully cognizant when he lights that cigarette that he is making a decision involving potential health risks. And Ms Car-driver knows she is placing herself at considerable risk of injury or death when she drives to work, or when she drives unbelted. When you next find yourself at a traffic light and look over to see an unbelted driver who is smoking a cigarette you will be looking at someone in touch with the dangerous side of things.

For the idea of voluntary risk to make much sense risk-takers must not only self-reflect on what they are doing nearly all the time, they must know the alternatives to what they are doing and be able to assess the comparative consequences of each course of action. At first glance it appears our smoker's alternatives are clear and easy to evaluate: smoke and die sooner, or not smoke and die later. But smoking is more complex than that. Smoking, smokers say, is a way to relax, a way to relieve stress by claiming for oneself a few minutes in which one concentrates intensely on the self. So a truly rational smoker must also realize that exercising, meditating, drinking alcohol, and eating right are alternative methods of relieving stress; the list could be much longer of course. So the conscious choice is quite complex. It is so complex in fact that if smokers actually were all that conscious of what they were doing they would never smoke – not because they would realize the danger, but because they would be continually busy evaluating the alternatives. In fact, it is highly likely that people smoke because they do not see better alternatives to that particular activity. A process of consciousness is involved, certainly, but hardly the one entailed in usual conceptions of the voluntary.

Be that as it may, mere awareness that there is a choice to make is not enough to constitute voluntariness. There must also be meaningful, even extensive, understanding of the risks and benefits of each alternative. Starr argues that presented with a set of alternatives, the individual weighs those options against one another in a cost–benefit analysis. This implies that the individual is able to evaluate alternatives. Recognition of potential risks and benefits is not equivalent to the comprehension and application of that information. A systematic evaluation of risks and benefits implies a level of technical understanding that allows people to discriminate among assorted options. Individuals cannot 'choose,' and thereby consent to, risks they do not understand.

Thus, 'voluntariness' means more than a cost–benefit analysis among a range of alternatives. 'Voluntary' risk assumes a fundamental state of awareness. It includes knowing that a risk-decision is being made; it includes awareness of a range of alternatives among which to choose, most especially awareness of the appropriate alternative set necessary for comparison; and it includes the technical knowledge necessary to weigh those alternatives against one another. Only if all three criteria – consciousness, choice, and evaluation – are met can an activity be deemed 'voluntary.' What goes unremarked is that cultural and structural factors shape each of these elements, so making use of the term 'voluntary' in any context is questionable.

CULTURAL SHAPERS

Consciousness, choice, and evaluation are constrained by the context in which risk-decisions occur. Risk perception happens only after it has filtered through a cognitive veil of norms, values, and beliefs that constitute the culture of a particular group – in fact, risk is experienced through the physical objects that symbolize and embody those commonly held beliefs. In both cases, cultural forces influence the ability to discern risk.

By these remarks we do not mean to say, as too many have, that there is no objective risk or that risk objects are only social constructions. That mistake happens on the polemical right and the epistemological postmodern left, the members of which form an odd alliance in analysis as each asserts that culture mediates risk to such a radical degree that danger is not real.

But cultural mediation undermines 'voluntariness' in several ways. First, cultural mediation highlights particular activities and objects as potentially dangerous while marking others as safe, leading people to assume a natural or inherent state of risk or non-risk in particular situations. Second, it leaves a large portion of activities and/or objects unmarked as neither dangerous nor safe. This may preclude the recognition of both risk-decisions and viable choices by making some risks or safety measures unrecognizable as such. Culture predisposes people to view certain things as alternatives, while others are beyond our sphere of attention. Depending on the culture in which you live, you have predetermined choice-sets available to you (that is, certain cultures use certain transportation methods while others do not, so depending on where you live, you are measuring the risks of only a limited number of alternatives against one another, while others never really cross your mind because they are not culturally available). In the United States, for example, people are concerned mostly with automobile, train, and air travel, while other countries rely on different transportation methods and thus perceive and measure transportation risks differently. Public transportation does not seriously figure in most Americans' transportation risk-calculus; in other countries it would top the list. When we talk about air traffic safety, we do so in terms of the major alternatives. We say it is statistically 'safer than' riding in a car, because that is the main alternative in a country whose transportation policy and industry have been controlled by automobile companies.[8] Culture thus sets the menu of choices so that one's ability to see particular objects or activities as viable alternatives is highly constrained.

Each culture defines danger and safety in specific ways, so certain activities are deemed risky while others are considered safe. The individual's ability to recognize potential risk depends largely on the cultural definitions of safety and danger. If an activity is inherently safe or dangerous, every culture (and thus every individual) would define it as such. But that is not the case.[9] 'Recreational risks,' such as those posed by bullfighting, auto racing, judo, bungee jumping, and cliff diving vary from culture to culture.[10] While Americans consider bungee jumping an acceptable recreational risk, they scoff at Pamplona's annual 'Running of the Bulls' in which participants are sometimes gored while attempting to outrun a stampede. Americans call Pamplona enthusiasts 'crazy,' then strap elastic cords to their ankles and jump from the nearest bridge.

Cultural mediation has important consequences for risk perception, legitimacy, and the exercise of power. There is considerable variation in the extent to which people believe and trust elites charged with protecting them. There is similarly wide variation across cultures in the extent to which actual democracy is thought to be a productive aspect of risk-decisions. Some powerbrokers and organizations are accorded more influence than others in shaping what is considered acceptable risk. Deeming an activity 'safe' (or safe enough) influences even the perception that a risk-decision is being made at all.

Consider automobile travel. People climb into their cars every day, rarely if ever thinking about the exorbitant numbers of fatalities occurring each year on America's highways. Driving is commonplace in American culture, and its dangers are largely overlooked. Moreover, meaningful public transportation finds no champion among influential politicians and has been massively defeated by powerful corporate interests. We turn the ignition key without considering that there could be an alternative to a known deathtrap. The day a teenager receives her driver's license is considered a day of celebration, as part of a rite of passage into adulthood. It is not frowned upon as the beginning of innumerable risk-decisions and situations, but rather as the start of a positive part of the adult experience.[11] The idea that there are safer ways to transport ourselves is not even on the menu.

Breaks in the cultural fabric, disruptions of routine, and inadvertent breaching experiments give us pause to ponder the danger of activities previously taken for granted. When laws are passed requiring seat belts something previously taken for granted must be reassessed. Driving by a grisly accident occasions the thought, 'there must be a better way.' When high-level decision-makers are found to lie or to falsely assert with certainty that something is safe, we take a moment to withdraw just a bit of legitimacy, a cognitive click of the tongue that vaguely recognizes that closed systems create closed minds.

A technology's novelty is another way that culture shapes our menu of risk choices. There is sometimes a liability of newness with technology.[12] The newer an activity, the more likely that people's attention is focused on the danger involved. Over time, as a product or activity becomes embedded in the cultural fabric of a society, it becomes more taken for granted, something people participate in without forethought of risk or danger. Automobiles are so commonplace in contemporary American culture that it is hard to imagine fear or reluctance to use them. Yet, when the car was first introduced to Americans in 1894, long after its general acceptance in Europe, there was tremendous skepticism regarding its safety and utility. Newspapers described it as 'the last call of the wild' and 'the world's most exciting sport,' characterizations fueled by the country's unpaved roads and considerably more developed trolley and railway systems.[13] Cultural mediation not only affects the ability to discern risk, it also affects the perception of options. Each risk-decision involves a range of alternatives among which the individual chooses. Viable choices are not readily apparent, but instead are a preconceived and prepackaged set of acceptable solutions for a particular situation. While each situation has countless options, only a minute subset are ever considered possible. Membership in this range immediately gives an alternative preference over those not culturally prescribed. Options perceived as acceptable, viable, and rational are more likely to be chosen than those that seem irrational, unusual, or unconventional.

This form of cultural mediation is an instance of risk 'framing.' Experimental research shows that the way alternatives are presented can significantly influence an individual's choice.[14] One way of understanding this 'cultural framing' of alternatives is that it distorts how decisions are made. But the effects of framing are so strong that it may be more helpful to see those frames as the decision itself. After all, people may worry and fret and think about the future, all of which we might call calculation, but they do not calculate in anything like the sense of economic theory. What they do, sometimes, is worry and think about the context, about how one way of acting is going to fit with their lives, or whether it is going to make someone mad, or make someone money. It is, indeed, the context or frame that is the thing that people make calculations (worry, fret, predict) about and not a moment in time that social scientists might like to call a 'decision.'

Consider executives who must travel from New York to Chicago for a business meeting. There are innumerable ways to get there. They may drive, take a commercial flight, take a commuter flight, take a bus, take a train, ride a bicycle, hitchhike, ride a camel, take a jitney, run, and so forth. Yet when executives plan trips, they consider only a small fraction of possibilities: driving, taking a commercial flight, taking a commuter flight, chartering a flight, taking a train, or taking a bus. They have been socialized to perceive this subset as 'viable transportation for business trips.' Actually, evaluating even that large a range of alternatives is unlikely. Were they to stop to think about it, they might be able to weigh each alternative on grounds of time, cost, safety, and convenience; they might then choose the best alternative from among this group. But that analysis happens only in economics textbooks, not in real life. It is a normative prescription for one particular, narrow kind of rationality. While they may have the cognitive capacity to perform such calculative feats, executive culture rules out of consideration alternatives that their culture deems unreasonable or inefficient. Further, no one else they know would even think of taking anything but an airplane. They may have a flash of fear in which they think of the latest airplane crash, but even if the thought stays with them through the day they will not cancel the flight, or ride a camel, because there is no choice.

Or consider popular consumption. As a product or activity gains wider acceptance, it is more likely to become part of the social fabric of a group. It not only exists within the cultural framework, but begins to shape that framework. The executives discussed above will certainly fly from New York to Chicago. Not only is flying among a prescribed set of alternatives, but it sits atop this range of options as the most practical. Because flying transports people more quickly than alternatives, it has become the business transportation of choice in American culture. Consequently, businesses assume the convenience and cost of commercial and commuter aviation, and schedule their activities accordingly. It is not unreasonable for a firm in Chicago to demand a New York executive's presence at a meeting the following morning. Commercial aviation's place as culturally approved business transportation has shaped the way Americans do business, further shaping individual choice. Patterns of popular consumption give particular technologies a dominant position among viable alternatives, which is then reflected in day-to-day routines. These technologies become so ingrained in cultural practice that they preclude personal assessment.

Again, it may be possible for executives, or any flyers, to perform the economist's fantasy. But perceptions of airline travel are filtered through a veil of norms, values, and beliefs. Weary travelers rely on a culturally prescribed subset of alternatives, unwittingly eliminating most or even all options. More broadly, business people do not make decisions in such an individualistically rational manner. Theories about decision-making provide precious little illumination of such processes. Rather than thinking about costs and benefits of flying or not, businesspeople are simply doing business. They do not decide to fly or not to fly. They do their work, and the work is comprised of other executives, who are also looking sideways for cues about what to do. People forfeit the opportunity to weigh each alternative within their own value systems, depending instead on the cultural criteria of danger and safety reflected in the framing of alternatives, consumption patterns, and daily cultural routines. Should we set ourselves the task of explaining business travelers' decisions, we would do best to attend to the network of affiliations, and the power relations, in which they are embedded. For it is those relationships that set the cognitive menu that makes it look as if there is a choice between flying or not.

STRUCTURAL SHAPERS

Social structure also mediates 'voluntariness,' creating, shaping, and limiting menus of choice. Examples of the structural mediation of risk are the 'knowledge gaps' that separate people both vertically and horizontally. A more complex division of labor and more abstruse technologies mean that deep technical understanding is limited to ever smaller segments of the population, a *technorati* of people who are highly trained and who speak esoteric languages (see also the chapter in this volume by William Freudenburg). Knowledge gaps emerge between experts and non-experts, informed and uninformed, or indeed between anyone in different structural locations.[15]

Vertical knowledge gaps contribute to viable options being kept off the menu in the first place. People's locations in divisions of labor – especially organizational divisions of labor – are the source of these gaps, which determine what is considered possible at all. Knowledge gaps influence what people recognize as options, some of which may be safer or more efficient. People unacquainted with the production of mountain-climbing equipment may not know that several types of cord exist. They simply buy the type of cord available at the nearest specialty store. They rely on knowledgeable salespeople, technical magazines, and popular advertising to cross the vertical knowledge gaps that limit their own technical expertise. Similarly, we have no choice but to trust airline mechanics, air-traffic controllers, pilots, and airline executives because they are in unique positions to know how aircraft are supposed to function. We do not have the inclination, which is to say the motive and opportunity, to protect ourselves in the skies.

Knowledge gaps prevent all but a small elite from taking part in production decisions. The majority of citizens are partitioned from the organizational, political, and regulatory decision-making that creates automobiles, cigarettes, mountain-climbing cords, junk bonds, heart bypasses, and so forth. For all the talk in the risk literature about 'The Public,' and for all the presumptions of democracy in Western societies, the general public has little to do with which risks are pursued in its name. 'The People,' rather, 'choose' among a highly truncated, certainly constructed, menu of products and technologies that have made it through the production process. The criteria for what gets fed into the process itself – and thus shapes later alternatives – have more to do with marketing, environmental neglect, profit rates, and consolidation of power than anything else. The alternatives that remain on the design-room floor, or stay locked in an alternative imagination, because of red tape, limited funding, expert dissensus, or elite interests do not make it onto the public's menu.

Consider smokers. Until manufacturers introduced low-tar cigarettes onto the market, smokers probably were not aware that such an alternative was available, let alone in early stages of production. Similarly, people unacquainted with automobile safety design were unaware that air bags were a viable safety device until they became an option in some cars. Today, air bags are installed in nearly all new cars, yet bureaucratic red tape, production pressure, or budget constraints could have consigned them to oblivion. People would continue driving cars without air bags, 'voluntarily' undertaking the risks therein, unaware that those risks could have prevented them from being delivered to the showroom. Moreover, the automobile companies fought tooth and nail to prevent safety belts and airbags. Tobacco executives knew a long time ago that their product caused death and destruction and so went to great lengths to limit options that the public might have considered relevant.

The ability to weigh and evaluate alternatives depends on social structure. 'Voluntary' risk assumes a cost–benefit analysis in which people optimize preferences, yet insufficient technical knowledge makes the evaluation of relative costs and benefits impossible. Technically impenetrable choices may as well not exist, because people must be able to place each option within a framework of utility or else there is little sense in speaking of choice at all. People without power lack the opportunity to optimize choices by weighing a broad range of alternatives. It is analogous to someone visiting a restaurant in a foreign country and discovering that the menu is written entirely in an unknown language, except for a single item. Or, to exploit our flying executives one more time, the range of alternatives they really can consider includes a commercial, commuter, or chartered flight. They must evaluate these options in a cost–benefit analysis measuring speed, comfort, efficiency, and safety. Their technical knowledge of these options is limited (especially where safety records are concerned), so they depend on information sources such as television news to bridge vertical knowledge gaps. If a major airplane accident has just occurred, they may avoid a particular airline, airport, or type of aircraft depending on who they perceive is responsible for the crash. They are unlikely, however, to avoid flying altogether. If no accident has occurred recently, they are in general wholly without safety information. They may choose a commuter flight because it is affiliated with a major airline, unaware that commuter services are not actually run by the parent corporation and operate under weaker government safety regulations. Only someone versed in commercial aviation – the *technorati* again – would be aware that a commuter service affiliated with a major airline has its own pilots, crews, training procedures, and safety standards.

Finally, structural mediation impedes the process of risk assessment by creating horizontal knowledge gaps. These fractures occur both within and among organizations, scientific communities, and their corollary regulatory agencies, when expertise, research and/ or control is confined to a small part of a complex system and expert dissensus separates ideological camps.[16] Horizontal gaps restrict the ability to assess risk by obstructing control-group consensus. Fractures within the expert system heighten, rather than alleviate, the lack of technical knowledge by presenting contradictory evidence on what is risky and what is not. Decision-making is reduced to choosing which group or agency to trust, as experts air disputes before a relatively uninformed public. When experts disagree on the effects of smoking, the individual's cost–benefit analysis is clouded. The decision to fly is likewise garbled by competing safety claims of airlines, government regulators, and consumer-watchdog groups.

CONCLUSION

'Voluntariness' is a widely used concept in the literature on risk. The term is critical, as it is often invoked to settle issues of accountability and responsibility. A closer examination of the term 'voluntary risk' reveals three central elements: consciousness, choice, and evaluation. Yet, each of these elements is significantly restricted by cultural and structural factors. Indeed menus of choice constitute the context within which people take their chances, and those menus often leave precious little room for actual choice. These menus rule in and rule out some alternatives as possible; the very idea that something is an alternative to something else depends on the menu in which the choice is situated. By thus situating items (that is, possibilities) on the menu, culture and social structure set the terms by which something is defined as a meaningful alternative. It is the social context, the menu of choice, that we need theories of, not some disembodied, disembedded pretend-decision that rational theory prescribes should be made according to criteria that are usually impossible in the real world.

Rational models of behavior should not be completely jettisoned. Rational theories are indeed quite useful, but in highly delimited contexts (see also the chapter by Ortwin Renn, Carlo Jaeger, Eugene Rosa, and Thomas Webler in this volume). The emphasis here is on things that do not happen, thoughts that do not occur, options that are not available. Of course, it is true that culture and structure enable social action, creating whatever degrees of freedom and choice one may enjoy. Together they are society. But all that exists is not all that can be. By thinking of and finding out about things that do not happen we can explore a wider range of alternatives than we presently see. What is outside the radar of possibility that we think about? What things can we not do?

Partly, this expanded conception of choice entails imagining counterfactual experiences. But we do not advocate merely playing ethereal mindgames. Alternatives rise and are defeated. The winnowing of choice possibilities is itself a social construction, naturally. It is in that winnowing, and what is left after the forces of history and society have exerted their inexorable power, that we will find the origins of menus of choice.

Cultural rules deem certain risks acceptable and frame the perception of alternatives. Popular acceptance of a technology imputes legitimacy, and therefore biases individual decisions. It also constrains individual conception of alternatives not available. A product, activity, or safety device absent from the cultural framework is less likely to be imagined, pursued, or demanded. The cultural definition of acceptable risk thus limits risk perception. Personal value systems become secondary to larger cultural evaluations of risk, danger, and safety.

Structural mediation refers to knowledge gaps that occur both within the scientific community, regulatory agencies, and organizations, as well as between these controlling groups and the general population. Increasing innovation and specialization limit both individual risk assessment and organizational consensus. Expert dissensus and popular ignorance have become the norm in the technological age, as they must. Arguing that people voluntarily choose a particular activity, and thereby consent to its risk, fails to account for insufficient technical knowledge.

It also fails to account for the important fact that one of the things that experts do is keep others from interfering with what they consider to be within their legitimate purview of decision. Individual cost–benefit analysis relies on the communication of technical expertise. Unable to overcome structurally induced confusion, ignorance, or apathy, people cannot fully recognize risk, viable alternatives, or relative costs and benefits. In the light of theories suggesting that mounting complexity increases the risk inherent in certain technologies, knowledge gaps become especially troubling.[17] As specialization increases, some kinds of danger increase while individual awareness of that danger decreases. Experts become increasingly capable of creating mass horrors, and yet the very specialization that allows such feats delimits the degree to which even they understand their own creations. The 'General Public' in all this becomes just an obscure concept in quaint theories of democracy. It may make more sense to speak of powerbrokers, experts, and victims.

We need a reconceptualization of 'voluntary' and 'involuntary' risk and corollary assumptions about accountability and responsibility. The concept of 'voluntariness' has existed in a vacuum, removed from its context within technologically based, expert-dependent culture. Cultural and structural mediation place pure risk assessment beyond the reach of anyone, and certainly beyond local populations that end up with gasoline leaks under their neighborhoods, or peasants with chemically seared lungs, or subsistence fishers and hunters whose prey becomes blackened with oil. While 'voluntary' risk implies a knowledgeable citizenry consciously choosing among a wide range of suitable alternatives, this is rarely the case. Cultural and structural mediation prevents many individuals from discerning risk-decisions, recognizing their alternatives, or weighing those alternatives intelligently. The menus of choice are not of their own construction.

A reasonable question to ask is whether individuals should be held accountable for undertaking risk activities. Explicitly theorizing menus of choice would require re-evaluating notions of personal choice, free will, and individual responsibility. Social scientists should turn their attention toward studying the elements of social life that constrain and restrict choice and understanding, rather than deny their existence behind a veil of 'voluntary' choice.

Menus of choice are socially constructed, but the key constructors are organizations, elites, and experts, not the hapless public. There is a photograph of a man fishing in a pond while wearing a surgeon's mask. He covers his face because he fears the radioactivity from the now dead, yet forever alive, Chernobyl nuclear-power plant. He knows the fish might be dangerous, contaminated with cesium, but he explains to the photographer that 17 people will share the catch and so whatever risk there is will be spread among them.[18] It is a harrowing picture, and one that easily leads to thoughts of the utter irrationality in the poor man's head. But such talk would miss more encompassing issues, would miss how his menus of choice were constructed by others. The fellow, and his comrades, needed to eat. Their geographic mobility and social mobility are related, because like all poor people their movement is restricted. Organizations created Chernobyl, and bureaucrats proclaimed it all safe. Our unfortunate fisher had no choice in the writing of that menu.

We can suggest several directions for further research. First is the examination of structural knowledge gaps, as well as the communication systems that attempt to overcome them. Has technological innovation eclipsed the ability of current communication systems to process information? Research should also abandon 'voluntariness' as a criterion for categorizing risk, and seek out other characteristics around which to erect typologies. Such characteristics should be of the contexts within which things happen that we call decisions. Categorization could hinge on technical complexity – revealing how well individuals and control groups comprehend and control the danger of a particular activity, and how much information must be processed to ensure a minimum level of understanding among all those affected by an innovation. A risk typology could also rest on levels of cultural mediation. It would help to recognize that some risks are unrecognizable, so deeply embedded in a society's culture that they are invisible. A systematic analysis of cultural mediation would begin to reveal these risks and provide the opportunity to re-evaluate their existence. We should move away from 'voluntariness' as a yardstick for responsibility, and move toward more thorough investigations of organizational, scientific, and political accountability. The very idea of voluntary risk imputes chimerical powers of choice to individuals. It thereby shifts responsibility for risk and danger from those who create it to those who bear it.

While people sometimes make relatively informed choices between sets of alternatives, we must be careful not to exaggerate choice among culturally constructed and structurally constrained sets into voluntariness. Inadequate communication of information across knowledge gaps, as well as the social construction of risk activities and their alternatives, undermines traditional notions of free will and personal choice. There may be considerable freedom to choose among items on any particular menu, but that very freedom may lead us away from theorizing the cultural and structural mediation of risk in technologically advanced societies. We have enough theories of how individuals pick something from a menu of danger. What we need now are theories of the menu itself.

NOTES

1. For a different use of these same concepts see B. Mintz and M. Schwartz, *Power Structure of American Business* (Chicago: University of Chicago Press, 1985).
2. C. Starr, 'Social Benefit Versus Technological Risk,' *Science*, 165 (1969): 1232–8.
3. See, for example, H. Nowotny, 'Scientific Purity and Nuclear Danger,' pp. 243–64 in E. Mendelsohn, P. Weingart, and R. Whitely, eds, *The Social Production of Scientific Knowledge* (Boston, MA: D. Reidel, 1977); S. Rayner and R. Cantor, 'How Fair is Safe Enough? The Cultural Approach to Social Technology Choice,' *Risk Analysis*, 7(1) (1987): 3–9; R. Kasperson, O. Renn, P. Slovic, H. Brown, J. Emel, and R. Goble, J. Kasperson, and S. Ratick, 'The Social Amplification of Risk: A Conceptual Framework,' *Risk Analysis*, 8(2) (1988): 177–87; and W. Freudenburg and S. Pastor, 'Public Responses to Technological Risks: Toward a Sociological Perspective,' *Sociological Quarterly*, 33(3) (1992): 389–412.
4. B. Fischhoff, P. Slovic, S. Lichtenstein, S. Read, and B. Combs, 'How Safe is Safe Enough? A Psychometric Study of Attitudes Toward Technological Risks and Benefits,' *Policy Sciences*, 9 (1978): 127–52; C. Perrow, *Normal Accidents* (New York: Basic Books, 1984).
5. L. Clarke, 'Explaining Choices Among Technological Risks,' *Social Problems*, 35(1) (1988): 501–14.
6. J. Gusfield, *The Culture of Public Problems: Drinking-Driving and the Symbolic Order* (Chicago: University of Chicago Press, 1981); T. Pinch, J. Trevor, and W. Bijker, 'The Social Construction of Facts and Artifacts: Or, How the Sociology of Science and the Sociology of Technology Might Benefit Each Other,' *Social Studies of Science*, 18(2) (1988): 147–67;

R. Stallings, 'Media Discourse and the Social Construction of Risk,' *Social Problems*, 37(1) (1990): 80–95; and S. Hilgartner, 'The Social Construction of Risk Objects: Or, How to Pry Open Networks of Risk,' pp. 39–53 in J. Short and L. Clarke, eds, *Organizations, Uncertainties, and Risk* (Boulder, CO: Westview Press, 1989).

 7. W. Freudenburg, 'Risk and Recreancy: Weber, the Division of Labor, and the Rationality of Risk Perceptions,' *Social Forces*, 71(4) (1993): 909–32.

 8. G. Yago, *The Decline of Transit: Urban Transportation in German and US Cities, 1900–1970* (New York: Cambridge University Press, 1984).

 9. J. Jasper, 'The Political Life Cycle of Technological Controversies,' *Social Forces*, 68(2) (1988): 357–77.

10. Freudenburg and Paster, 'Public Responses to Technological Risks.'

11. P. Rothe, *Beyond Traffic Safety* (New Brunswick, NJ: Transaction, 1994).

12. We borrow this term from A. Stinchcombe, 'Social Structure and Organizations,' pp. 142–93 in J. March, *Handbook of Organizations* (Chicago: Rand McNally, 1965).

13. K. Jackson, *Crabgrass Frontier: The Suburbanization of the United States* (New York: Oxford University Press, 1985), pp. 159.

14. S. Lichtenstein and P. Slovic, 'Reversals of Preference Between Bids and Choices in Gambling Decisions,' *Journal of Experimental Psychology*, 89(1) (1971): 46–55; P. Slovic and S. Lichtenstein, 'Preference Reversals: A Broader Perspective,' *American Economic Review*, 72(4) (1983): 596–605; and A. Tversky and D. Kahneman, 'The Framing of Decisions and the Psychology of Choice,' *Science*, 211 (1981): 453–8.

15. See, for instance, A. Mazur, 'Disputes Between Experts,' *Minerva*, 11(2) (1973): 243–62 and C. Heimer, 'Social Structure, Psychology, and the Estimation of Risk,' *Annual Review of Sociology*, 14 (1988): 491–519.

16. S. Plous, 'Biases in the Assimilation of Technological Breakdowns: Do Accidents Make Us Safer?' *Journal of Applied Social Psychology*, 21(13) (1991): 1058–82.

17. Perrow, *Normal Accidents* and S. Sagan, *The Limits of Safety: Organizations, Accidents, and Nuclear Weapons* (Princeton, NJ: Princeton University Press, 1993).

18. Reported by Rolf Lidskog at the workshop from which this volume originates.

Part III
Theoretical Extensions of the Risk Society

4 Dealing with Environmental Risks in Reflexive Modernity

Joris Hogenboom, Arthur P. J. Mol, and Gert Spaargaren

INTRODUCTION

Since the early 1970s sociologists have been attempting to incorporate environmental questions into social theory. The main objective of these efforts has been to gain a better understanding of the birth and development of environmental issues in society and the way society changes in dealing with them. During the 1970s and early 1980s the debate between distinct schools of thought in what we would now label environmental sociology focused on the main institutional dimensions of modern society that should be held responsible for the environmental crisis. To some extent this phase of intellectual development can be interpreted as the environmental 'application' of a more general sociological debate dating back to the 1960s that concentrated on questions relating to whether industrialism, capitalism, or surveillance was the common denominator characterizing modern Western societies.[1]

The past decade has seen a new turn in discussions concerning the relationship between the institutional dimensions of modern society and the environmental problematique in the form of a broader and more general sociological debate on *reflexive modernization*. We contend that this perspective offers considerable promise for analyzing how modern Western societies cope with environmental risks. Though the contributors to the theory of reflexive modernization are quite heterogeneous, they all take the basic idea of 'the modernization of modernity' as both an analytical and normative point of departure. Solutions to the detrimental consequences of modernization (among which environmental risks have a prominent place) are to be found in a radicalization of, rather than a breaking away from, modern institutions and practices. In this respect, reflexive modernization contradicts theories of counter productivity that – parallel to the dominant view of environmental movements in the 1970s and 1980s in most Western countries – stressed the need for a distinct break with modern (industrial) society by arguing for a process of demodernization. On a general and rather abstract level the environmental question has played an important role in developing the core ideas of the theory of reflexive modernization as it interprets the environment as one of the crucial issues around which social transformations take place.[2] According to the theory of reflexive modernization we now live in an era 'beyond left and right' in which emancipatory politics are losing their dominant position in framing societal controversies and developments. In their place 'life politics' or risk controversies ascend as central axes around which social transformations take place.[3] Notwithstanding the centrality of risks, the theory of reflexive modernization should not be interpreted as a social theory of the environment because its scope is much broader and its analysis of environmental risks rather superficial. We think – and this is the main objective of this chapter – that the theory of reflexive modernization may offer an inspiring theoretical framework for analyzing how contemporary modern societies deal (and change in dealing) with the environmental crisis. Furthermore, by focusing exclusively on the environment we may contribute to a more refined interpretation – and 'application' – of the rather broad category of reflexive modernization.

To substantiate the theory of reflexive modernization in an environmental way we make – often implicitly, sometimes explicitly – use of two recent and influential contributions to environmental sociology: the theory of ecological modernization and the theory of risk society. Both perspectives can be treated as being consistent with some of the core ideas of the theory of reflexive modernization and we will use these two partly contrasting frameworks to develop a more comprehensive understanding of how society deals with environmental questions in an age of reflexive modernity. In doing so we will especially focus on the role of science and politics. These two institutions seem crucial to processes of risk interpretation and environmental reform and are undergoing radical transformations in the age of reflexive modernity. Before turning our attention to these two issues we begin with a short introduction to the theories of reflexive modernization, ecological modernization, and risk society.

REFLEXIVE MODERNIZATION, ECOLOGICAL MODERNIZATION AND RISK SOCIETY

If Ulrich Beck did not invent the concept of reflexive modernization, he certainly was responsible for centering it in present-day social theory in his book *Risikogesellschaft*.[4] Originally published in 1986, it became influential in (environmental) sociology during the 1990s especially after its translation into English in 1992. In this work Beck develops a theory about the evolution of the modern order in which the initial process of modernization that converted agrarian society into industrial society will be completed by the transformation of industrial society into risk society.[5] In the first phase of *simple modernization* continuing economic and technological developments result in growing prosperity and welfare. However, the increasing production of goods is accompanied by the expansion and movement to the fore of previously unrecognized social, economic and ecological risks. In this second phase of reflexive modernization these negative side-effects become dominant. Reflexive modernization means in the first place the 'self-confrontation' of modern society with the negative consequences of modernization. While controversies concerning the distribution of goods and prosperity are crucial to the constitution of industrial society, the transition to the risk society is characterized by conflicts regarding risks. Risks transcend into a dominant feature of everyday life, engendering paralyzing feelings of anxiety among large groups of individuals. Furthermore, the risks produced by modern institutions strike these very institutions like a boomerang. Social controversies about environmental and technological risks are in essence conflicts about the social and economic consequences of risk management, and can become a major threat to the responsible institutions.

Thus, in what Beck refers to as an 'empirically oriented projective social theory,' reflexive modernization is put on a par with the birth of risk society and refers to a condition in which progress can turn into self-destruction. However, apocalyptic as his analysis seems, Beck's rather indistinct exposition leaves room for a slightly more optimistic scenario, one in which modern society may be able to ward off its self-destruction by way of self-criticism and renewal. This apparent paradox implies that though science and technology are held to a high degree of responsibility for the emergence of the risk society, they are simultaneously seen as indispensable institutions to overcome it. Scientific rationality takes a key position in perceiving negative side-effects, criticizing practices, and indicating alternatives. This capacity should include a process of *reflexive scientization* in which scientific rationality is critically applied to demystify the foundations of its own negative consequences. In any case, all possible routes out of the risk society imply the further modernization of rationality and modern institutions.[6]

Anthony Giddens unmistakably feels affinity with Beck's work, but his contribution to the debate on reflexive modernization is quite distinct.[7] He parallels Beck to a considerable extent in emphasizing the changing 'risk profile' of modern society. Giddens notes that scientific and technological developments have reduced many premodern risks like famine and natural disasters, but are at the same time jointly responsible for the emergence of new types of ecological risks. However, Giddens deviates from Beck's apocalyptic risk society scenario and gives a much more nuanced interpretation of present-day processes of globalization as well as the changing position and role of both science and experts in modern society. Furthermore, he extensively explores the consequences for the constitution of everyday practices and the feelings of security and trust among individuals.

In contrast to premodern times, Giddens asserts, contemporary daily practices are constantly evaluated and modified in the light of a continuous flow of incoming information stemming from expert systems. Instead of following relatively durable life patterns, as was the case in tradition, individuals must actively shape their own lives, often by choosing from a plurality of options. Furthermore, they have to do so in circumstances where no certainties can be obtained about the conditions for and consequences of their decisions, since expert knowledge on which they depend is always open to revision. The concept of 'reflexivity' for Giddens thus means that the idea of a continuous rationalization and control of material processes and social practices, central to the Enlightenment, comes to an end. Science becomes disenchanted and scientific authority makes way for an 'institutionalization of doubt.' At the same time, trust in expert systems is a necessary part of daily life, and a fragile phenomenon in the modern era when lay people must deal with conflicting knowledge claims and competing experts. Giddens' work provides a rich theoretical entrance to study contemporary feelings of anxiety and insecurity in relation to the changing character of science and expert systems, and to incorporate trust as a central issue.[8]

Although Beck and Giddens elaborate on reflexive modernization as a general theory of social continuity and change in modern society, the ecological question is interpreted as one of the most pressing social problems that brings about such transformations. Environmental issues – in particular risks with global range and 'high consequences' – place the more general features of reflexive modernity most clearly in the fore. Such concerns contribute to the disenchantment of science and technology, the widespread diffusion of insecurity and anxiety throughout society, the necessity for everyone to choose from different options regarding questions of how to live, the lay public's dependency on recondite expertise, and the importance of public trust in the expertise required for maintaining ontological security.

Although many of these elements as such do not appear in the theory of ecological modernization, the latter can nevertheless be placed in the same theoretical tradition as the elaborations of Beck and Giddens on reflexive modernization. Ecological modernization focuses less on questions of risks in everyday life and trust vested in expert systems, but rather concentrates on issues concerning transformations of production and consumption processes induced by ecological considerations. Its central concepts and premises are allied to those of Beck's more optimistic views on modern society surmounting ecological risks. At the same time, ecological modernization offers a more profound analysis of how modern society repairs the so-called structural design faults of modernity that give rise to the environmental crisis. Ecological modernization theorists such as Joseph Huber and Martin Jänicke maintain that we can already analyze some of the starting institutional transformations for overcoming these flaws being actively and reflexively shaped by governments, corporations, environmental movements, and individual citizens. Science and technology, as well as the modernization of environmental politics, are key movers in this (reflexive) process of ecological reform, one that implies a radical restructuring of social processes of production and consumption in accordance with criteria of ecological rationality.

From this summary we may conclude that the theory of ecological modernization focuses predominantly on institutional reflexivity, while Beck and especially Giddens pay much more attention to reflexivity in everyday life. Furthermore, both Giddens and (most prominently) Beck analyze in detail the disenchantment of science and the negative side-effects of technological developments, while ecological modernization theorists stress the role of science in the emergence of an ecological rationality. Thus, both theories are partially equipped – and are to some extent complementary – for studying social phenomena related to reflexive modernization. Although there exists some tension between the more apocalyptic undertones in risk society *vis-à-vis* the more positive perspective of ecological modernization, they do not contradict each other as fundamentally as is sometimes stated. They share – in contrast to proponents of environmental de- and postmodernization schools of thought – the commitment that all ways out of the ecological crisis will lead more deeply into modernity.

ENVIRONMENTAL RISKS AND THE CHANGING ROLE OF SCIENCE

Within the environmental sciences and politics the notion of risk has been developed mainly in accordance with a technological, natural science-based, approach. Conceptualizing environmental problems in terms of risks that can be quantified and assessed scientifically has become, for instance, very prominent in Dutch environmental politics. This so-called risk approach (*risicobenadering*) has evolved as an instrument to provide policy-makers with a strong (that is unquestionable) scientific basis for determining environmental standards through which to legitimate tough regulatory measures.

Although the natural science-based risk approach has been important for environmental politics since the early 1970s, most commentators and policy-makers agree that the process of dealing with risks is much more complicated than is suggested by the conventional model of 'policy-makers adhering to natural science-based facts.' This customary approach is unacceptable as a normative framework for policy-making due to its denial of the social character of risk policies. Additionally, it is unsuitable for its task because it underplays the ambiguities that are inherently connected to modern science and technology in an age of reflexive modernity. Critics of natural science-based risk models often present a (strong) constructivist approach to risk as a radical alternative. In this section we will, against the background of the theory of reflexive modernization, discuss some of the main problems encountered when assessing environmental risks from either a natural science perspective or a strong constructivist approach. The extensive debate on environmental risks that has developed within the social sciences in recent years provides a promising point of departure for our discussion.

Social Sciences and Environmental Risks

One could almost pose that a whole new discipline – which can be referred to as social studies of risk – has arisen complete with its own concepts, theories, working groups, and journals. This discipline encompasses more conventional areas of inquiry such as sociology, psychology, anthropology, and political science. Notwithstanding the differences among the various perspectives, these social science approaches converge in their denunciation of risk as 'a certain calculable possibility that a certain negative effect will occur' – as is the explicit definition employed by practitioners of natural science-based risk assessment. The former group focuses on the social processes by which individuals and social institutions observe, perceive, define, and experience risks, both inside and outside official politics. While from the start social science studies of risks have examined mainly technological and natural risks, gradually the environment has moved to the center of attention. Here, environmental issues are not analyzed primarily as self-evident problems stemming from social institutions and actions, nor is the main emphasis on possible ways to handle these dilemmas in modern society. Rather, the perception and delineation of environmental issues by different groups in society and the controversies between social actors concerning definitions of and responses to risks are given pivotal position. The role of science in processes of risk interpretation provides one of the most important focal points in social studies of risk.

The first observation that might be drawn from this body of literature concerns the broad spectrum of risk dimensions found to contribute to the meaning of risk. From diverging and sometimes conflicting approaches, psychologists, sociologists, and anthropologists have stressed different elements in this respect. Psychologists were the first to point to the importance of such features as 'controllability' and 'voluntariness' and they also found personal characteristics (e.g. gender, education) to be key determinants of risk perception.[9] Sociologists and anthropologists have taken as their task the development of a more 'contextual approach' of risk perception, one that incorporates cultural values, social circumstances, and social interactions into the frame of analysis.[10] Without discussing nuances, we can identify two relevant conclusions from this research. First, differences in risk perception between the lay public and the scientific community cannot simply be contrasted in terms of rationality and irrationality (as is often suggested in public debates). Second, a singularly (or even predominantly) natural science-based approach cannot provide an adequate understanding of risks because it denies important and legitimate dimensions grounded in social relations and other experiential parameters.

Risk assessments are confronted with many scientific uncertainties, for example about possible impacts, exposure pathways, dose-effect relations, and extrapolations from laboratory experiments to real-world situations. Most natural scientists have no problems interpreting scientific uncertainties as relevant social dimensions of their evaluations. Assessing risks under these circumstances means making assumptions and choices that are strongly connected with social considerations and values. Notwithstanding the importance of dealing with these uncertainties in scientific analyses, the involvement of social considerations in risk assessments cannot be reduced to mere uncertainties. Risk definitions vary due to the different social and political assumptions embedded within natural scientists' models. To analyze risks experts simply *have* to make assumptions about the social and natural world, for instance which possible effects are important and which groups of people and regions of the world may be affected.[11] This means that 'objective risks' as such do not exist. Instead, we often observe different experts posing a wide range of conflicting claims about the 'real risk.' When experts maintain that their risk analyses are value-free and purely scientific, and the lay public is confronted with contradictory signals, problems in risk communication will intensify.[12]

Following theorists of reflexive modernization, controversies around objectivity, certainty, and the diversity of knowledge claims in risk debates are connected with a more general characteristic of modern science. As Giddens illuminates, doubt and skepticism – implying that all knowledge can be revised in the light of new information – have always been a major driving force in enlarging scientific knowledge and are consequently at the origin of the Enlightenment's assertions to certainty.[13] Paradoxically, while doubt is the condition for providing certainty, it is exactly the radicalization of this principle in late modernity that has raised ambiguity and uncertainty in debates on risk and the environment. This incertitude, and the involvement of social dimensions in risk assessment, point to the limits of scientific rationality (see also the chapter by Ortwin Renn, Carlo Jaeger, Eugene Rosa, and Thomas Webler in this volume).

This awareness becomes even clearer when we switch our attention from the evaluation of risk as a scientific activity to the role this type of research plays in society. Risks are assessed by science, but not simply adopted by social institutions. Risk definition is a complex social process that involves many actors: risk-producing institutions, groups of people confronting risks, government agencies, scientists, and environmental organizations. Each of these entities has particular interests and tries to influence risk definition and control in accordance with its unique perspective. As Beck stresses, risk conflicts are to a large extent struggles regarding social and economic risks – for affected groups as well as for risk producers – that result from environmental risk management and control. In risk controversies agents use scientific findings and uncertainties as important resources. This feature not only influences risk definitions, but also brings science in its 'contested' role of authority further to the centre of attention. In the Netherlands, for example, there are some small groups (e.g. the Dutch branch of the Heidelberg Appeal), as well as 'individual experts,' active in the environmental field who systematically attack the scientific foundations of policy interventions. Global climate change and the contribution of manure to acidification are two domains in which these actors have operated with relative success. More influential, however, is a report by the prestigious Scientific Council for Government Policy (WRR) in which it was claimed that no 'hard scientific core' exists on which environmental politics can be founded.

According to the Council, a broad diversity of normative and political considerations present in society, as well as existing scientific uncertainties (which will continue to exist), hinder an unambiguous interpretation of the concept of sustainability necessary to build effective environmental policy. WRR argues in favor of the acceptance and further development of a plurality of views concerning sustainability, each connected with diverging visions of how to deal with environmental facts, uncertainties, and social and environmental risks. Obviously, each interpretation generates different options for policy scenarios and related environmental quality.[14] It is the political debate among these divergent views that informs processes leading to the adoption of concrete environmental policy programs. This point of view was used to attack the no less distinguished Dutch National Environmental Planning Agency (RIVM), as well as Professor Johannes Opschoor, a leading Dutch environmental economist. RIVM and Opschoor acknowledged the social dimensions of setting environmental standards and making environmental risk assessments, but refused to concede that this gave natural scientific inquiries any less decisive value in claims-making regarding the environment, ecological disruption, and desired amenity qualities. Both the policy body and the economist asserted that natural scientific knowledge can help in discriminating between conflicting environmental story lines and between different policy programs. Or as van Hengel and Gremmen assert: 'Sustainability can be considered as a universal, rational norm, whose cognitive delineation can in principle be deduced from normatively-informed scientific knowledge about the environment.'[15]

Risk Society and Constructivism

The contested role of science in dealing with environmental risks in late modernity is especially emphasized in Ulrich Beck's theory of risk society. Beck stresses the thoroughly social character of risk definitions, with social agents attempting to define risks according to their own prerogatives. Science – and especially the mechanism of emphasizing scientific uncertainties – is used as a resource to achieve economic and political ends. By strenuously questioning the role of science and technology in the context of his concept of 'organized irresponsibility,' Beck seems to have paved the way for a new round of debate on the role of these mechanisms of modernity.[16] Furthermore, we can observe that in the sociology of science argumentation concerning the so-called 'constructivist perspective' on science and the environment has become very prominent. Environmental sociologist Peter Dickens contends the stronger constructivist perspectives are easily moving from the late-modern idea that no absolute certainties exist to the proposition that 'the environment is a purely social construction . . . simply a product of language, discourse and power-plays.'[17] In fact, this form of social constructivism reduces nature and reality to human knowledge about it – it *only* exists as a product of knowledge. In our view three basic ideas of constructivist perspectives should be distinguished.

First, constructivists stress the idea that human knowledge about reality is always created in social processes, and consequently that reality is variously understood in different societies and social groups.

This is basically what Hannigan illustrates and analyzes in his book on environmental sociology.[18] Second, some constructivists emphasize that because of the social embeddedness of knowledge, no 'true knowledge' is possible and that, by implication, no distinction can be made between more or less 'objective' or 'true' understandings of reality. Finally, strong constructivism asserts that reality only exists, and only has impacts on society, if and so far as we come to understand it socially.

We think constructivists have important contributions to make regarding the first point, that is in evaluating the origin of knowledge and how societies develop a specific understanding of the natural and social world. However, from analysis of the social embeddedness of knowledge we can and should not conclude that all knowledge is equally true and that, associated with diverging knowledge claims, multiple realities exist. Nature and environmental damage exist independently of human knowledge about it. It should be stressed that although knowledge is socially constructed and all knowledge claims are permanently open to revision, this concession does not imply the absence of systemic knowledge.

While Beck's emphasis on the social character of the processes that contribute to risk definitions and the declining authority of science seem in agreement with a (strong) social constructivist position, the 'other side of Beck' appears to reflect a strong 'realist' approach.[19] In outlining his perspective of reflexive modernization, he asserts that the risk society comes into being 'unknown and unseen,' without human beings noticing it.[20] He strongly discriminates between reflexivity and reflection. Reflexivity means that:

> [M]odernization undercuts modernization unintended and unseen, and therefore also reflection-free, with the force of autonomized modernization ... [T]his can quite well take place without reflection, beyond knowledge and consciousness. Reflexivity of modernity can lead to reflection on the self-dissolution and self-endangerment of industrial society, but it need not do so.[21]

How reflexive modernization in Beck's sense can occur without reflection is not clear to us. We would maintain that environmental issues in most cases only become socially relevant (as a source for concern and a driving force for social change) when acknowledged by human beings. Correspondingly, dangers to industrial society can only start to dominate public and private debates and conflicts (as Beck puts it) when they are *perceived* as potential dangers.

Both sides of Beck, contradictory as they are, underestimate the central position of expertise in modern societies dealing with environmental risks, be it no longer with the authority natural sciences had during the phase of 'simple modernization.' However, in contrast to the 1960s and early 1970s, today this central role of scientific expertise in dealing with environmental risks can no longer be reduced to an overall negative contribution – as Beck sketches in his account of the 'blindness' of science to the risks it has itself created to a large extent. Such an Ellulian interpretation disregards the increasingly essential role that contemporary science plays in risk observation, contra-expertise, and risk reduction.

ENVIRONMENTAL RISKS AND THE MODERNIZATION OF POLITICS

As suggested at the onset of this chapter, coping with environmental risks in an age of late or reflexive modernity is also related to what might be called the end of traditional politics. Traditional politics is characterized by the central position of conventional institutions of the nation-state (e.g. state bureaucracy, political parties, and parliament) and focus on the dominant political controversies involving the distribution of welfare. The theory of reflexive modernization emphasizes transformations in these dominant institutions and distributional political controversies. Furthermore, corresponding to our earlier discussion, environmental risks are assigned a crucial role in this process of political transformation. With regard to the diminishing importance of distributional conflicts Giddens has articulated the emergence of life politics of which environmental issues are a part, while Beck points at partly similar modifications in stressing the political emergence of risk issues and the decreasing attention devoted to customary questions concerning economic distributions (the allocation of 'goods').[22] The diminishing relevance of class divisions goes together with the disappearing traditional political classifications of left and right so often analyzed by contemporary social scientists and political commentators. Issues of life politics and risks cannot divide political parties and social groups along the same lines as distributional conflicts have done in the last century, although it does not mean that environmental risks are distributed equally over the world.

These contemporary political controversies give rise to novel ways, strategies, and institutions to deal with them. Before addressing in more detail the changes regarding the principal institutions and the political 'mechanisms' for managing these new dominant political controversies, we will briefly address what we have elsewhere labeled the 'modernization of politics.' In proceeding along these lines we will concentrate on the modernization of politics related to only one – albeit essential – issue of life politics, namely questions of ecological risks.

During the early 1980s, against a background of economic decline and more than a decade after the establishment of various new political institutions designed to mitigate the problems that emerged during the so-called first wave of environmental concern, the state in a number of industrialized countries came under indictment for its inability and ineffectiveness to regulate and control sources of ecological deterioration. It was especially the theory of state failure that delivered the charge of incompetence against the modern state.[23] Although the environment was not the only realm on which the state was believed to fail in fulfilling its obligations, it was this policy domain that came under scrutiny as one of the prime and most controversial areas, especially with the emergence of a second wave of environmental concern in the late 1980s. Two lines of clarification were put forward to understand the 'logic' of state failure.

The first component of this argument relied heavily on neo-Marxist and critical theory to claim that the capacity of the state in capitalist society to regulate the negative side-effects of economic processes was limited. This specific position of the 'capitalist state' would eventually result in severe problems of legitimacy and effectiveness, especially in times of economic decline. The second element of this argument took a more historical perspective. While the nation-state is still held accountable for solving most of the social and environmental abuses within its territory, its powers to actually do so are undermined, and to some extent wither away, due to what Giddens describes as 'the intensification of worldwide social relations which link distant localities in such a way that local happenings are shaped by events occurring many miles away and vice versa.'[24] Global economic, political, and cultural processes contribute both to the (perception of) failure of the nation-state to act effectively in protecting its territory from environmental deterioration and to difficulties in legitimizing its actions. These inadequacies are all the more true for environmental problems that have a strong supra-national dimension, either because pollutants cross borders or because the causes of degradation are closely interrelated with supra-national economic processes.

This 'crisis of the welfare state' crystallized into a 'modernization of politics' to cope with tendencies of state failure regarding, among others, continuing environmental deterioration. This 'modernization of politics' should, of course, not be analyzed purely as the sole result of intentional strategies in and by state institutions. By shaping new types of cooperation and reforming daily routines, other social actors have actively contributed to the origination, construction, and specific design of novel political structures. We will elaborate here on two 'modernization strategies,' specifically the modernization of conventional politics and the emergence of subpolitics.

Modernization of Conventional Politics

The modernization of conventional politics, or political modernization as it is often labeled in the literature on ecological modernization, starts from two cross-cutting premises: the role of the state is essential on ecological questions, but its performance up until now has been highly questionable.[25] Although, following the argumentation of state failure, ecological modernization theorists are critical of the role of a strong bureaucratic state in the redirection of processes of production and consumption, they do not deny the state's indispensable role in environmental management, as some of the theory's critics would have it.[26] Rather, the state should modernize its environmental involvement basically in two ways.

First, some tasks, responsibilities, and incentives for environmental restructuring and reform can and should shift from the state to the market. Economic mechanisms (often but not always developed and introduced – directly or indirectly – by the government) can be redesigned, introduced, and activated to let them work in the direction of less pollution and more efficient use of natural resources. For instance, ecological taxation, levies, value-added differentiation, and charges create economic distinctions in products and production processes on ecological grounds. Besides these government-installed market dynamics, private economic actors become involved in triggering environmental reform, for example when customers and consumers demand the certification of products and processes, insurance companies and credit institutions ask for environmental audits of industrial producers, industries compete on environmental performance, and producers search for niche markets predicated upon high standards of ecological accountability. The envisaged net result is more efficient and effective environmental reform, as well as the alleviation of some of the state's environmental responsibilities. By utilizing market dynamics to promote environmental reform and by leaving less – albeit essential – elements of environmental policy-making to central (and localized) governmental bodies, the state is prevented from becoming an environmental Leviathan.[27]

Second, in those areas where the state continues to fulfill a central role, its hierarchical and centralized functions should be abandoned. Following the movement toward growing complexity, the creation of global economic interdependencies, the need to adapt environmental programs to local circumstances, and the necessity for flexibility in environmental planning, state environmental policy changes from curative and reactive to preventive. In other words, there is a transition away from 'closed' to participatory policy-making, from centralized to decentralized state institutions, from prescribing the means of environmental reform to the creation of mechanisms that establish standards and norms but leave specific measures and strategies to the polluters, and from dirigistic governance to the formulation of favorable conditions for environmental reform by enterprises. This transformation is often referred to as reflexive governance, communicative governance, or consensual steering.[28] Examples of this new approach can be found in Dutch environmental policy with respect to industrial production. Environmental authorities in the Netherlands have facilitated the emergence of the so-called 'target-group approach,' the expanded use of voluntary agreements (over 100 were put in place between 1987 and 1994), the widespread diffusion of environmental management and auditing systems and eco-labeling schemes, and the development of an integrated region-oriented approach (for instance as now applies in the industrial areas of Rotterdam/Rijnmond and Sas van Gent-Terneuzen). In a comparative study of Denmark, Austria, and the Netherlands we found that this approach is not limited to the Dutch context, although it appears in different forms under distinct 'policy styles,' political cultures, or national traditions.[29]

We can summarize criticism of these processes of political modernization in three points. First, the effectiveness of such actions is more than incidentally questioned, as is the assumption that political modernization is an answer to state failure. Although the fierce opposition to these political innovations in the Netherlands and elsewhere – especially by environmental non-governmental organizations (NGOs), legal experts, and some factions within the bureaucracy – has partially diminished, allegations concerning effectiveness regularly reappear. Second, the democratic outlook of these new forms of policy-making is challenged because in practical application legislative bodies often play a very limited role and environmental NGOs are set aside as part of the effort to create consensus. Third, while we welcome in general these innovations in policy style, taken together with the introduction of market mechanisms in environmental reform there is the danger of a withering away of the central state in setting the agenda, standards, goals and long-term strategies for safeguarding environmental quality. We can indeed identify such tendencies in Dutch policy-making in which the central state is withdrawing into a more facilitating than norm-setting role, leaving the major controversies for the municipalities and provinces. Political modernization should not mean that the traditional command-and-control approach is completely discarded. Rather, the conventional tools must function as important sticks and safety nets in those – still numerous – situations in which this new consensual policy style stalls or fails, and market dynamics prove to be inadequate or insufficient.

ENVIRONMENTAL 'SUBPOLITICS'

A second innovation accompanies the modernization of conventional environmental politics, namely the emergence of so-called environmental 'subpolitics.'[30] In a number of cases the core political institutions of parliament, bureaucracy, and political parties are no longer considered adequate to deal with environmental risks. Especially in instances where governmental policy (1) remains restricted to natural science-based approaches toward environmental risks, leaving questions of public perceptions, norms, and values unaddressed, (2) is immobilized by internal conflicts of interest, and (3) proves to be too bureaucratic, rigid, and universal to meet the complex diversity of society–nature interactions, state policy is increasingly criticized and environmental politics are triggered by other actors outside these traditional institutions. The proposed dumping of the Shell oil platform *Brent Spar* in 1995 is the most cited example of – in this case even international – subpolitical decision-making. Greenpeace International, numerous motorists passing Shell gas stations, and some ministers acting on private grounds (although announced publicly) to prevent the dumping, paralyzed for two weeks the Dutch and British governments (the home countries of the multinational company). The *Brent Spar* controversy is generally put forward as a singular case of subpolitics. While the international character and the high mediagenics contributed to this perception and interpretation of exceptional quality, the principle of environmental politics operating outside traditional institutions and with unusual actors is becoming widespread and multiform. By analyzing a few Dutch examples of subpolitics on the institutional and individual levels we aim to show both the diversity and the extensive diffusion of this novel approach to contesting environmental claims.

In the Netherlands and some other countries a tendency is emerging where environmental negotiations are taking place between environmental NGOs and business representatives, bypassing the government. Because of dissatisfaction with governmental pesticide policy, Friends of the Earth Netherlands in 1994 negotiated agreements with potato farmers to reduce their use of agro-chemicals. Similar examples can be found in, for instance, the United States where in 1986 – in reaction to the stagnation of pesticide policy – a coalition of environmental and consumer organizations and pesticide producers almost succeeded in getting a bill on pesticide reduction and innovation accepted by Congress.[31] For a considerable time the World Wildlife Fund (WWF) has regularly marketed its *Panda* logo by negotiating with producers to use it on environmentally sound products and services. The prevalence of environmental subpolitics is also exemplified by the influential Dutch environmental NGO *Stichting Natuur en Milieu (SNM)* that negotiated in 1997 an agreement with Shell to reduce greenhouse-gas emissions beyond the level required by the government. Obviously, it is no longer sufficient for industries to follow only governmental standards; they also have to take non-state environmental requirements into account.

A second domain in which we witness environmental subpolitics is the so-called environmental cooperatives of farmers. In this instance, regional forms of cooperation are used to integrate environmental protection into agricultural practices and to encourage farmers to take collective responsibility for fulfilling environmental targets. This approach can be seen as a type of self-regulation, one in which the 'market' of nature and environment is better articulated. These initiatives are a reaction to rather rigid and undifferentiated governmental policies that were not adapted to local conditions. Additionally, these local associations meet a consumer demand for locally produced food with short and 'verifiable' product chains between producer and consumer.

Of a quite distinct order is the subpolitical intervention of individual citizens in securing safe drinking water. The Netherlands is well known for its high-quality drinking water, delivered to all households and safeguarded by an impressive expert system of highly qualified scientists and technologists, a network of advanced purification technologies, and a series of preventive environmental policies from the central and regional governments. Still, a growing group of consumers is alarmed by reports about water quality threats and distrusts the safety claims put forward by this expert system. Citizens take their own subpolitical measures. They exclusively use bottled water for drinking and cooking, buy additionally purified water in health food stores and some supermarkets, and install activated carbon filters on their home taps. In 1988, over 150 000 Dutch consumers no longer relied on conventional sources of drinking water and this number has increased over the past decade.[32] These practices, strongly influenced by proprietors with a commercial interest, might jeopardize the existing expert system for providing safe drinking water.

A further form of subpolitical arrangements evident in the Netherlands is the so-called 'ecoteams,' each comprising a group of approximately ten households and organized on the street or neighborhood level. The idea was strongly influenced and triggered by both severe criticism of the slow progress and meager results of governmental environmental policy and the emerging conviction that individual households are important contributors to environmental problems. Members of these ecoteams monitor their own environmental impacts, discuss the results regularly with their neighbors, and exchange experiences and advice to lower the impact of each household. This monitoring is not restricted to the use of water, gas, and electricity, but also includes different streams of waste, mobility, washing behavior, and internal reuse. At the moment there are about 2000 ecoteams in the Netherlands, a figure that contrasts sharply with the original goal of 140 000 by 1997. Nonetheless, this institutionalized form of social control has penetrated into the center of private life and is being coordinated by an international NGO with national branches. Recently, some Dutch provincial governments have decided to stimulate and financially support these initiatives.

CONCLUSION

In this chapter we have used the theories of ecological modernization and the risk society to understand and interpret the changing role of science and politics in dealing with environmental risks in an era of reflexive modernization. At first glance, and especially in the initial contributions to these traditions, both theories contrast sharply on both the role of science and technology and the political innovations required to deal with environmental risks.[33] We have elaborated elsewhere on these differences.[34] More recent extensions of these theories, however, show a growing correspondence, especially regarding political innovations, and it is on these contributions to environmental sociology that we try to evaluate the changing role of politics and science in dealing with environmental risks.

The examples of subpolitical environmental reform we described serve to illustrate that conventional political institutions and actors no longer have a monopoly on political decision-making and environmental politics.[35] In this sense, political modernization and subpolitics should not be seen as two completely different alternatives – related to distinct social theories – to conventional politics, but rather as two variants that are directly in line with each other and even partly overlap.[36] In most cases these innovations construct creative new answers to the challenges of late modernity in which the traditional position of the nation-state is compromised. But when related to environmental politics, the following points should be kept in mind.

First, these innovations do not imply a withering away of conventional political institutions concerned with environmental reform. As we have argued before, with respect to a broad number of environmental risks, the nation-state remains the most important normative and regulative institution.[37] It is especially within the framework set and controlled by the nation-state that these innovations show their advantages as 'alternatives.' No matter how 'contested' the nation-state's environmental efforts are, an atrophication of its environmental role would strongly affect the relative successes of these novel developments.

Second, several disadvantages can be related to certain forms of political innovation. From our examples we can mention the potential undermining of 'conventional' expert systems as in the case of drinking water and the colonization of the life-world, not by the imperatives of state and market as Jürgen Habermas has theorized upon, but by ecoteams from the life-world. Furthermore, there is a lack of democratic control and a neglect of certain societal interests in cases of political modernization and negotiated subpolitical agreements between NGOs and business. We indicate these drawbacks not so much to stress the shortcomings, or even dangers, of such activities. Rather, we should assess the modernization of environmental politics with a set of criteria that looks beyond narrow ecological effectiveness.

Third, it is useful to reflect on the changing role of science and technology in late modernity in instances in which environmental issues are involved. Most forms of subpolitics and political modernization rely as much on modern science and technology as more customary ways of environmental reform. In this sense, these alternatives do not provide an answer to Beck's radical criticism of the role of science and technology in environmental politics. Ecoteams, as an example of citizen organizations motivated to contribute to environmental reform, are not to be interpreted as soft and 'small-is-beautiful' groups at the periphery of societal development that are worried about plastic bags and are fighting for appropriate technology windmills. These activists are knowledgeable and capable agents who are engaged in environmental auditing schemes and energy exchange coefficients of different materials, and they negotiate with public utilities on favorable conditions for selling back energy produced by their technologically advanced windmills. Also, consumers who no longer rely on the central drinking-water system, simply cannot opt for consumption practices in which expert knowledge is abandoned. Instead of the more conventional, centralized source of expertise they depend on purification technologies at the tap or purveyors of bottled water, both of which are equally related to modern science and technology.

Finally, the former conclusion does not mean that the societal position of science and technology remains unaltered under conditions of reflexive modernity. As we have described in this chapter, the authority of scientific expertise to provide certainties has been diminished in both public debates and private life. This knowledge system will never return to its 'original' Enlightenment character.

58

Nonetheless, we should not exaggerate the transformations in the role of science in dealing with environmental risks. Society has not turned its back on science and expertise in addressing environmental concerns. Furthermore, scientific knowledge and modern technology have proved not to be a static and monolithic block, but are reflexively modified and increasingly relate to solutions to environmental questions, and not only or mainly to the origination of environmental catastrophes. Related to both of these observations is that the public's ambiguous attitude concerning scientific expertise is not consistent across all environmental risks and under all social conditions. The so-called high-consequence risks – most prominently global warming and genetic engineering – as well as threats directly affecting everyday life such as food safety (e.g. mad cow disease) and contaminated drinking water, contribute to this perception of a radically different public role for science. Simultaneously, less mediagenic and science-challenging hazards – for example, water pollution, soil degradation, noise, solid waste, acidification, and even ozone layer depletion – are environmental problems that continue to be treated in more or less the 'normal' way. Elaborations on this 'contextuality' of the changing role of science in dealing with environmental risks may enrich theories of reflexive modernization.

NOTES

1. For a more extensive discussion of these theoretical issues in environmental sociology, see A. Mol, *The Refinement of Production: Ecological Modernization Theory and the Chemical Industry* (Utrecht: Jan van Arkel/ International Books, 1995) and G. Spaargaren, *The Ecological Modernization of Production and Consumption: Essays in Environmental Sociology* (Wageningen: Wageningen Agricultural University, 1997).
2. Elsewhere we have pointed to the considerable attention paid to environmental issues in sociological theories of reflexive modernization, especially when compared to the rather peripheral position of these questions in mainstream sociological theory before the late 1980s. See, in particular, Mol, *The Refinement of Production* and Spaargaren, *The Ecological Modernization of Production and Consumption*.
3. A. Giddens, *Beyond Left and Right: The Future of Radical Politics* (Cambridge: Polity Press, 1994).
4. U. Beck, *Risk Society: Toward a New Modernity* (London: Sage, 1992).
5. In his book *Risk Society* Beck situates the start of this second transformation in the 1970s, but in later contributions he is less clear

concerning the question of whether he is describing present developments or a potential future scenario.

6. Importantly, Beck diverges from the position articulated by Zygmunt Bauman. Bauman argues that the theory of the risk society implies that modern institutions are fundamentally incapable of overcoming the ecological crisis and that a movement away from modern institutions – towards de- or post-modernity – remains the only option. See Z. Bauman, *Postmodern Ethics* (Oxford: Basil Blackwell, 1993).

7. A. Giddens, *The Consequences of Modernity* (Cambridge: Polity Press, 1990) and his 'Living in a Post-Traditional Society,' pp. 56–109 in U. Beck, A. Giddens, and S. Lash, *Reflexive Modernization: Politics, Tradition, and Aesthetics in the Modern Social Order* (Cambridge: Polity Press, 1994).

8. We have used Giddens' framework for empirical studies of present-day feelings of anxiety and insecurity concerning environmental risks affecting daily life in relation to expert systems on drinking water and sun bathing. See J. Hogenboom, *Environmental Risk and Everyday Life: The Constitution of Daily Practices Connected with Environmental Risks*, unpublished PhD thesis, Wageningen Agricultural University, forthcoming.

9. See, for example, B. Fischhoff, P. Slovic, S. Lichtenstein, S. Read, and B. Combs, 'How Safe is Safe Enough? A Psychometric Study of Attitudes Towards Technological Risks and Benefits,' *Policy Sciences*, 9 (1978): 127–52 and P. Slovic, 'Perception of Risk: Reflections on the Psychometric Paradigm,' pp. 117–52 in S. Krimsky and D. Golding, eds, *Social Theories of Risk* (Westport, CT: Praeger, 1992).

10. Krimsky and Golding, *Social Theories of Risk*; J. Brown, ed., *Environmental Threats: Perception, Analysis, and Management* (London: Belhaven Press, 1989); M. Douglas, *Risk Acceptability According to the Social Sciences* (New York: Russell Sage Foundation, 1985); and O. Renn and E. Swaton, 'Psychological and Sociological Approaches to the Study of Risk Perception,' *Environment International*, 10 (1984): 557–75.

11. For example, B. Wynne, 'Frameworks of Rationality in Risk Management: Towards the Testing of Naïve Sociology,' pp. 33–47 in Brown, *Environmental Threats*; B. Wynne, 'May the Sheep Safely Graze? A Reflexive View of the Expert–Lay Knowledge Divide,' pp. 44–83 in S. Lash, B. Szerszynski, and B. Wynne, eds, *Risk, Environment, and Modernity: Towards a New Ecology* (Cambridge: Polity Press, 1996).

12. For a broad analysis of this issue see A. Irwin, *Citizen Science: A Study of People, Expertise, and Sustainable Development* (London: Routledge, 1995).

13. Giddens, *The Consequences of Modernity* and his 'Living in a Post-Traditional Society.'

14. WRR, *Duurzame risico's: Een blijvend gegeven*, WRR-rapport #44 (Den Haag: SDU, 1994).

15. E. Van Hengel and B. Gremmen 'Milieugebruiksruimte: Tussen Natuurwet en Conventie,' *Kennis en Methode*, 11(3) (1995): 277–303.

16. U. Beck, *Ecological Politics in an Age of Risk* (Cambridge: Polity Press, 1995).

17. P. Dickens, *Reconstructing Nature: Alienation, Emancipation, and the Division of Labour* (London: Routledge, 1996).
18. J. Hannigan, *Environmental Sociology: A Social Constructivist Perspective* (London: Routledge, 1996).
19. Staunch defenders of objectivist or realist approaches are also making use of certain elements advanced by the same Ulrich Beck.
20. U. Beck, 'The Reinvention of Politics: Towards a Theory of Reflexive Modernization,' pp. 1–55 in Beck et al., *Reflexive Modernization*, and his 'Replies and Critiques: Self-Dissolution and Self-Endangerment of Industrial Society: What Does This Mean?' pp. 174–83 in the same volume.
21. Ibid., pp. 176–7.
22. Life politics, as Giddens stresses, can be interpreted as a combination involving both a renewal of the political agenda and a different way of dealing with political questions. These processes are evident in observations that traditional party and bureaucratic politics are now becoming less important in favor of politics at the level of the individual (though deeply intruded by globalizing influences) and involve more ethical considerations of life, death, and lifestyle. See A. Giddens, *Modernity and Self-Identity: Self and Society in the Late Modern Age* (Cambridge: Polity Press, 1991), pp. 214ff.
23. M. Jänicke, *Staatsversagen: Die Ohnmacht der Politik in der Industriegesellschaft* (Munich: Piper, 1986).
24. Giddens, *The Consequences of Modernity*, p. 64.
25. M. Jänicke, 'Über ökologische und politische Modernisierungen,' *Zeitschrift für Umweltpolitik und Umweltrecht*, 16(2) (1993): 159–75. See also Mol, *The Refinement of Production* and Spaargaren, *The Ecological Modernization of Production and Consumption*.
26. The bureaucratic environmental policy of the 1970s and 1980s is regarded as inflexible, economically inefficient, and unjust. These conventional forms of intervention slow down rather than propel technological innovation. Such measures are unable to control the billions of material and energy transmutations that occur each day and are incapable of stimulating progressive environmental behavior by companies. See Jänicke, *Staatsversagen* and J. Huber, *Unternehmen Umwelt: Weichenstellungen für eine ökologische Marktwirtschaft* (Frankfurt am Main: Fisher, 1991).
27. R. Paehlke and D. Torgerson, eds, *Managing Leviathan: Environmental Politics and the Administrative State* (London: Belhaven, 1990).
28. K. LeBlansch, *Milieuzorg in bedrijven: Overheidssturing in het perspectief van de verinnerlijkingsbeleidslijn* (Amsterdam: Thesis Publishers, 1996).
29. A. Mol, V. Lauber, M. Enevoldsen, and J. Landman, *Joint Environmental Policy-Making in Comparative Perspective*, paper presented at the Greening of Industry Conference, Heidelberg, November 1996.
30. Beck, 'The Reinvention of Politics.'
31. C. Bosso, 'Transforming Adversaries into Collaborators: Interest Groups and the Regulation of Chemical Pesticides,' *Policy Sciences*, 21(1) (1988): 3–22 and A. Nownes, 'Interest Groups and the Regulation of Pesticides: Congress, Coalitions, and Closure,' *Policy Sciences*, 24(1) (1991): 1–18.

32. A. Mol and G. Spaargaren, 'Environment, Modernity, and the Risk Society: The Apocalyptic Horizon of Environmental Reform,' *International Sociology*, 8(4) (1993): 431–59.
33. Beck, *Risk Society* and J. Huber, *Die Regenbogengesellschaft: Ökologie und Sozialpolitik* (Frankfurt am Main: Fisher Verlag, 1985).
34. Mol and Spaargaren, 'Environment, Modernity, and the Risk Society.'
35. For instance, industrial customers, insurance companies, credit providers, certification organizations, branch associations, and even trade unions often play similar roles in subpolitical environmental reform.
36. Political modernization is viewed as being in line with ecological modernization, while subpolitics finds its origins and closest affinity with the theory of the risk society.
37. Mol and Spaargaren, 'Environment, Modernity, and the Risk Society.'

5 The 'Risk Society' Reconsidered: Recreancy, the Division of Labor, and Risks to the Social Fabric

William R. Freudenburg

INTRODUCTION

Due in part to the important work of Ulrich Beck and Anthony Giddens, a good deal of attention has been devoted to the concept of the 'risk society.' To date, however, most of this interest has focused on recent and dramatic forms of risk – such as the potential for nuclear or other forms of annihilation – which tend not to be socially divisive at the subnational level. Today, despite the breaking-up of the former Soviet block, these risks cannot be ruled out. Still, perhaps the relaxation of former Cold War animosities may make it easier for sociologists to focus on different types of risks, namely those that, while less dramatic, may be more insidious, more invidious, and ultimately more influential in the lives of most ordinary people. These risks may also be more corrosive for industrial societies as a whole. This chapter argues that the more salient risks for modern (and postmodern) societies are those that derive from increasing specialization and division of labor. These interlinked processes contribute to growing susceptibility to the risks and rewards of interdependence and give rise to a context in which the ability of people to exert meaningful social control over the 'responsible' specialists has declined substantially.

Sociologically speaking, the late-twentieth century has brought a 'risk society' not just through the potential wartime use of weapons, but also through 'peaceable' activities, such as the production, testing, and management of nuclear technologies and their wastes. Yet the problem is by no means limited to nuclear risks; instead we are experiencing the emergence of what Kai Erikson has termed 'a new species of trouble' with a widening range of non-nuclear technologies, involving hazardous chemicals, facilities, transportation technologies, and many of the other controversial components of contemporary industrialization.[1]

These pervasive yet 'everyday' risks highlight a serious flaw in Durkheim's conception of the division of labor in society, in part because of a widespread failure to recognize the present-day implications of Weber's insights into what it means to say that we live in a 'rationalized,' technological world. In statistical terms, the risks of death have been dropping significantly for more than a century. During that same time, however, there has been a dramatic growth of societal interdependence, and hence of the potential for *recreancy* – the failure of institutional actors to carry out their responsibilities with the degree of vigor necessary to merit the societal trust they enjoy. Furthermore, as the process has advanced, there has been a substantial decline in the ability of the broader society to assure that its specialists do indeed serve the interests of the larger collectivity, and that its 'responsible officials' do indeed act responsibly.

The process also highlights a problem articulated by Jürgen Habermas among others – specifically the dilemma of a societal distribution of assets that is unequal, yet accepted as legitimate.[2] For much of the period after World War II, the problem tended to recede from sight – not simply because of the growth in prosperity, but also due to growing evidence of scientific-technological prowess, and because people who had concerns about any given technology could often be isolated as 'extremists' and characterized as being opposed to science and technology more generally. As we enter the twenty-first century, however, the problems associated with recreancy have become sufficiently widespread to reveal the underlying contradictions. Even conservative or 'mainstream' citizens are increasingly beginning to conclude that they may actually be opposed to scientific-technological activities as a whole. While there is growing evidence of the inadequacies in the institutions we have inherited from the past, there remains a need to devote much more attention to the development of societal institutions that might be better adapted to the needs of the future.

WHICH 'RISK SOCIETY' IS THIS?

In 1933, the official guidebook to the Chicago 'Century of Progress' International Exhibition offered a bold proclamation: 'Science Finds – Industry Applies – Man Conforms.' After another half century of 'progress,' however, the relationships no longer seem quite so straightforward. In a book that became quite influential in the United States and elsewhere during the 1980s, a prominent political scientist and anthropologist would ask, 'What are Americans afraid of? Nothing much, really, except the food they eat, the water they drink, the air they breathe, the land they live on, and the energy they use.'[3] Within the next dozen years, two internationally respected sociologists – Anthony Giddens and Ulrich Beck – would be proclaiming that the anticipated 'Century of Progress' had led us instead to what Beck has termed the 'risk society.'[4]

In some ways, such a proclamation would need to be seen as paradoxical. By many measures, science and industry have achieved great success in reducing risks over the course of the twentieth century. Due in part to scientific and technological successes in battling death and disease, people in the industrialized societies are now living significantly longer, healthier, and safer lives. Still, as any number of social commentators have noted, neither men nor women today show much interest in 'conforming' to the dictates of science and/or technology. Instead, whether scientists and industry are searching for oil offshore or attempting to dispose of nuclear or other wastes onshore, their efforts now seem less likely to be welcomed with open arms than to open the public policy equivalent of armed warfare.

Nonetheless, these types of concerns do not seem to loom large among the risks identified by Giddens and Beck, in spite of the attention that Giddens, in particular, places on the forms of trust accorded to technical specialists. Instead, the two theorists have chosen to place greater emphasis on what Giddens calls 'truly formidable,' global-scale risks, ranging from nuclear warfare and nuclear winter to 'chemical pollution of the seas sufficient to destroy the phytoplankton that renews much of the oxygen in the atmosphere.'[5] For Beck, similarly, special attention is devoted to 'uncontrollable consequences' or threats, for which 'measures for the "rational" control of results are to the unleashed consequences what a bicycle brake is to a jetliner.'[6]

While these distinguished theorists are to be commended for

recognizing the importance of risk in contemporary societies, this chapter contends that the sociologically significant aspects of the emerging 'risk society' are actually quite different from the ones Giddens and Beck emphasize, coming significantly closer to the types of problems previously identified by sociologists such as James Short.[7] In fact, my argument can be grounded in the understanding of 'rationality' that Max Weber put forth far earlier. As will be spelled out in greater detail in the following discussion, I see a need for sociologists to focus not just on risks that are massive and uncontrollable, but also on those that are more mundane – yet which simply fail to be controlled. We also need to consider the ways in which these failures create strains in the social fabric, and in the process undermine the legitimacy of the broader social order.

For Beck, for example, 'the litmus test' is 'the lack of insurance protection.' As he puts it, 'nuclear, chemical, and ecological threats destroy the . . . principal pillars of insurance.'[8] This litmus test, unfortunately, would miss many of the cases that form a key focus for a growing number of scholars – including not just James Short, Kai Erikson, and myself, but also a significant number of other American environmental sociologists.[9] In many of the cases these researchers have studied, the *availability* of insurance was not the problem. Insurance was readily acquirable or even in place; indeed, insurance companies may even have joined in the effort to undermine the legitimacy or 'standing' of victims as part of concerted efforts to reduce the companies' liability after an accident had occurred. But if the availability of insurance is not the key consideration, what is? As I will try to illustrate, the central issue has less to do with the accessibility of financial or business *in*surance, *per se,* than with the small but significant fraction of cases in which business was executed in a manner that offered too little *as*surance that public health and safety would be protected.

UNDERSTANDING PUBLIC REACTIONS TO TECHNOLOGICAL RISKS

To return to my starting point, part of what puzzles so many observers about the growing sense of public concern toward risks is the fact that, by most straightforward indicators, the twentieth century has been a time of unprecedented progress in improving human welfare. As illustrated by the downward sloping trend line in

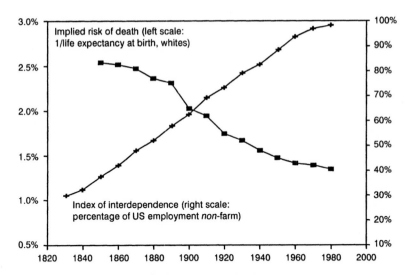

Figure 5.1 US experience with the technological risk crossover

Figure 5.1, the risks that have been the traditional focus of science and technology – the risks of death, as measured by life expectancy figures – have gone down markedly over the course of the past two centuries, declining by roughly 50 percent in the case of the United States, and showing similar patterns in many of the other industrialized nations.

Perhaps it is partly in response to this paradox that commentators such as Beck and Giddens have emphasized the potential for risks that, in effect, could involve utter catastrophe – for example, the collapse of economic growth mechanisms, the rise of totalitarian power, the onset of nuclear or other large-scale warfare, and the occurrence of outright ecological disaster.[10] These are such spectacular risks that it is possible to argue that concern over such 'high-consequence risks . . . transcends all values and all exclusionary divisions of power.'[11]

To a certain extent, moreover, such arguments are quite plausible. All of us who value life on earth have a shared interest, after all, in reducing the risks of nuclear conflagration or ecological catastrophe. When examined more closely, however, the arguments become less credible. In focusing on the dramatic or even the hyperbolic risks, commentators such as Giddens and Beck are largely overlooking those types of technological and environmental risks that are less spectacular, but that in many ways are more insidious – and more socially significant.

Over half a century has now passed since the last use of nuclear weapons in warfare, and yet the recent era has had hundreds of thousands of examples of innocent civilians who have been harmed by 'peaceable' nuclear tests – on both sides of the former Iron Curtain. In addition, much as Durkheim would have argued, the specter of shadowy 'enemies' with nuclear weapons actually did a good deal to *increase* social cohesion, at least within national societies. However, as Short, Erikson, and others have reminded us, the 'peaceable' testing and commercialization of the atom have often done just the opposite, often putting the social fabric itself at risk.[12]

The difference is not necessarily in the industry or the activity, but in the nature of their focus. As a useful simplification, Giddens and Beck tend to emphasize the potential for nuclear technologies to lead to widespread and catastrophic harm – Beck's *Risk Society*, after all, was conceived in part under the cloud of fallout from Chernobyl. In contrast, research conducted in the United States on nuclear risks has typically examined the more structured or differentiated forms of risk, such as those that are disproportionately concentrated around the sites of nuclear facilities.[13] My personal orientation in this respect reflects my belief that the socially significant risks may have to do not just with the threat of nuclear weapons being used against all of us by those we see as our enemies. Instead, my concern also includes the less dramatic, but far more socially divisive, threats that 'ordinary' nuclear technology poses for some of us, due in large part to the actions of those who claim to be our friends. In other words, for most individuals and societies of the industrialized world, the forms of risk that may ultimately prove to have the greatest salience – at least most of the time – may be precisely the opposite of those Giddens and Beck emphasize. The most socially relevant threats may prove to be precisely those risks that do *not* 'transcend all values and all exclusionary divisions of power.'

To understand this point more fully, it is helpful to avoid (or to correct) a widespread but fundamental misunderstanding about what it means to say we live in an 'advanced, technological society.' The corrective can be found in an observation made initially three-quarters of a century ago by Max Weber, one of the earliest and most articulate proponents of 'intellectualized rationality.'[14] In his famous lecture on 'Science as a Vocation,' Weber discussed a question that was evidently a source of confusion for many of his students, as well as for many who were to follow. What does it mean, Weber had been asked, to say that we live in a world of 'intellectualized rationalization'?

> Does it mean that we, today . . . have a greater knowledge of the conditions of life under which we exist than has an American Indian or a Hottentot? Hardly. Unless he is a physicist, one who rides on the streetcar has no idea how the car happened to get into motion. And he does not need to know. He is satisfied that he may 'count' on the behavior of the streetcar, and he orients his conducts according to this expectation; but he knows nothing about what it takes to produce such a car so that it can move. The savage knows incomparably more about his tools.[15]

Instead, Weber continued, intellectualization and rationalization mean 'the world is disenchanted. One need no longer have recourse to magical means,' because 'one can, in principle, master all things by calculation.'[16]

Yet the availability of this option 'in principle' clearly does not mean that the average individual – or indeed, perhaps *any* individual – will be able to 'master all things by calculation.' Instead, the expectation is that *someone* will be performing the necessary calculations – and that the relevant person will be doing the counting in a way that can be 'counted on.' Yet it may be precisely this expectation that becomes increasingly problematic as the societal division of labor grows more complex.

In emphasizing the forms of risk that 'transcend all values and all exclusionary divisions of power,' Giddens and Beck are in some ways paralleling the work on the division of labor in society by Emile Durkheim.[17] When he first called attention to the phenomenon, Durkheim referred approvingly to what he called 'organic solidarity.' With increased specialization, he argued, different kinds of people come to need each other just as much as do the different organs of the body; the heart cannot live without the brain or stomach, for example, and the stomach is not viable on its own. While the interdependence may be real, however, the analogy to the social order has often proved to be problematic. Unlike stomachs, after all, humans have the capacity to discern specialized interests that differ from the objectives or needs of the broader collectivity.

Durkheim did not directly address the troublesome implications of this capacity. Instead, he resorted to an argument that claimed, in essence, such problems were unthinkable. He wrote, 'The different parts of the aggregate, because they fill different functions, cannot easily be separated.'[18] Elsewhere, he advanced a similar assertion, specifically that 'the division of labor . . . more and more, fills the role that was formerly filled by the common conscience.'[19]

To be fair, it can be argued that, to a very great extent, something looking very much like Durkheim's vision has indeed come to pass in the industrialized nations of the world. Not just industry, but the larger society within which industrial activities have developed, is now characterized by an elaborate and delicately choreographed division of labor. Moreover, in this system the vast majority of specialists – at least the vast majority of the time – carry out their specialized duties with an appropriate and even impressive degree of skill and care.

At the same time, however, the world that is emerging around us includes a small but significant number of instances where the filling of functions has proved not to be so automatic. Instead, the very interdependencies of our ever more complex social systems appear to have increased our susceptibility to cases where some key portions of the system – some 'vital organs' to use the Durkheimian metaphor – cannot be safely 'counted on.' Paradoxically, in other words, the very division of labor that permits many of the achievements of advanced industrial societies may also have the potential to become one of the most serious sources of risk and vulnerability. This is due precisely to the small but non-zero probability that specialized individuals and/or organizations will *fail* to transcend their own interests.

What may actually be the most socially salient change in today's 'risk society' is something that has been far less dramatic, yet far more pervasive, than the 'truly formidable' or uninsurable risks that Giddens and Beck emphasize. What may have changed, as indicated in Figure 5.1, is the *form* of risk that is most socially relevant. Industrialized societies, I am suggesting, may have experienced a 'risk crossover.' While there have been substantial strides in reducing the traditional forms of risk – specifically those involving the statistical threat of death – this progress has been achieved, in part, at the expense of *increases* in another form of risk, relating to social control over an increasingly complex division of labor. To put the matter another way, the highly specialized division of labor in industrialized societies has helped to permit a substantial decrease in the risk of death, but it has done so at a cost – a paradoxical cost of substantially increased vulnerability to the very interdependencies that also make the system work.

Based on these points, then, what does it mean to say that we live in an 'advanced, technological' society – does it mean that we 'know more' today than did our great-great-grandparents? Collectively, of course, we do. Individually, however – to return again to Weber's point – we actually know far *less* today than did previous generations about the tools and technologies on which we depend.

In the early 1800s, the vast majority of the people in the world (the figure was over 80 percent in the case of the United States) were engaged in producing their own food. The life they lived was often difficult, and few of the more affluent persons of today would truly want to trade places with them. Still, for the most part, those relatively self-sufficient people were capable of repairing – or even of building from scratch – virtually all of the tools and technologies upon which they relied. By contrast, the contemporary world is so specialized that even a Nobel laureate is likely to have little more than a rudimentary understanding of the tools and technologies that surround us all, from airliners to ignition systems, and from computers to corporate structures.

Far more than was the case for our great-great-grandparents, in other words, we tend to be not so much in control of as *dependent upon* our technology – and hence, we must rely as well on whole armies of specialists, most of whom we will never meet, let alone be able to control. For most of us, most of the time, we do find that we *can* depend on our technologies and the people who are responsible for them. For instance, millions of people travel annually by jet aircraft that, while amazingly complex in both organizational and technological terms, nevertheless manage to fly long distances and land quite safely. Despite our *generally* positive experiences, however, the case studies described elsewhere in this volume demonstrate that the exceptions can be genuinely troubling.

One of the reasons for this unease is that our increases in *technical* control have come about, in part, at the cost of decreases in *social* control. In this sense, too, we are very much unlike our great-great-grandparents. In the relatively few cases where they needed to buy an item of technology from someone else, it was often from a 'someone' with whom they were personally familiar, or at least would know how to find if something went wrong. Today, by contrast, not only do we have more interdependence but we also have less ability to monitor or to control the countless specialists upon whom we depend. Today's citizens often discover that when something goes wrong – be it a car or a computer or a chemical – the 'responsible' person or organization can prove almost impossible to find.

I am not arguing that such failures are truly pervasive. My own belief is that cases of 'things going wrong' are still more the exception than the rule, and by a considerable margin. In the relatively small number of cases where such failure does occur, however, they may be no less troubling because they are relatively rare. Instead, as Paul Slovic reminds us, these few but salient failures help to illustrate what he calls the 'asymmetry principle.' This principle expresses the notion that trust is far easier to destroy than to build.[20] If an accountant steals from you even once, after all, that single trust-destroying event is not likely to be forgotten, despite the fact that the same accountant had not stolen from you in the past. Furthermore, this breach of confidence will have persistent consequences even if the accountant chooses not to repeat the theft the next year – or for that matter, the next year and each successive year. Such experiences, though they are undoubtedly rare, represent what Slovic calls 'signal' events – they send a signal that the system may not be as trustworthy as we would all want to believe.

Using a very simple index of interdependence, based on the proportion of Americans *not* involved in growing their own food, the upward sloping trend line in Figure 5.1 illustrates the 'risk crossover' that I have been discussing. As is evident from the diagram, during the very era when society has been enjoying a substantial decline in the risks that have been the traditional focus of the scientific community – namely the risks of death – there has been a substantial increase in levels of interdependence, and hence of the potential for failures related to interdependence itself. The problem, to return to my earlier point, involves what I have termed *recreancy* – in essence, the failure of experts or specialized organizations to execute properly responsibilities to the broader collectivity with which they have been implicitly or explicitly entrusted.[21]

The word comes from the Latin roots *re-* (back) and *credere* (to entrust), and the technical use of the term is analogous to one of its two dictionary meanings, involving a retrogression or failure to follow through on a duty or a trust. The term is likely to be unfamiliar to most readers, but there is a simple reason for its use. We need a specialized word if we intend to refer to behaviors of institutions or organizations (as well as of individuals), and, importantly, to keep attention focused on the facts instead of the emotions. The reasons for this novel expression quickly become clear upon reflection and provide insights that may tell us something about the societal importance of trustworthiness. Virtually all of the common words in the English language with comparable meanings have come over time to take on a heavily negative set of connotations. To say, for example, that a technical specialist is responsible, competent, or trustworthy is to offer at least a mild compliment. However, to accuse that same person of being *ir*responsible, *in*competent, or of having shown a 'betrayal' of trust is to level a very serious charge indeed. While 'recreancy' may not be an everyday term, the necessity for such a word grows quite directly out of the need to avoid the emotional and/or legal connotations of the available alternatives.

How important is recreancy? At least in terms of public concerns over risk, recreancy proves to be far more important than most of the factors that have typically been stressed in the many editorials written in recent years about the mass media and the public. One recent review, for example, finds that, of 15 studies designed to test empirically the hypothesis that environmental risk concerns will be predicted by a lack of technical information, only four support it. Interestingly, seven studies reported significant findings in the opposite direction.[22] In another example, Salamone and Sandman found similarly little support for the common belief that 'exaggerated' media reports can be blamed for increased public concerns about risks.[23] While researchers with considerable experience coding qualitative data often agreed that media reports were biased, they evidenced remarkably little agreement even on something as basic as the *direction* of the partiality.[24]

By contrast to public knowledge levels and media coverage recreancy and trustworthiness have been shown by systematic research to be key factors behind the increasingly toxic social chemistry that has been associated with an ever-increasing range of technologies. In my own analysis of attitudes towards a proposed low-level nuclear waste facility, for example, I found that socio-demographic variables were only weak predictors of attitudes. Such factors as age, occupation, and so forth were associated with differences of only 7–15 percent in levels of public support for the proposed facility. Even values-based and/or ideological items were associated with differences of only 10–25 percent. By contrast, three measures of recreancy were each associated with a difference of 40–60+ percent. In regression analyses, the recreancy variables alone more than tripled the amount of variance explained by the socio-demographic and the ideological variables combined. The growth in interdependence – and in the risks of recreancy – appears to be among the reasons why trust and trustworthiness have been found to be key variables in an increasing number of other studies as well.[25]

CONCLUSION

The challenge we face is a delicate one and involves a kind of balancing act. We need to encourage the promising growth in sociological enthusiasm for understanding the 'risk society' that has been kindled by the work of Anthony Giddens and Ulrich Beck. At the same time, we need to proceed without falling prey to the somewhat simplified and mistaken understanding that these theorists and their followers have tended to develop about the true sociological and societal significance of risk. Given trends toward further increases in the division of labor in society – in the absence of comparable expansion of the capacities of industrialized societies to exert effective social control over their specialized and often virtually autonomous institutions – that challenge is likely to become all the more important as the world crosses the threshold to a new millennium.

Yet it is important that we embrace this challenge. After all, while sociology has a great deal to offer to the study of risk, the study of risk also has a great deal to offer to sociology. For the longer-term good of both the discipline and society in general we need to work toward the realization of that full potential.

Before we will be able to make real progress in moving toward this objective, however, it will be necessary for sociology to go beyond the initially encouraging – but ultimately unsatisfactory – efforts made to date. It is even possible to offer a suggestion as to how greater progress can be achieved. There may well be a need to shift attention from the work of theorists who are currently better-known toward the research of a growing number of other sociologists (some of whom are contributors to this volume) who may ultimately be seen to have known better.

ACKNOWLEDGEMENTS

The author thanks Maurie Cohen and an anonymous reviewer for their helpful comments and suggestions.

NOTES

1. K. Erikson, *A New Species of Trouble: Explorations in Disaster, Trauma, and Community* (New York: W. W. Norton, 1994).
2. J. Habermas, *Toward a Rational Society* (New York: Beacon, 1970).
3. M. Douglas and A. Wildavsky, *Risk and Culture: An Essay on the Selection of Technological and Environmental Dangers* (Berkeley: University of California Press, 1982).
4. A. Giddens, *The Consequences of Modernity* (Cambridge: Polity Press, 1990); U. Beck, *Risk Society: Toward a New Modernity* (London: Sage, 1992). See also Beck's *Ecological Enlightenment: Essays on the Politics of Risk* (Atlantic Highlands, NJ: Humanities Press, 1995).
5. Giddens, *The Consequences of Modernity*, p. 125.
6. Beck, *Ecological Enlightenment*, p. 127.
7. J. Short, 'The Social Fabric at Risk: Toward the Social Transformation of Risk Analysis,' *American Sociological Review*, 49(6) (1984): 711–25.
8. Beck, *Ecological Enlightenment*, p. 127.
9. Short, 'The Social Fabric at Risk,' and Erikson, *A New Species of Trouble*. See also, K. Erikson, 'Toxic Reckoning: Business Faces a New Kind of Fear,' *Harvard Business Review*, 68(1) (1990): 119–26 and W. Freudenburg, 'Risk and Recreancy: Weber, the Division of Labor, and the Rationality of Risk Perceptions,' *Social Forces*, 71(4) (1993): 909–32. See also the works of many of the other American contributors to this volume.
10. Giddens, *The Consequences of Modernity*, p. 171.
11. Ibid., p. 154.
12. See Short, 'The Social Fabric at Risk' and his 'Defining, Explaining, and Managing Risk,' pp. 3–23 in J. Short and L. Clarke, eds, *Organizations, Uncertainties, and Risk* (Boulder, CO: Westview Press, 1992). Refer also to Erikson, *A New Species of Trouble*.
13. See, for example, W. Freudenburg and T. Jones, 'Attitudes and Stress in the Presence of Technological Risk: A Test of the Supreme Court Hypothesis,' *Social Forces*, 69(4) (1991): 1143–68 and Freudenburg, 'Risk and Recreancy.'
14. M. Weber, 'Science as a Vocation,' pp. 129–56 in H. Gerth and C. Mills, eds, *From Max Weber: Essays in Sociology* (Oxford: Oxford University Press, 1918 [1946]).
15. Ibid., pp. 138–9.
16. Ibid.
17. E. Durkheim, *The Division of Labor in Society* (New York: Free Press, 1893 [1933]).

18. Ibid., p. 149.
19. Ibid., p. 173.
20. P. Slovic, 'Perceived Risk, Trust, and Democracy,' *Risk Analysis*, 13(6) (1993): 675–82.
21. Freudenburg, 'Risk and Recreancy.'
22. D. Davidson and W. Freudenburg, 'Gender and Environmental Risk Concerns: An Empirical Reexamination,' *Environment and Behavior*, 28(3) (1996): 302–39.
23. K. Salamone and P. Sandman, *Newspaper Coverage of the Diamond Shamrock Dioxin Controversy: How Much Content is Alarming, Reassuring, or Intermediate?* (New Brunswick, NJ: Rutgers University, Environmental Communication Research Program, 1991).
24. For further studies that provide potential explanations for the underlying reasons, see W. Freudenburg, C. Coleman, J. Gonzales, and C. Helgeland, 'Media Coverage of Hazard Events: Analyzing the Assumptions,' *Risk Analysis*, 16(1) (1996): 31–42 and A. Gunther, 'Biased Press or Biased Public: Attitudes toward Media Coverage of Social Groups,' *Public Opinion Quarterly*, 56(2) (1992): 147–67.
25. For further discussion of this research refer to Freudenburg, 'Risk and Recreancy.'

Part IV
Empirical Assessments of Reflexive Modernization

6 'Outsiders Just Don't Understand': Personalization of Risk and the Boundary Between Modernity and Postmodernity
Michael R. Edelstein

INTRODUCTION

Contamination became a widely recognized facet of modern reality in the 1970s after such events as the discovery of buried hazardous wastes at Love Canal in Niagara Falls, New York and the spread of dioxin following an explosion at a pharmaceutical plant in Seveso, Italy. In these instances, reflecting chronic and acute cases of contamination, residents were relocated and permanent 'dead zones' were created on the landscape. Based upon such events, contamination emerged as the prototypical 'new species of trouble,' challenging modernity and forcing the transition toward a new postmodern society.[1] Here it is argued that an understanding of this transition can be drawn from the experience of pollution's victims. Using observations derived from empirical studies of the contamination experience, it is possible to confirm the largely European sociological representation of postmodernity, as depicted by Ulrich Beck's theory of the 'risk society.'[2] At the same time, limits to the risk-society formulation also become apparent.

According to Beck, postmodernity results from reflexive modernity – that is postmodernity is in part a reaction to the hazardous consequences of modernity. While modernity's organizing principle was to conquer the human condition of scarcity, postmodern people confront the risks caused by modern society in the form of its systems and technology. In this sense, human society, rather than nature, has become the source of danger. Reflecting the new obsession with risk, questions of threat and hazard insinuate themselves into all facets of life, through the air we breathe, the water we drink, the food we eat, as well as through procreation and health and through transportation and shelter. As a result, people are continually confronted with new kinds of risk choices and risk tradeoffs, becoming burdened with unprecedented responsibilities for differentiating between what is safe and hazardous in the face of inherent uncertainty. Unlike the general acceptance of risk that characterized modernity, aversion to risk becomes the postmodern preoccupation.

SOCIAL PROCESS OCCURS IN AN ECO-HISTORICAL CONTEXT

This changed meaning of risk reflects the contemporary direct and vicarious experience of environmental contamination conceptualized in Figure 6.1.[3] Here we see the psychosocial impacts of contamination as occurring along a dynamic continuum from personal to societal. Simultaneously, independently, and synergistically, the contamination events affect the individual, the family, the relational group, the involved institutions, the community, and the society. These impacts are further understood in historical and ecological context as threats to place.

The psychosocial process is well-illustrated by the Love Canal event. Focusing upon the individual, we find the oft-noted example of Lois Gibbs, the leader of the Love Canal Homeowner's Association, transformed by the incident from a shy, family-oriented housewife to a national figure.[4] Although unique in many respects, Gibbs is the prototypical community leader – her experience is recapitulated in community after community across the United States and beyond.[5] Through her biography we can see the extraordinary challenge to the toxic victim and activist. But this story is not just about an individual. It includes the familial strains her activism caused in her relationship with her first husband and for her children, her organizational activities within the Love Canal neighborhood, her confrontations with government officials over differing interpretations of safety, impact, and required assistance, and local, citywide, state, and national dynamics that helped define a societal response to contamination in the United States. These activities

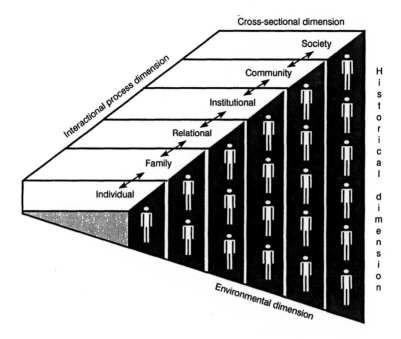

Figure 6.1 Contamination as a psychosocial process in an ecohistorical context

inspired Congress to adopt the Comprehensive Environmental Response, Compensation, and Liability Act (CERCLA) – better known as Superfund – to enable the government to act quickly to address contamination problems. In sum, the dynamics of Love Canal incorporated all these dimensions of social interaction.

Such social dynamics occur within an ecological context. The perceived contamination of the environment simultaneously overlays and underlies the quality of social interaction at each level of process.[6] The more aware and sensitive people are to their biophysical surround, the more directly they are impacted by the quality and attributes of the environmental context. However, even undetected and unknown environmental forces may exert great influence over social process. A defined contamination event will influence various media (air, soil, and water) within a neighborhood, region, or other spatial context of place. People will respond according to the boundaries of the event, their watershed, airshed, odorshed, or other cognitive means of delineating how personal and threatening

an event promises to be. For example, at Love Canal, the realization that industrial wastes were buried beneath the surface of an
unfinished canal was the serendipitous result of a search for the
source of contamination found in the nearby Niagara River. This
discovery unleashed several years of intense debate over the degree of hazard, the extent of cleanup required, and the actions
necessary to protect residents. Illustrative was the conflict between
public authorities and local residents concerning the exposure
pathways and their linkages to illness. The relevant governmental
body, the New York State Department of Health, failed to find
any relationship between proximity to Love Canal and higher incidence of disease, implying, accordingly, that there was no evidence
of a negative health effect from the canal. In response, residents
conducted health surveys indicating the incidents of cancer and other
diseases in the community. With the help of Beverly Paigen, a professional cancer researcher, local activists overlaid their results onto
a map.[7] This innovative methodology showed that disease incidence
correlated with proximity, not to the canal *per se*, but rather to
swales – ditches and underground watercourses – that drained from
the canal and traversed the community.[8]

The historical dimension also defines the evolution of the community's relationship to place over time by describing a chronology
of locally important milestone events related to the contamination.
The combined 'ecohistorical context' defines meaning in that setting. While the presence of a long-forgotten, partially constructed
canal built by an entrepreneur named Love had been a surprise to
most residents of the LaSalle neighborhood of Niagara Falls, once
labeled, the Love Canal became significant to the city's subsequent
identity. Under the 'principle of perpetual jeopardy,' once a loca-
tion is labeled as contaminated, is the site of a hazardous facility,
or is even considered as a potentially suitable site for future waste-
disposal activities, it is stigmatized for desirable land uses.[9] Under
such circumstances, the particular place becomes attractive only
for ill-founded or risky facilities. Accordingly, we would expect that
already-contaminated Niagara Falls would attract proposals for
additional hazards and that regulators would find such applications
within an already-tainted community to be 'permitable.' Indeed,
Love Canal appears to have had a lasting impact upon Niagara
Falls' identity. For example, the CECOS corporation successfully
located a major sanitary landfill and five successive hazardous waste-
disposal facilities in the center of the community, creating a hill of

debris visible throughout the essentially flat city. While there was some opposition to these installations, they met with a general sense of public resignation. It was not until the mid-1980s, after CECOS announced plans to build a sixth facility at its waste complex, that a community consensus began to form in opposition to the proposal. It was time, people seemed to be saying, to overturn Niagara Falls' legacy of environmental hazards that began with Love Canal. A line was needed between the contaminated past and a desired alternative, unstigmatized future founded upon tourism. It was, after all, the Falls, and not Love Canal and other scars of the industrial era, for which the community wanted to be known.[10] This social and eco-historical frame helps to explain the common experience of contamination victims that 'outsiders just don't understand.'

OUTSIDERS JUST DON'T UNDERSTAND

A nearly universal complaint from residents of contaminated communities is that outsiders – those never personally victimized by toxic contamination – do not understand them. This failure to share an appreciation for the plight of contamination victims compounds their adversity. In fact, many of the most disturbing impacts of these events result from the insider–outsider dialectic. Within the empirical literature, there is a strong convergence regarding the effects of toxic victimization and the resulting conflicts. These patterns of identified impacts confirm key tenets of the postmodern 'risk society' thesis.

Psychosocial impacts associated with contamination begin at the point that people learn they are exposed to contaminants, understand the implications to be negative, and accept this undesired change of circumstances as reality. Thus, as boundaries of the contamination are drawn, the people thought to be at risk from exposure will view it differently from those for whom it is merely a distant, abstract problem. Bounding defines the potential victims, who are likely to attend closely to information bearing on their risk and prospects. For individuals outside the boundaries, the contamination is someone else's problem. Here we see the nexus of the insider–outsider dichotomy.

Once there is an acceptance of toxic victimization, the costs of the risk society are proven to be severe. Victims are pulled into the vortex of the contamination experience, ripped from the moorings that help them to establish a secure and stable perspective on the world. This period of turbulence contrasts sharply with any previous period of solidity in the victims' lives. Contamination, once accepted as reality, frequently shatters the basic sense of balance and certainty of everyday life. There may be changes in the activities that are engaged in and the ways that a person feels about him or herself, others, and the surrounding world. There are serious ramifications for family and other relationships. As old relational networks (family, friends, co-workers) fail to help, offer support, or even understand the victims' experiences, a forced dependence emerges upon institutions for assistance and experts for information. To offset the disabling aspects of this dependency, individuals affected by contamination frequently band together to create local grassroots action groups that enable them to exert some control, find power, attain trusted information, and receive social support. Thus, contaminated communities often spawn nascent advocacy organizations to address the mutual concerns of proximate or interlinked residents. Such efforts are often unstable over time and relatively few become permanent fixtures of community life. Thus, a whole realignment of one's social and political world is often demanded of the contamination victim.[11]

Of course, not all potentially affected people believe in the threat of the contamination. Divergent information, uncertainty, differences in employment, education, or outlook, as well as differences in resources, lifestyles, and lifecycle frequently contribute to divisions between believers and non-believers in the perception of the contamination.[12] While the mobilized toxic activists fit the role predicted by the theory of the risk society, individuals engaging in denial, or those people not impaired in a clear and personal manner, continue to hold tenaciously to the old ways of modernity.

In sum, when toxic victims inevitably complain that outsiders do not understand their plight, what do they mean? Such victims have come to accept that they, and perhaps their family, home, and community as well, have been exposed to health-threatening environmental contamination. The step into this non-normative reality now separates their experience from that of friends, kin, co-workers, and even from the government officials with whom they must now deal, all of whom are still living in the previous reality of the 'non-contaminated' person. The result is an insider–outsider divide. Except for those neighbors or others who also perceive themselves to be toxic victims, most ordinary people are not privy to the meaning of contamination. They are ill-prepared to be supportive, informative, or helpful because their reality is drastically different.

This gap between insiders and outsiders may affect the ability of even purportedly objective observers to appreciate the victims' reality. Professional expertise may diverge from residents' local expertise. Technical knowledge is contextually very different from local knowledge.[13] Likewise, the researcher or theorist may have a different reality than their informants. As a case in point, 'acceptable risk' may be very different for the outside expert than for the prospective victim.

Three elements of normalcy are challenged by belief in contamination, creating the divide between believers and non-believers: the ability to cope with daily life, the pattern of activities that orders lifestyles (i.e. the behaviors that constitute daily life), and the existing set of assumptions about life in relation to place.[14] The following sections examine sequentially each of these elements.

Emotional Trauma and Ability to Cope

There is little that is not upsetting in the wake of learning about the contamination of one's self, family, and home. Victims may experience trauma at all levels of social process. At the individual level fear of illness, protectiveness for one's dependents, feelings of insecurity, and anger at the sources of threat or assistance are all to be expected. Disruption from the contamination, as well as all the accompanying life complications, is further compounded by efforts to cope with the changed situation. The result is that the accumulated stress may potentially cause damage to both psychological and physical health. The extent and effect of these impacts will vary within the community across individuals. The psychological stress from contamination has been found to be significant and long lasting. Furthermore, clinically defined and quantitatively measured psychopathology has been related to contamination.[15] We know relatively little about how to help people get past the shock of contamination and there is sparse evidence to suggest the disappearance of these impacts over time. In multiple ways then contamination produces comprehensive and often dramatic undesired changes for its victims.

Of course, such individual impacts are not easily separable from family responses. Adjustments to the contamination may render family life vulnerable. Activism in response to the threat often draws away from family time and energy. Blame and anger are frequently vented within the household circle. Pressures at the community level may be compounded by tension within the family, or in other related parts of victims' lives. Decisional dilemmas – most notably over whether to relocate or stay – are frequently the source of intra-family strife. These effects can be compounded by other life stressors that have nothing to do with contamination. Overall, family stress can affect relationships in both short-term and more permanent ways. The uncertainties inherent in most contamination scenarios invite additional opportunities for divergent interpretation and response. Conflict and controversy frequently divide communities in the wake of contamination, setting neighbor against neighbor. At the extreme, dissensus results in the formation of a 'corrosive community' that destroys previous elements of constructive community unity through a cycle of blame.[16]

Lifestyle Change

Beyond affecting how victims feel, the belief that contamination is dangerous, combined with the perception of exposure, is likely to produce fundamental lifestyle changes (i.e. normal patterns of activities). For affected individuals, daily lives may have to be modified to account for changes to their water source, diet, or other adjustments. These alterations may aid victims' ability to cope with the realities of contamination, but they also exact a drain on emotional and physical resources for daily life. Modifications of long-established daily routines are likely to serve as continual reminders of what has occurred. Other lifestyle changes arise from the need to attend frequent public meetings, to seek and receive government assistance, to engage in political activism, to resolve personal, family or community conflicts, to deal with media representatives, to develop new interpersonal relationships, and to acquire new technical skills and knowledge with which to better comprehend what has occurred. There is likely to be controversy about the physical reality and consequences of the contamination that will introduce uncertainty into daily life. In short, post-contamination lifestyles are likely to be different and stressful.[17]

The Lifescape

Contamination also has a way of stripping from people the core assumptions underpinning daily life – the lifescape. The lifescape reflects each individual's way of embodying a larger shared societal paradigm in the context of personal life. Contamination upsets the lifescape like the ball upsets bowling pins, resulting in a shift of basic understandings about life. People now come to see themselves as unfair victims of a dangerous condition caused by others. Toxic victims' perceptions of five core assumptions about life, central to our 'normal' way of thinking, are likely to be altered. Each of these lifescape shifts represents a loss of the cultural immunity that previously served as a protective shield.

First, toxic victims are likely to experience a change in the way they perceive their own personal health, as well as the health of family members. Gone is the presumption of health that characterizes normal thought.[18] Victims regularly reassess past and current health problems and come to see symptoms as potentially caused by the contamination. Patterns of health maladies may be identified for the person, the family, and for the community.[19] Fear of prospective health problems includes dread of cancer and impacts on children and grandchildren.[20] Because these conditions often have very long periods of latency, this transformation is protracted and recurrent.[21]

Second, toxic victims generally experience a loss of perceived control that they formerly assumed they held over their lives.[22] They realize that they were unable to avoid exposure to a contaminant, or to protect their family from such exposure. Furthermore, as the new realities of living in a contaminated community unfold, the victims now become enveloped in the uncertainty of the new situation. The resulting dependence upon experts, government officials, and attorneys brings on a feeling of disability due to the loss of control. No longer is the future seen as directed by their choice or custom. It is now out of their hands. Compounding this effect is the sense that evolving events follow a foreign logic that belies common sense. Instead of assuming a rosy future, prospects are now ominous.

Third, the victims' environment comes to be distrusted as a potential source of unseen threat. Local foodstuffs can no longer be eaten because they may be contaminated. Proximate bodies of water cannot be used any longer for recreation or drinking for the same reason. Place is now tainted. Nature is soiled and spoiled. The prospect of feeling secure in the future is hampered by concerns that other unseen dangers now lurk in the environment. As a result, despite the insecurity of one's current place, there is now distrust that other locales will harbor incubating contamination.[23]

Fourth, victims' homes likewise are redefined from places of security to places of danger. The psychological and financial value of the home becomes inverted. As a result of this changed understanding of place, contaminated houses are seen as unsellable and the victims become economically trapped. Frequently, as mobility becomes impaired, there is a corresponding desire to be relocated with the aid of government assistance. The bond to the home is severed in a way that is difficult to repair.[24]

Finally, contamination causes distrust. The fact that contamination is the result of human actions emerges as a central psychological attribute affecting the lifescape. Someone caused this event to happen. It was no accident. Similarly, there is distrust for those who failed to prevent the contamination and may subsequently prove unable to adequately remedy the threat. As William Freudenburg describes elsewhere in this volume, the inability of government to prevent and respond effectively exhibits 'recreancy,' a fundamental failure of institutions to carry out the missions with which they have been entrusted.[25] In this way, the polluters and the government both come to be distrusted. Furthermore, reeling from their victimization, the casualties of contamination readily come to see others in a suspicious light. The fact that outsiders – those who have never experienced contamination – do not readily understand why victims of contamination are so affected results in their frequently being unsupportive, unreasonable, or blaming. Accordingly, victims may feel isolated and abandoned. The climate of distrust is compounded by community conflict over the costs, severity, or boundaries of the contamination. Such feelings are further fed by environmental stigma.

ENVIRONMENTAL STIGMA

The perceptual divide between victims and non-believers is perhaps best captured by the occurrence of environmental stigma. This phenomenon involves the tendency for contaminated environments – settings, places, objects, non-human lifeforms, as well as people and everything associated with them – to become devalued and discredited.[26] Environmental stigma is evident, for example, in situations where feared environmental conditions pertain, as with 'contaminated' places, media (soil, air, water), substances, and products (e.g. milk, apples, meat, wine). An anticipatory stigma may be created when a future hazard threatens a place or community, as with the proposed siting of a hazardous facility. I have argued that environmental stigma is an inherent property of toxic contamination.

When environmental stigma is operative not only do outsiders seek to avoid contact with the tainted community, but the residents of the area bounded by perceived contamination are also seen as being contaminated. Thus, the social dynamics of contamination involve direct social stigma against victims, as well as secondary stigma, such as loss of property value or inability to sell or rent one's home. Because stigma effects are dependent upon the visibility of the mark or stigmatizing characteristics, the more that a contamination event is publicized, the more stigma occurs. As a result, there is a direct tension between the need for toxic victims to make their concerns public so as to attract help and their need to be private to avoid attention and, therefore, not be identified as contaminated. This bind is only one of several that affect contaminated communities. A final issue with environmental stigma is the active possibility that some communities are selected for contamination because they are already socially stigmatized.[27]

To summarize the argument so far, an expanding literature reveals convergent findings regarding the emotional, lifestyle, and lifescape impacts of contamination. The nature of these effects is to separate the perceived world of victims from that of non-victims, creating a serious insider–outsider gap. Using the social process model, we can see this breach as a reflection of the difference in perspective between individuals directly and locally affected by contamination and those living outside the boundaries of contamination and whose views reflect the cultural immunity of the larger society.

CULTURAL IMMUNITY AND THE RISK SOCIETY

Overall, the previous findings suggest that victims of contamination are plunged into a new reality, essentially the 'immiseration' predicted by Ulrich Beck in his thesis of the risk society.[28] However, also evident from community studies of toxic events is that the majority – the outsiders, disbelievers, or non-victims – continue to enjoy a cultural immunity from contamination, a perceptual blinder that allows people to stay the course of modernity. Specifically, the predicted societal shift away from the expectations of modernity, and toward the new reflexive consciousness of the postmodern risk society, is not borne out. Instead, the empirical evidence reveals that modernity continues to retain its tight grip over the daily reality of life. Modern people are extremely resistant to the idea that they themselves are personally threatened by contamination. A global and abstract awareness of environmental pollution problems does not loosen this hold. Rather, a personal confrontation with the contamination of place and person is required to make such abstractions real and to challenge a perception of personal impunity to ecological threat. We can see the enduring strength of this protection from environmental threat in the very experience of contamination.

The cultural immunity to contamination is first suggested by the violent readjustment demanded of its victims. Contamination unleashes a process of social and psychological turbulence that wrenches people out of the private sphere of modern everyday life.[29] Several dimensions of this 'turbulence theory' of transformation are informative for our understanding of cultural immunity.

First, modernity creates an insulating sphere through employment, consumerism, isolation within the nuclear family, extreme time pressure, media seduction, demands to relax and forget, and disconnection from community, polity, and nature. The normative lifestyle and lifescape does not recognize contamination as possible. In the course of ordinary, contemporary life, most people are concerned with home, family, work, entertainment, and immediate social circle – but not environmental risk – unless a particular hazard intrudes into their lives in a visible and believable fashion.

Second, it is not that contaminated communities are unknown. Quite to the contrary, the media have been saturated with the stories of victims of these untoward events, making Love Canal and other examples more vernacular than esoteric. But these familiar tragedies are bounded. They happen to others, not to oneself. Repeatedly, in my interviews with toxic victims, these individuals report that they had previously seen themselves as immune from such catastrophes: 'This was something that could happen to someone else, but I never thought it would happen to me.'

Finally, the subjects of toxic exposure believe that they have been unfairly victimized. In other words, they view contamination as unjust and consider that if justice were to prevail they would not have deserved their unfortunate fate. By extension, outsiders remain reasonably secure in their lifescape assumption of control. They see themselves as effectively immune to such disasters. Furthermore, the uncertainty that victims experience is not what one wishes to emulate.

Therefore, despite the fact that a heuristic understanding of toxic victimization has been widely spread by the media, and images of this experience are readily available, toxic victims do not seem prepared for their own transformation. Rather, it catches them by surprise. It is not until there is a clear discovery, announcement, or demonstration of contamination – making exposure to contaminants a personal issue – that there may be an acceptance of exposure and a resulting sense of victimization. Even afterward, there are likely to be some non-believers who deny the contamination.[30]

In this way, we see evidence of the persistence of modern values in the studies of contaminated communities. The 'Dominant Social Paradigm' of industrial society persists as a personal worldview, even in the face of evidence of widespread belief in the ideals of a 'new environmental paradigm.'[31] The shifts are in the realm of attitudes and broad policy intentions, but they intrude relatively little into the cocooned reality of everyday life. The lifestyle and lifescape are organized around a very different frame of reality than is the abstract sense of what should be. Thus, a transformation in values may not translate into a new way of life. Furthermore, given the absence of ecological literacy in modernity, people fail to comprehend the link between abstract environmental problems and personal vulnerability. Thus, even alarming environmental threats to the biosphere may not be seen as personally threatening.

IMPLICATIONS OF CULTURAL IMMUNITY TO ENVIRONMENTAL THREAT FOR THE RISK SOCIETY

European theory relating to contamination seems largely to have focused on societal levels of social process, whereas empirical studies emanating from the United States have tended to focus on individual, family, institutional/organizational, and community levels of process. The emergent discourse between these perspectives not only bridges methodology, but also levels of analysis. In particular, this chapter has contrasted this empirical tradition with Ulrich Beck's risk society theory. Beck views society as having become reflexive, reacting against the very risks introduced by modernity. According to this thesis, one would expect to find global, postmodern society to be obsessed with risk. However, as has already been noted, the empirical tradition does not confirm these expectations.

Even the construct of risk is itself suspect. An insurance term expropriated for rationalizing dangerous activities, risk was not traditionally a vernacular construct. In contradiction to the prediction that we have entered a 'risk society,' risk has still not emerged in common everyday language. For example, in my own interviews with toxic victims, the term was rarely mentioned. Not only does risk not appear to be a naive construct from their pre-contamination lifescape, but it is evident that victims now hold an 'all or none' view of environmental hazards that does not accept tradeoffs of costs and benefits, declarations of safety attested to by risk assessments, or compromises due to greater public goods.[32] It appears that risk is itself a technocratic concept that has made its way into social science jargon, research, and theory. The fact that conferences, professional organizations, government documents, books, and journals are devoted to risk suggests a professional rather than popular adoption of the construct.[33] Risk is the way 'outsiders' and experts think. It is, in itself, abstract, not personal.

Thus, while Beck's thesis raises the question of how much risk creeps into everyday existence, my interviews with more than a thousand people in diverse community settings tell me that risk is not a normative construct. People do not talk about risk. They are still in an individual and economic paradigm, at least until forced out by turbulence. Contrasted against the empirical evidence, the risk society formulation overstates risk aversion. There are indications that developments roughly congruent with the theory do exist in contaminated communities. But, as this chapter suggests, the reason outsiders do not understand the plight of these victims is because their lifescape is still rooted in modernity, not in the risk society. If the latter were true, the wider public would be empathetic and understanding of victims. They would also not be so severely shocked when they themselves come to be victims of contamination.

Beck is of course correct in his contention that risk has entered the life of the modern individual in myriad ways. A case in point is the so-called 'Not-In-My-Backyard,' or NIMBY, syndrome, a predictable defense of place against certain categories of stigmatizing events, such as waste or hazardous facilities in a local area. NIMBY exists as a collection of isolated parallel events in thousands of communities, where the more immediate dimensions of social process are evident. Yet, cumulatively, NIMBY has emerged as a rejection of hazardous technologies that has had a societal effect.[34] The impact on normative 'state-of-the-art' engineering approaches to problem-solving is notable. Thus, the abandonment of incineration as a technology for waste disposal in the United States, and the shift toward waste reduction and recycling, is a direct outcome of controversies over siting landfills and incinerators. Similarly, industrial ecology and the effort to avoid hazardous waste generation reflect the point at which corporations have been forced to abandon the assumption of easy and inexpensive waste disposal. Laws and regulation played a role in these shifts, but fear of community opposition has been a force in its own right. The very proliferation of grassroots organizations worldwide supports the central themes of the risk society.

While such examples support Beck's assertions, other risk examples appear to contradict it. For instance, the contemporary home-buyer confronts the need to test many facets of his or her new purchase before acquisition. But confronting risk in this context need not imply that threats are clearly recognized and personally feared. As has been widely reported, geologic radon has hardly been shown to motivate widespread voluntary protective action, despite its dreaded consequences and pervasiveness. The lack of personal aversion to radon may reflect the potential ease of remediating the hazard, the fact that it is a natural rather than human-caused hazard, or the reality that people are sufficiently mobile to dismiss risk associated with place. Most radon testing and mitigation is instead narrowly utilitarian and economic, reflecting the need to demonstrate lower radon levels to transfer property. Thus, it is prudent to test a new home for radon so that any corrective actions can be paid for by the seller. At least for radon, action is motivated by modern pragmatism rather than postmodern protective risk avoidance.[35] As the radon example suggests, a risk response may be the exception rather than the rule in the course of modern life.

If the risk society is not generally evident in American research at the individual, family, and community levels of society, might it be evident at the institutional/organizational and societal levels? Here it is necessary to turn to social critique rather than empirical research as the method. At first blush, there are many confirming observations that suggest a social transformation in response to technological risk. The 1992 Rio Earth Summit and global negotiations such as the 1997 Kyoto conference on climate change, the success of international environmental organizations, and the political rhetoric around much of the world point to an age of ecological thinking and reduction of environmental risk. Industrial ecology, green accounting, and ecological economics have made beachheads in a corporate world reeling from regulatory limitations.

But there is only so far that one can push the list of confirmatory developments in American and global corporately dominated society. The increasing omnipresence of free trade and finance, the ascendancy of the multinational corporation, and the feebleness of government actions (as opposed to words) indicate that we are far from a true shift toward a risk-reducing society. Rather, capitalism has moved to isolate itself from the grassroots and even national levels of political influence. In many ways, we have solidified modernity in an advanced stage of neo-colonialism rather than abandoning it in favor of a sustainability-driven vision. This new world order is moving to address the latent doubts about risk by controlling information and advertising, and by inducing a renewed interest in global consumerism, complete with its tradeoffs. In fact, we see contradictory but simultaneous trends in social process, suggesting an eventual confrontation between visions of grassroots sustainability and global capitalism.

Further, one can turn to the events of the 25th anniversary of Earth Day in the United States to see that even the consensus over environmental protection that had Republican President Richard Nixon signing landmark laws such as the National Environmental Policy Act has long slipped away. In the recent 104th Congress, under the rubric of 'The Contract with America,' Republicans controlling Congress attempted to destroy or erode key pieces of environmental legislation. While their success was only partial, they are still with us and – as was the case for ratification of the Kyoto climate accords – make progress very difficult. Their impacts will echo, as will those of the Reagan–Bush era before them, far into the future. Not only do such trends signal the absence of a risk society, but they portend a reinforcement of the modern belief that risk is a necessary consequence of economic growth and must therefore be accepted.[36]

In conclusion, turbulence theory suggests that one has to shake a person from the private sphere within which operative modernity provides insulation from the environment. Even when contamination is publicly recognized as a dominant attribute of place, most individuals treat it as an abstraction, a marginal, minority, and private experience for some unfortunate few. People's concerns are with home, family, work, entertainment, and immediate social circle – but not with risk from the environment – unless risk turbulence intrudes and catapults them into the postmodern mindset of the risk society by removing their protective sense of immunity. Accordingly, we can see an integral relationship between cultural immunity and the observation that outsiders just don't understand. If Americans appear not to live in a risk society, but rather the normal world of modernity, then we have an explanation for why outsiders just don't understand the experience of contamination. The insider–outsider boundary is precisely that between believers and disbelievers, between those accepting and those denying contamination as reality, between those having the luxury to put off worrying about abstract and remote problems and those grappling with immediate and personalized threats. The experience of the insider varies dramatically from that of the ordinary person living a normal life. Many impacts on victims are, in fact, associated with the stigmatizing or distinguishing marks of contamination due to this differentness. This observation merely underscores that the risk society is not a reality for the majority of people who continue to deny the potential that they might personally be affected by contamination. For the hypothesized shift to occur the cultural immunity against contamination must be overturned.

Of course, in acknowledging a partial disconfirmation of the risk society, one faces the old dilemma of whether to call the glass half full or half empty. Is the paradigm of modernity being transformed, or is the old paradigm successfully defending itself against anomalous challenges? How then does one fairly judge disconfirming observations about the risk society? One possibility is to cite cultural differences – for instance, that the Germans who provide the context for Beck's theorizing are somehow more environmentally conscious than others. There may be truth to this contention, but it does not fully account for the differences. The social critique, as represented by Beck's work, need not be literal to have a heuristic and provocative effect, showing where modern society is headed, even if there is not empirical proof that it has arrived. Social theory may show selective attention, much as empirical work reveals selective sampling. In either case, predictions are confirmed even if significant exceptions are missed. In the case of contamination, one must bridge the gap between insiders and outsiders even as one must note the boundaries surrounding the insiders' point of view.

ACKNOWLEDGEMENTS

I gratefully acknowledge the critical comments of Deborah Kleese, Duane Gill, and Maurie Cohen.

NOTES

1. K. Erikson, *A New Species of Trouble: Explorations in Disaster, Trauma, and Community* (New York: W. W. Norton, 1994).
2. U. Beck, *Risk Society: Towards a New Modernity* (London: Sage, 1992).
3. M. Edelstein, *Contaminated Communities: The Social and Psychological Impacts of Residential Toxic Exposure* (Boulder, CO: Westview Press, 1988).
4. L. Gibbs, *Love Canal: My Story* (Albany: State University of New York Press, 1982); A. Levine, *Love Canal: Science, Politics and People* (Lexington, MA: Lexington Press, 1982).
5. Edelstein, *Contaminated Communities*.
6. See S. Couch and J. S. Kroll-Smith, 'The Chronic Technical Disaster: Toward a Social Scientific Perspective,' *Social Science Quarterly*, 66(4) (1985): 564–75.
7. This approach has been termed 'local' or 'popular' epidemiology. See P. Brown and E. Mikkelsen, *No Safe Place: Toxic Waste, Leukemia, and Community Action* (Berkeley: University of California Press, 1990).
8. Levine, *Love Canal*; and Gibbs, *Love Canal*.
9. Edelstein, *Contaminated Communities*.
10. M. Edelstein, 'Psycho-social Impacts on Trial: The Case of Hazardous Waste Disposal,' pp. 153–76 in D. Peck, ed., *Psycho-social Effects of Hazardous Toxic Waste Disposal on Communities* (Springfield, IL: Charles Thomas, 1989) and M. Edelstein, 'When the Honeymoon is Over: Environmental Stigma and Distrust in the Siting of a Hazardous Waste Disposal Facility in Niagara Falls, New York,' *Research in Social Problems and Public Policy*, 5(1) (1993): 75–96.
11. M. Edelstein and A. Wandersman, 'Community Dynamics in Coping with Toxic Exposure,' pp. 69–112 in I. Altman and A. Wandersman, eds, *Neighborhood and Community Environments* (New York: Plenum Press, 1987) and Edelstein, *Contaminated Communities*.
12. M. Fowlkes and P. Miller, *Love Canal: The Social Construction of Disaster* (Washington, DC: Federal Emergency Management Agency, 1982).
13. M. Edelstein, 'Disabling Communities: The Impact of Regulatory Proceedings,' *Journal of Environmental Systems*, 16(2) (1986/87): 87–110; A. Irwin, *Citizen Science: A Study of People, Expertise, and Sustainable Development* (London: Routledge, 1995); and R. Sclove, *Democracy and Technology* (London: Guildford Press, 1995).
14. I refer to this latter element as the lifescape, or the cognitive or meaning component, of study. See my *Contaminated Communities* upon which the following portion of this chapter draws.

15. M. Gibbs, 'Psychological Dysfunction as a Consequence of Exposure to Toxics,' pp. 47–70 in A. Lebovitz, A. Baum, and J. Singer, eds, *Health Consequences of Exposure to Toxins* (Hillsdale, NJ: Lawrence Erlbaum Associates, 1986). See also L. Palinkas, J. Petterson, J. Russell, and M. Downs, 'Community Patterns of Psychiatric Disorders After the *Exxon Valdez* Oil Spill,' *American Journal of Psychiatry*, 150(10) (1993): 1517–23; and J. S. Picou, D. Gill, C. Dyer, and E. Curry, 'Disruption and Stress in an Alaskan Fishing Community: Initial and Continuing Impacts of the *Exxon Valdez* Oil Spill,' *Industrial Crisis Quarterly*, 6 (1992): 235–57.
16. See K. Erikson, *Everything in Its Path* (New York: Simon & Schuster, 1976); J. S. Kroll-Smith and S. Couch, *The Real Disaster is Above Ground: A Mine Fire and Social Conflict* (Lexington: University of Kentucky Press, 1990); A. Shkilnyk, *A Poison Stronger than Love* (New Haven, CT: Yale University Press, 1985); and W. Freudenburg and T. Jones, 'Attitudes and Stress in the Presence of a Technological Risk: A Test of the Supreme Court Hypothesis,' *Social Forces*, 69(4) (1991): 1143–68.
17. See also C. Dyer, D. Gill, and J. S. Picou, 'Social Disruption and the Valdez Oil Spill: Alaskan Natives in a Natural Resource Community,' *Sociological Spectrum*, 12(2) (1992): 105–26; Palinkas et al., 'Social, Cultural, and Psychological Impacts of the *Exxon Valdez* Oil Spill'; and Picou et al., 'Disruption and Stress in an Alaskan Fishing Community.'
18. See, for example, N. Weinstein, 'Optimistic Biases About Personal Risks,' *Science*, 246 (1989): 1232–3.
19. Brown and Mikkelsen, *No Safe Place*.
20. See, for example, S. Berman and A. Wandersman, 'Fear of Cancer and Knowledge of Cancer: A Review and Proposed Relevance to Hazardous Waste Siters,' *Social Science and Medicine*, 31(1) (1990): 81–90.
21. H. Vyner, *Invisible Trauma: The Psycho-social Effects of Invisible Environmental Contaminants* (Lexington, MA: Lexington Books, 1988).
22. See also A. Baum, R. Flemming, and J. Singer, 'Coping with Victimization by Technological Disaster,' *Journal of Social Issues*, 39(3) (1983): 117–38.
23. Edelstein, *Contaminated Communities*. See also B. McKibben, *The End of Nature* (New York: Anchor Books, 1989); M. Olsen, D. Lodwick, and R. Dunlap, *Viewing the World Ecologically* (Boulder, CO: Westview Press, 1992); and L. Milbrath, *Environmentalists: Vanguard for a New Society* (Albany: State University of New York Press, 1984).
24. M. Edelstein, 'Toxic Exposure and the Inversion of Home,' *Journal of Architecture and Planning Research*, 3 (1986): 237–51 and J. Fitchen, 'When Toxic Chemicals Pollute Residential Environments: The Cultural Meanings of Home and Homeownership,' *Human Organization*, 48(4) (1989): 313–24.
25. See also W. Freudenburg, 'Risk and Recreancy: Weber, the Division of Labor, and the Rationality of Risk Perceptions,' *Social Forces*, 71(4) (1993): 909–32.
26. My notion of environmental stigma is developed from the work of Erving Goffman, *Stigma: Notes on the Management of Spoiled Identities*

(Englewood Cliffs, NJ: Prentice-Hall, 1963). See also E. Jones, A. Farina, A. Hastorf, H. Markus, D. Miller, and R. Scott, *Social Stigma: The Psychology of Marked Relationships* (New York: W. H. Freeman, 1984); Edelstein, *Contaminated Communities*; M. Edelstein, 'Ecological Threats and Spoiled Identities: Radon Gas and Environmental Stigma,' pp. 205–26 in S. Couch and J. S. Kroll-Smith, eds, *Communities at Risk: Community Responses to Technological Hazards* (New York: Peter Lang, 1991); Edelstein, 'Mitigating Environmental Stigma and Loss of Trust in the Siting of Hazardous Facilities'; and Edelstein, 'Crying Over Spoiled Milk: Contamination, Visibility, and Expectation in Environmental Stigma,' Paper presented at the Annenberg Conference on Risk, Media, and Stigma, 23 March 1997, Philadelphia.

27. See, for example, R. Bullard, *Dumping in Dixie: Race, Class, and Environmental Quality* (Boulder, CO: Westview Press, 1990).

28. Beck, *Risk Society.*

29. Edelstein and Wandersman, 'Community Dynamics in Coping with Toxic Exposure' and Edelstein, *Contaminated Communities.*

30. Fowlkes and Miller, *Love Canal.*

31. See Olsen et al., *Viewing the World Ecologically* and Milbrath, *Environmentalists.*

32. Edelstein, *Contaminated Communities.*

33. M. Edelstein, 'Public and Private Perceptions of Risk,' pp. 60–4 in T. Burke, N. Tran, J. Roemer, and C. Henry, eds, *Regulating Risk: The Science and Politics of Risk* (Washington, DC: The International Life Systems Institute Press, 1993).

34. M. Edelstein, 'The Psychological Basis for the "NIMBY" Response,' pp. 271–8 in J. Andrews, L. Askew, J. Bucsela, D. Hoffman, B. Johnson, and C. Xintaras, eds, *Proceedings of the Fourth National Environmental Health Conference: Environmental Issues – Today's Challenge for the Future* (Washington, DC: Department of Health and Human Services, Public Health Service, November, 1990).

35. M. Edelstein and W. Makofske, *Radon's Deadly Daughters: Science, Environmental Policy, and the Politics of Risk* (Lanham, MD: Rowman & Littlefield, 1998).

36. Olsen, et al., *Viewing the World Ecologically* and Milbrath, *Environmentalists.*

7 The *Exxon Valdez* Disaster as Localized Environmental Catastrophe: *Dis*similarities to Risk Society Theory

J. Steven Picou and Duane A. Gill

> This... transformation of threats to nature from culture into threats to the social, economic, and political order is the concrete challenge of the present and the future.
>
> Ulrich Beck, *Risk Society*

INTRODUCTION

Contemporary social theorists have begun to devote increasing attention to the sources, nature, and consequences of ecological degradation in the modern world.[1] This work has begun to amend the historically conditioned social science view of the natural environment as an 'objective reality.' The pre-existing perspective legitimized opportunities for control by human social organization and created a theoretical void concerning the social risks posed by massive environmental catastrophes and global environmental damage.[2] As such, recent conceptualizations of the environment–society relationship have provided both theoretical and empirical direction regarding the economic, social, and psychological consequences of contamination to the biosphere. The emergence of environmental harm as a barometer for the distribution of technological risks represents a paradigmatic shift in social theory to a more 'analytical heuristic' concern with global environmental degradation and its attendant social consequences. Although the latter issue is inextricably interwoven with postmodern thought, several European sociologists have begun to focus on technological risk and catastrophe, as well as on the emergence of a modern 'consciousness of threat,' as one perspective for explaining the demise of classical industrial society.[3]

In particular, the German sociologist Ulrich Beck argues that the broad contours of this social malaise of modernity include a variety of known risks, dangers, and impacts produced by industrial society and transformed through the process of 'reflexive modernization.' This transformation signals that, ultimately, the entire planet may succumb to the 'juggernaut of modernity,' the runaway train that leads down the 'road to hell.'[4] Toxicity in modernity is more threatening and ominous because it introduces new forms of uncertainty, posing decisive risks to humans which are irreversible and cumulative, and environmental degradation that can be disastrous in scope. These modern risks are often both physically and socially invisible, therefore inviting debate and conflict over the calculation of alleged impacts and damage claims.[5]

Beck also asserts that through a process of so-called 'organized irresponsibility' the institutions and calculus of classical industrial society fail to restore catastrophic damage in the risk society. The insecurity of the present is further elaborated by ongoing scientific debate and social criticism, mediated by reflexive modernization, which results in the unbinding of both science and politics. As Beck suggests, until now, 'sociology . . . has not asked what the threat of self-annihilation means to society.'[6] In his writings, environmental degradation becomes the focal point for a theory of modern society. This theoretical development out of European sociology is relevant to American environmental sociology, particularly that line of research concerned with the social effects of human-caused environmental contamination.[7]

As outlined in this volume's introductory chapter, environmental sociology in the United States has been rather atheoretical in its development through its failure to address adequately environmental degradation and to build a theoretical consensus.[8] Although issues of political economy, environmental values, social movements, and environmental attitudes have traditionally provided the content of courses on environmental sociology in American universities, none of these approaches conceptually integrates social structure and change with the biophysical environment.[9] Indeed, one can argue that the significance of the social is completely overlooked in environmental risk assessments that, as Beck asserts, '[R]esult in a sometimes trivial and meaningless discussion of nature without people.'[10]

John Hannigan criticizes this 'nonreflexive realist' position and proposes in its place a social constructivist paradigm for environmental degradation and the emergence of social movements around such issues.[11] Given that ecological consciousness and action show variation over the course of time, Hannigan argues that 'environmental problems do not materialize by themselves; rather they must be "constructed" by individuals or organizations who define pollution ... as worrisome and seek to do something about it.'[12] Hannigan applies his constructivist model to environmental problems, communications, science, and risks through case studies of acid rain, biodiversity loss, and biotechnology, providing a conceptual framework for environmental sociology. However, this model ignores any realist account of environmental degradation and is limited by an 'oversocialized' conception of the environment.[13]

A more 'reflexive realist' view recognizes that the physical destruction of the environment can be empirically measured and scientifically monitored, thus avoiding an extreme form of naive constructivism. Both perspectives – constructivist and realist – are relevant and necessary for understanding the human consequences of environmental degradation. We need to view the physical deterioration of the natural environment, the social construction of this demise, and the subsequent consequences for the human community within a dynamic socio-cultural context. Culturally based relationships between the biophysical environment and human communities connect realist and constructivist positions. As Szerszynski and his collaborators have recently noted, risk society is characterized by 'the problematization of objective physical-biological dangers.'[14]

Contamination of the biophysical environment results in 'a social crisis in the relationship to nature.'[15] Risk society theory frames this crisis in terms of localized hazards and reinterprets them through global concepts such as 'organized irresponsibility,' 'anxiety community,' and 'reflexive modernization.' In this chapter, we will review selected themes from these macro-theoretical concepts and contrast them with data from a more localized catastrophic event.

The verification of elements of risk society theory for environmental catastrophes should provide important information for understanding social change in late modernity. As such, the remainder of this chapter will focus on an evaluation of the appropriateness of selected themes from Beck's theoretical approach for explaining community responses to catastrophic environmental degradation. Specifically, we will use longitudinal social impact data from the 1989 *Exxon Valdez* oil spill to illuminate the utility (and indeed non-utility)

of themes from risk society theory for explaining community responses to the most environmentally destructive oil spill in North
American history.

ENVIRONMENTAL CATASTROPHE AS TECHNOLOGICAL DISASTER

Beck elaborates a model of social change that moves from premodern through classical modern to late-modern society.[16] This global
model identifies a historical shift from natural hazards to technological hazards for the risk society, as well as a corresponding
transformation from local to global threats. Beck is rather ada-
mant about the dire invisible, irremediable, and irreversible consequences of catastrophes arising from chemical, nuclear, and genetic
technologies. Risks emanating from these industrial activities are
also socially explosive and contribute to organized public mobilization efforts.

This perspective has commonalities with recent social science
research concerning technological disasters in the United States.
In particular, case studies of localized contamination have docu-
mented social conflict and disruption, psychological pathology, and
negative health impacts.[17] These slowly evolving 'chronic technical
disasters' and more sudden 'technological disasters' typically result
in toxic contamination of the environment through organizational
agency and involve the identification of a principle responsible party
for legal reparations.[18] Researchers have debated the utility of distinguishing technological disasters from natural disasters and it is
increasingly apparent that untoward events resulting from the failure of technology are coming to occupy key theoretical and empirical
positions among scholars working in this field.

Although any type of disaster may impair a social system's ability to maintain biological survival, social order, social meanings,
and social interaction, research has revealed some fundamental
differences between the consequences of natural and technological
disasters. Erikson describes these technological catastrophes as a
'new species of trouble,' in that these events 'contaminate rather
than damage; pollute, befoul, and taint rather than just create wreck-
age' and 'scare human beings in new and special ways.'[19]

Whereas the literature defines events such as floods, volcanic
eruptions, earthquakes, hurricanes, drought, blizzards, and torna-

does as disasters caused by 'nature' or 'acts of God,' the causes of technological disasters are frequently traced to human culpability or technological malfunction. Natural disasters involve a lack of control over processes perceived to be beyond human dominion, while technological disasters engender a loss of control over technical processes generally thought to be subject to management. Accordingly, technological disasters involve the identification of certain entities that can be blamed and held accountable for malfeasance. It is also worthwhile to observe that historical experiences with natural disasters have led communities to develop emergency preparedness and planning procedures, as well as disaster subcultures (sets of cultural defenses grounded in knowledge, norms, values, and technology) with which to respond to hazardous situations arising from the forces of nature. Society cannot wholly prevent adversity from such sources, but it can anticipate, predict, prepare, defend, and recover from nature's most extreme environmental events.[20] In contrast, we tend to perceive technological disasters as preventable and thus the organizations whose actions are ultimately responsible for these situations rarely anticipate them in advance. Government has certain responsibilities in all untoward events, but the plot thickens when industrial corporations become the focus of public blame and acrimony. The complexity of organizational and technological operations, combined with the secretiveness in which many firms shroud their manufacturing operations, confounds local efforts to prepare for a technological disaster.[21]

Because toxic contamination threatens assumptions about environmental safety, technological disasters frequently sever the relationship between people and the natural environment. This loss of 'lifescape' (i.e. the personal security of the biophysical surround) leads to the erosion of institutional trust among victims.[22] Natural disasters produce obvious physical damage to the built environment (e.g. buildings, roadways, bridges), but communities typically rebuild and recover quickly.[23] However, many technological disasters do not result in physical damage to infrastructure, but rather contaminate the local ecology. We cannot observe these agents through conventional means and, as Vyner notes, 'it is quite impossible for humans to determine if and when they are being exposed.'[24] The intractability of these events is further compounded when physicians using sophisticated equipment are unable to confirm cases of exposure. The undetectability of contaminants and the complex etiology of resulting health effects contribute to lingering uncertainty concerning the personal threats of exposure (see also the chapter by Michael Edelstein in this volume).

Within this milieu of indeterminacy, potential victims often advance rival interpretations of the situation. Kroll-Smith and Couch observe that, 'What emerges are competing views of the same local world: It is dangerous and uninhabitable; you should be concerned. No, the environment is safe and habitable; you should get control of yourself.'[25] Contamination engenders numerous risks – for instance to family and personal health, financial security, social relationships – and creates considerable distress among victims as they respond as best they can to these novel threats.[26]

As researchers have frequently observed, natural disasters follow a predictable pattern in which a community moves from a state of equilibrium through a series of stages: warning, threat, impact, inventory, rescue, remedy, recovery, and rehabilitation.[27] Technological disasters rarely follow such a linear pattern. Although some of these events have an identifiable beginning (e.g. Three Mile Island, Chernobyl, Bhopal), others originate long before people develop an awareness of a specific problem. Many instances of slow-onset chemical contamination, in which hazardous substances can remain buried underground and can seep slowly into homes and water sources over extended periods of time, fall into this latter category. Kroll-Smith and Couch contend that such cases of contamination 'trap portions of the population in the warning, threat, and impact stages.'[28] Efforts to secure assistance and gain recompense after a technological disaster typically require affected communities to enter into class-action litigation. Responsible organizations generally react defensively and attempt to minimize the perceived amount of damage for which they (and their insurers) could be financially liable. Protracted legal wrangling and processes of restoration following technological disasters may continue for decades and this creates ambiguous endings and deprives individuals of a sense of event closure.[29] These unsettling features usually give rise to a subsequent disaster – an emergent stressor that victims continue to experience over time. Such secondary disasters keep people locked into a state of long-term distress by evoking recurrent reminders of the original event and perpetuating incertitude regarding future outcomes. In short, this chronic pattern creates a 'corrosive community,' an important analogue to Beck's concept of the 'anxiety community.'[30]

The corrosive community is characterized by the deterioration of social relationships resulting from apprehension, fear, anger, confusion, and stress. This breakdown of the social fabric occurs in a milieu of anxiety and unease, facilitated by competing definitions of contamination, environmental damage, and pending threats. Victims also become distrustful of institutional offers of compensation and support. In some cases, as occurred at the infamous Love Canal, the community consequences of technological disasters are ultimate – residents disappear, although homes and buildings might remain intact.

This point is instructive because it suggests that American environmental sociologists have independently been investigating the outcomes of Beck's notion of 'localized self-annihilation,' providing micro-level evidence of themes found in contemporary social theoretical literature. In the following section we outline some of the global concepts from risk society theory that are relevant to environmental sociologists' empirical understandings of technological disasters.

CATASTROPHE IN MODERNITY: COMMUNITY IN RISK SOCIETY

Technological disasters are clearly part of the landscape of the twenty-first century. The modern age signals a shift in the nature of risk. 'Modernity is risk culture' and the acknowledgment of late and high modernity phases, or even a postmodern society, identifies a sociological concern with the 'unthinkable' or the 'dark side' of progress. This theme is embodied in the recent work of both Ulrich Beck and Anthony Giddens, who pose the 'risk of societal self-annihilation' and a social dynamic that creates doubt regarding incalculable high-consequence risks as characteristics of the present era. 'Risk society is catastrophic society' and Beck distinguishes a class of novel, contemporary hazards that are different from the natural disasters which have customarily threatened humanity.[31]

Beck's conceptualization of catastrophe is global in scope. Modern concerns such as anthropogenic climate change and ozone depletion have a holistic impact on all organic matter and extend across both time and space to encompass distant others and future generations. Importantly, these new threats preclude the provision of compensation for victims (or at least make this task very difficult given prevailing institutional mechanisms).[32] Such situations are technological breakdowns that harm the physical environment in

largely invisible and unknown ways. Accountability for the social
problem of environmental degradation cannot be determined and
victims confront corporate, government, and legal institutions engaged in weaving webs of 'organized irresponsibility.'[33]

Although for Beck catastrophes are supra-national, he notes that
the social risks of late modernity have both short- and long-term
consequences for plants, animals, and people. Furthermore, in building his theory of risk society he uses the chronic mercury
contamination of Villa Parisi (Brazil) and the explosive industrial
accident at Bhopal (India) to illustrate actual technological disasters in developing countries.[34] Elsewhere, he evokes Chernobyl as
the classic example of the tendency of the risk society for self-
annihilation.[35] Beck has also written that the risks of modernity
can be geographically localized and forecasts their unpredictable
social consequences to be tortuous.[36] He describes the emergence
of a 'solidarity of anxiety' among victims and how such a condition
contributes to the 'anxiety community.' Beck skirts the details concerning the anxiety community because, in his estimation, the ability
of such a collectivity to withstand stress and not self-destruct is
unknown. As he observes, 'anxiety has not been a foundation for
rational action.'[37]

Beck's theoretical treatment contains occasional reference to more
situated contexts. Specifically for our current purposes we suggest
a more focused definition of catastrophe, relative to the concept
of disaster. Furthermore, Beck's notion of the anxiety community,
and his subsequent questions regarding this construct, suggests that
environmental disasters may very well range in scope from ultimate global self-annihilation to instances of smaller-scale destruction.
The accumulation of thousands of small-scale incidents of environmental harm could give rise to a pattern of collective anxiety in
the culture of the risk society. Accordingly, an understanding of
localized catastrophes and their social impacts, as well as the identification of either mobilized 'anxiety' or depressed 'corrosive'
communities and subsequent patterns of social change, provides a
pathway for verifying empirically aspects of Beck's theoretical work.

We are particularly interested in several of Beck's macro-level
themes and his occasional examples of concrete, localized catastrophes. Our discussion will attempt to bridge these abstract
theoretical concerns to the micro-context of the 1989 *Exxon Valdez*
oil spill in Alaska. This objective is, at best, a hazardous undertaking. Nonetheless, Beck describes the articulation of risk society as

containing 'some empirically oriented, projective social theory without any methodological safeguards,' and such a statement suggests relevance to the social impacts of localized environmental destruction. We derive some middle-range interpretations of risk society theory and contrast these themes with data on the *Exxon Valdez* disaster.

Beck's notion of catastrophe connotes an unthinkable and irreversible risk of environmental harm that threatens the lives and livelihoods of present and future generations of people, flora, fauna, air, water, and soil. Researchers have traditionally viewed the concept of 'catastrophe' in terms of extreme events in which the vast majority of residents of an area suffer dislocation. The incident disrupts normal, everyday routines for an extended period of time and strains the local social and cultural infrastructure with continuing threats to vulnerable human groups.[38] In short, we can differentiate catastrophes from disasters by the fact that they produce social damage for entire communities and this impairment can persist over an extended period of time.

Localized environmental catastrophes are highly probable in the risk society. Concrete experiences of technological failure from Chernobyl, Bhopal, Three Mile Island, and Love Canal, as well as a host of other less ignoble places, alert us to the possibility of the 'ultimate catastrophe,' that is the destruction of all organic life on the planet. However, the global risk society – particularly in a post-Cold War era – will in all likelihood come about through the accumulation of an ever-growing number of smaller-scale incidents. The proliferation of novel threats will occur within situated sociocultural contexts engaging in processes of reflexive modernization and producing communities that are self-conscious of present and impending dangers.[39]

For Beck, it is this 'reflexivity of self-destruction' that drives people together, generating a 'solidarity of anxiety.' At this point, Beck becomes rather vague about the nature of the anxiety community. Initially, it seems to be a critical prerequisite for political action (i.e., a response of reflexive modernization), yet he acknowledges that it is unclear how such mobilization will occur.[40]

The important question at present is whether the anxiety community associated with the risk society is able to mobilize residents for collective action. Alternatively, will it generate a pattern of local social fragmentation and distress? Studies of the community impacts of technological disasters in the United States point to an important parallel with the concept of the corrosive community.

This socially destructive process tends to emerge during the aftermath of technological disasters, thereby denying the possibility of recovery or mobilization for recovery. Such collectivities are characterized by: (1) the ambiguity of biophysical damage, (2) the likelihood of a debilitating (rather than a therapeutic) process of social response, and (3) the overall tendency toward socio-cultural disruption.[41] In contrast to the solidarity of Beck's anxiety community, the conflict, uncertainty, fear, and distrust in the corrosive community loom as the 'tortuous' path for localized victims traumatized by these untoward events.

We turn our attention toward exploring these themes in the light of data on the social impacts from the *Exxon Valdez* accident. This examination will give a hearing to people Beck describes evocatively as the 'voices of the side-effects,' in this case those individuals who bear the risks of the sprawling technical system responsible for the global transport of oil. Industry experts estimated that an oil spill of catastrophic proportions would occur in Alaska only once every 227 years.[42] However, this low probability event did take place and it had profound consequences for the three small communities in the surrounding vicinity that are economically and culturally dependent on renewable natural resources.[43]

THE *EXXON VALDEZ* DISASTER AS LOCALIZED CATASTROPHE

On March 24, 1989, the supertanker *Exxon Valdez* ran aground on Bligh Reef in Prince William Sound off the southcentral coast of Alaska resulting in an oil spill that caused extensive ecological damage. The vessel released over 11 million gallons of crude oil that over the course of the following weeks and months inundated a vast intertidal area and eventually spread south into the Gulf of Alaska. Alyeska, the consortium of multinational oil companies that operates the pipeline and the oil transport facility located in the coastal town of Valdez, was responsible for containing the spillage. Corporate officials, however, missed numerous opportunities to limit the effects of the accident within the first 72 hours due to inadequate communications and a lack of readily available equipment. Ultimately, the initial organizational response proved to be a complete failure. Ensuing storms and high seas over the next three-month period washed oil across approximately 1900 kilometers of rugged Alaskan coastline. Controversial clean-up methods, including the use of hot water and chemical detergents, resulted in further damage to the surrounding ecological resources and alarmed local residents.

Because the oil spill occurred during the season of greatest biological productivity, it had an immediate and devastating effect on both the natural environment and the human communities that rely on the region's renewable natural resources. The casualty list of most visible damage included more than 250 000 seabirds, 144 bald eagles, approximately 3500 sea otters, 300 seals, and 22 whales. Furthermore, marine scientists have linked declines in populations of pink salmon and herring to destruction of the bioregion's food chain and to contamination of spawning areas.[44]

Needless to say, the oil spill severely impaired the isolated local communities that are economically dependent on commercial fishing. Furthermore, the Prince William Sound area is home to several groupings of Alaska Natives, and village life, largely arranged around the subsistence gathering of fish and wild game, was severely disrupted.[45] These local residents could not conduct their traditional harvests of herring, seal, salmon, and clams because of fears of contamination (and a state-imposed moratorium). We have elsewhere described these settlements as *renewable resource communities,* that is localities with cultural, social, and economic structures organized around the collection and exchange of renewable natural resources.[46] There are three such communities in Prince William Sound – two Alaska Native villages (Chenega Bay and Tatitlek) with populations of less than one hundred persons and a primarily non-Alaska Native town (Cordova) comprising approximately 2500 people. All three communities are located in an extremely remote area and are accessible only by airplane or boat. Given their distinct dependence on renewable natural resources, these communities are extremely vulnerable to perturbations of the biophysical environment. In addition to its obvious immediate social dislocation, the oil posed longer-term threats to the cultural and economic viability of these communities due to the damage suffffered by local biota.

Commercial fishers in Prince William Sound have experienced a succession of unusual seasons since the accident. State authorities canceled the annual herring season five times during the seven years following the oil spill. Although there was a limited herring harvest in 1997, prospects for the recovery of this fishery remain uncertain. Pink salmon have experienced sporadic returns during most years since the accident and the stability of this species is questionable. Among local residents, economic hardships resulting from disruption of commercial fishing and uncertainty regarding resource recovery have contributed to ongoing cultural, social, and psychological stress.

The *Exxon Valdez* oil spill exemplified the basic features of a localized technological catastrophe for these Prince William Sound communities. The accident was the result of a loss of control over complex organizational and technical activities involving corporate, political, and societal arrangements.[47] The public variously assigned blame to the tanker captain, Exxon, Alyeska, oil corporations, and government agencies.[48] Litigants (many from the Prince William Sound communities) filed hundreds of lawsuits and the legal proceedings will likely continue well into the next century.[49] The biophysical damage stemming from the oil spill directly disrupted local environment–community relationships. Differing definitions of the amount of ecological damage, the threat to future economic viability, and the legal responsibility of corporate and government actors created deep schisms and sharp conflicts. Some community members earned considerable sums of money working on the clean-up during the oil spill's immediate aftermath, while other local residents did not, would not, or could not gain employment. Such inequity intensified internal disputes.[50]

For many local residents, the early announcements of a catastrophic oil spill virtually within sight of their homes served to give the event an identifiable beginning. However, few people living in the Prince William Sound area have experienced a sense of closure and, indeed, the accident's residual effects continue to take their toll. The aftermath of the oil spill, in the form of failed fisheries and protracted litigation, have contributed to a continuing pattern of social anxiety and distress. Over the past eight years, we have used survey and ethnographic methods to systematically collect data in several Alaskan communities on the accident's social impacts. In the following section, we draw upon this research to highlight selected themes in Beck's risk society theory.[51]

*DIS*SIMILARITIES TO REFLEXIVE MODERNIZATION: SCIENCE, COUNTER-SCIENCE, AND ORGANIZED IRRESPONSIBILITY

The extent of the ecological damage caused by the *Exxon Valdez* oil spill has been the subject of numerous scientific debates that continue to be socially constructed nearly a decade after the actual event. Although it is indisputable that the *Exxon Valdez* spilled more than 11 million gallons of oil into Prince William Sound, it has been impossible to apply rigorous scientific models to determine unambiguously the accident's immediate and continuing ecological damages. This feature has given Exxon, the principle responsible party, a moral and legal rhetoric to avoid ultimate accountability.[52] During the four years following the oil spill, a judicially ordered moratorium prevented data pertaining to biological effects from being publicly released and this caused many local residents to question both the legal and scientific rationale for perpetuating uncertainty. Once researchers working for the state and federal governments made public their initial findings at an Anchorage symposium early in 1993, Exxon utilized one month later the annual meeting of an industrial research association, the American Society of Tests and Measurements, to present and promote the results of its own studies. While the evidence aired at the Anchorage conference described a pattern of serious – albeit in certain instances uneven and indistinct – damage, Exxon's investigations suggested that the oil spill had minimal, if any, ecological impacts.[53] More recently, a researcher who was working under Exxon sponsorship, suggested that because of 'environmental advocacy,' early calculations overestimated the oil spill's impacts, thereby exaggerating Exxon's moral and legal obligations. This assertion appeared in a peer-reviewed academic journal, adding credibility to the oil company's assessments of the damage caused by the accident.[54]

The socially constructed 'spill science,' or research into the event's effects premised on preconceptions, resulted in two distinct – and contradictory – bodies of purportedly objective data. Ott describes this incompatible discourse in the following manner:

> Something went terribly wrong with 'science' in the aftermath of the *Exxon Valdez* oil spill as illustrated by the extreme differences in the findings of key studies between government and industry. These differences are symptomatic of underlying problems with the scientific and regulatory processes that were designed to produce quality science.[55]

After the *Exxon Valdez* accident, as has become routine for large oil spills, the federal and state trustees for natural resources and the principle responsible party (i.e. Exxon) designed and executed studies to collect data to support their partisan positions. For the government, the claim was that the spillage injured resources and the relevant agencies conducted research to determine the extent of those damages. In contrast, Exxon held the position that resources may have been impaired, but natural recovery would be rapid and the company (and its contractors) proceeded to determine what and how much was unharmed to minimize its liability.[56]

For many residents of the Prince William Sound area this pattern of science and counter-science continues to be disconcerting and frustrating. A leading marine scientist residing in Cordova noted:

> The local people do not understand the complexity of determining spill impacts on the salmon and herring fisheries. There has been more variation in catch totals in the years preceding the spill than the years since the spill. So how can you absolutely say that poor salmon runs are due to the spill?[57]

Local residents interpreted this spill science as politics and the resulting litigation, in Beck's terminology, as 'institutional political discourse.' The following statements by Cordova residents illustrate this point:

> The whole mess – the spill, studies of impacts and the lawsuit – is all about money. Exxon's too powerful and rich – they will buy their own science and through their PR [public relations] make it real. We are just a gnat on an elephant's leg.

> I don't understand why scientific information hasn't been released. Decisions are being made that could be clarified by information.

> I think that it is all politics. Exxon is not really out to pay for what it has done. Exxon will fill a few pockets to avoid paying. It has also made money as a tax write-off.

> Exxon and politicians put pressure on the news media to suppress the news. What they claim to be real is not. It's all hype to make money.

Spill science created a sense of distrust among local residents. Many Cordovans soon after the accident became sensitive to this loss of control and lack of institutional trust. For example, a majority of respondents from a community-wide survey expressed skepticism about Exxon's ability and willingness to clean up the oil spill, the science of ecological damage assessment, and the legal system set up to distribute compensation. In August 1989, only five months after the accident, roughly seven out of ten Cordovans felt that the legal system would not require Exxon to conduct a satisfactory clean-up. Furthermore, 83 percent of our respondents thought that the company had publicly presented misinformation, 55 percent opined that Exxon was not telling the truth, and 51 percent asserted that there was a lack of public information about the oil spill and its ecological impacts. Most residents also maintained that Exxon's activities following the accident and the ensuing clean-up reflected 'legal advice' rather than a sincere effort to restore Prince William Sound and the surrounding vicinity.

This disenchantment with institutional responsibility is further reinforced by the survey data in Table 7.1. We found that the overwhelming majority of both community residents and commercial fishers were dissatisfied with corporate, government, scientific, legal, and media responses to the oil spill. Perhaps surprisingly, only one out of three respondents expressed satisfaction with local government activities, suggesting estrangement from both primary and secondary institutions responsible for managing risks associated with the local transport of oil. The pattern of organized irresponsibility observed by local residents, as well as issues of uncertainty associated with incomplete scientific accounts of ecological damages, contributed to a loss of institutional trust among community residents.

These observations also relate to the 'unbinding of science' that Beck discusses as part of the process of reflexive modernization. For the *Exxon Valdez* oil spill, competing social constructions of ecological damage were correlated with institutional interests and local residents quickly lost faith in science's ability to measure impacts objectively. For many of our respondents the ecological damage and the long-term threat to Prince William Sound was obvious and logical. The community-wide consensus regarding dissatisfaction with the accounts emanating from the full range of institutional actors is clearly indicative of a lack of trust in experts and their relevant support systems. This pattern of 'social recreancy' deters participation in community social movements and restricts the emergence of the subpolitical structures Beck foresees as emerging out of the anxiety community.

Table 7.1 Community satisfaction with institutional truth regarding the *Exxon Valdez* oil spill in Cordova, Alaska, 1992

	Total community	Commercial fishers
Federal government	14.9	8.3
Alaska state government	14.1	14.6
Alyeska Corporation	5.2	2.1
Exxon Corporation	6.1	2.7
VECO Clean-Up Corporation	6.3	0.0
United States Coast Guard	31.9	17.0
Local government	30.4	22.9
Scientists	19.9	20.5
Lawyers	8.5	8.7
Local newspapers	26.5	23.4

*DIS*SIMILARITIES TO THE ANXIETY COMMUNITY: SOLIDARITY OR CONFLICT?

Although the *Exxon Valdez* oil spill did not pose a direct threat to the human residents of Prince William Sound, it placed in jeopardy the viability of Alaska Native subsistence culture and the economic resources of commercial fishers. Local renewable resource communities faced both immediate and long-term ecological damage from the unknown consequences arising from the sizeable release of 'a toxic, persistent chemical' in waters so necessary for their way of life.[58] One Alaska Native stated, '[The spill] is hurting more than anything else we ever experienced. Its like losing everything you had.'[59]

The late Chief Walter Meganack, a widely respected Alaska Native elder, expressed the trauma of the unthinkable in the following manner:

> The excitement of the season had just begun, and then, we heard the news, oil in the water, lots of oil killing lots of water. It's too shocking to understand. Never in the millennium of our tradition have we thought it possible for the water to die, but it's true.[60]

Residents active in the local fisheries also felt immediately the impact of the oil spill. Following exceptional seasons during the two years prior to the accident, many commercial fishers invested their profits in additional capital equipment (e.g. boats, electronic equipment, nets). One of our respondents remarked in 1995:

I made a lot of money in [19]88, so I bought a warehouse to start a new business, a new boat, and a pick-up truck. In six years I've lost everything – three [fishing] permits, the boats, the warehouse, my wife, my family – everything! I don't think I'll get anything from the court, either – if I do its way too late to help me.

Some especially prescient local residents began to recognize the seriousness and the enduring quality of the oil spill's economic impacts as early as 1992. Several of them described to us the financial dislocation that the accident produced:

Since the spill I've lost a house in Montana, a lot in Montana, a new fishing boat, 25-foot Boston Whaler, 21-foot Munson Aluminum, 15-foot Boston Whaler, boat trailers, all my savings and my credit. Need I say more?

Cordova is suffering economic disaster at this time and is causing extreme hardships here. These surveys do not accurately portray the fear and despair that many of us are feeling. We have always been highly independent and now seem to have no control over our lives.

Since 1985 my husband and I have fought very hard to get ahead. We have worked very hard to get ahead. In 1988 we had $180,000 saved to build a new boat and since that time we have had to sell everything – crab pots, property, one boat – just to stay afloat which we are not. Last year we couldn't even make our [fishing] permit payment for the first time since we got it in 1985. Fishing is only opened half as much. We just can't make it.

Our survey data from 1995 reveals that from 1990 to 1994 the per capita economic loss (projected less actual earnings) for local commercial fishers was nearly $215 000. This continuing economic loss spiral severely affected the fishing economy of Cordova and is a major source of continuing social disruption and mental health impairment in the community.[61]

Beck acknowledges that anxiety communities are stressed. He also notes that it is an empirical question whether or not these communities can withstand stress, become politically mobilized, organize, and exert a reflexive political force. Table 7.2 addresses this theme by providing insight into the patterns of oil spill-related stress in Cordova over the last eight years. Data pertaining to the

Table 7.2 Intrusive stress and avoidance behavior scale means for the *Exxon Valdez* oil spill in Cordova, Alaska, 1989–97

	Intrusive stress	Avoidance behavior
Cordova community		
1989 (n = 117)	16.5	11.1
1990 (n = 68)	10.1	9.6
1991 (n = 221)	9.4	7.3
1992 (n = 151)	8.5	8.1
Cordova Commercial Fishers		
1989 (n = 49)	19.3	12.1
1990 (n = 27)	10.1	9.7
1991 (n = 73)	13.1	10.1
1992 (n = 48)	11.8	11.4
1995 (n = 88)	13.2	13.0
1997 (n = 65)	13.1	11.3
Cordova Alaska Natives		
1991 (n = 62)	13.4	11.5
1992 (n = 40)	14.6	10.7
Clinical cases[1]		
Clinical patients (symptoms due to bereavement from death of a parent 3–6 weeks after death)	21.6	n.a.
Clinical patients (6 months after therapy for symptoms due to bereavement from death of parent)	13.8	n.a.
Rape victims (2 years after incident)	11.4	n.a.

1. Data for clinical patients obtained from Howowitz (1976) and data for rape victims obtained from Seidner et al. (1988).

'impact of events' scale are available for the entire community and two high-impact groups: commercial fishers and Alaska Natives. The impact of events scale is a standardized psychological scale that measures two components of stress: (1) intrusive thoughts and recurrent images of a traumatic event, and (2) active attempts to avoid discussions or reminders of a traumatic event. This scale uses a specific event, in this case the *Exxon Valdez* disaster, to identify oil spill-related stress responses.[62] As noted, intrusive stress refers to the extent to which individuals endure recurrent memories of troublesome events. This component of the scale is informative because the frequent mental repetition of distressing experiences over long periods of time may indicate an increased vulnerability to disease progression and the deterioration of both physical and mental health.[63]

Table 7.2 clearly reveals a chronic pattern of collective stress. However, as presented these measures may not capture the full dimensions of the anxiety community because groups within such aggregates are affected differently. For instance, commercial fishers and Alaska Natives – two groups intimately linked to local environmental systems – experienced higher levels of intrusive stress. These incidences of stress among Cordovans appear substantial when contrasted to clinical patients (e.g. rape victims), further underscoring the scope of the chronic, debilitating consequences of this event for local communities.

Social disruption and psychological stress from the accident also affected utilization patterns for mental health facilities in the Prince William Sound area. Rates of mental health and alcohol counseling during the post-accident period in two local clinics (Cordova and Valdez) were significantly higher than those recorded for the pre-oil spill years. Despite this trend, mental health service delivery was severely restricted after 1989 by high personnel turnover (during an eight-year period Cordova's mental health center had five directors and over 14 staff members) due to heavy client loads and 'professional burnout.' Such evidence raises questions about whether anxiety communities are able to mitigate the long-term collective stress produced by technological catastrophes solely with local resources.

As previously described, event-related stress characterizes most communities that have suffered the effects of technological failures. In the case of the *Exxon Valdez* oil spill we have been concerned primarily with the psychological symptomology of members of vulnerable groups. We collected psychological data for commercial fishers in Cordova in July 1995 and included in our survey instrument items designed to ascertain respondents' psychological symptoms and interpersonal relationships.[64]

The results reveal that commercial fishers experienced relatively high levels of psychopathology – 20 percent of our sample evidenced severe anxiety and we classified 40 percent as having severe depression. Six years after the oil spill, we found 37 percent of commercial fishers had symptoms of spill-related Post-Traumatic Stress Disorder (PTSD). PTSD is a psychological disorder that identifies a delayed response to a traumatic event characterized by intrusive thoughts and images, avoidance behaviors, and hyper-vigilant reactions. These psychological symptoms result from a specific traumatizing event. Even more significant was the finding that one out of every two commercial fishers manifested either severe depression, PTSD, or a combination of these symptoms of psychological impairment.

The identification of severe depression and PTSD among commercial fishers provides an indication that within the anxiety community, serious emotional disorders are associated with vulnerable groups and this may preclude the emergence of collective political responses. Furthermore, our data identify two additional factors that may limit the politicization of the anxiety community, specifically the breakdown of social support systems and severe economic dislocation.

We found that commercial fishers who experienced severe depression and PTSD encountered difficulty with their interpersonal relations. Problems with relatives and within families were correlated with severe levels of psychopathology. Additionally, commercial fishers with severe levels of depression and PTSD also reported deterioration of their physical health since the oil spill.

These results clearly suggest that residents of anxiety communities may be preoccupied with resolving internal social conflicts, grappling with economic losses, and (for some) dealing with the effects of severe psychopathology. Beck notes that in risk society the 'quality of community begins to change' – indeed, our analysis of data from the *Exxon Valdez* accident suggests that the quality of community deteriorates sharply in the aftermath of an environmentally destructive event and the transformed collectivity resembles more the conflict-based corrosive community than it does the politically charged anxiety community.[65] This situation is apparent from our respondents' descriptions of community changes over a seven-year period:

> It is not the same small town with everyone pulling for each other. Now we are small groups going our own ways. Some old timers just couldn't handle the aftermath and moved away. The new people mostly seem to want to make a pocket full of money and leave for somewhere else.

> The oil spill has permanently changed our lifestyle, our community will never be the same. There is a different feeling to me; more stress, less open, less everyone helping each other. The community does not feel as safe.

The food prices are atrociously high. Thirty families have moved away. People are drinking more – more alcoholism and more fights. Some friendships are only seasonal now.

More harsh feelings. More separation of the town. Oil spill issues have affected the community.

My husband got cancer three months after the spill. We believe that the stress from the oil spill caused cancer. There are many cancer cases in Cordova. The oil spill divided a lot of people, and it also reunited a lot of friendships. The spillionaires [residents who made sizable sums of money during the accident's immediate aftermath] caused a lot of resentment between those who helped and those who did not. Prices of groceries doubled and never went back down.

The town remains split because of the spill and those who made too much money from it. Also, a lot of people have died – seems like more than usual – stress?

Everyone got along well before, but now the city government and everybody else are fighting. There is a lot of bickering in the community.

When asked this question, my immediate response is tears welling up. I don't know why, but the pain and loss I felt two years ago can suddenly come forth. The spill and the subsequent disfunctionalism of many people in this town feels like a horrible killing cancer has been planted in our community and I feel ineffectual in bringing a positive change. I even feel a diminished energy to seek solutions.

The people in Cordova used to be so upbeat, but now they're so negative. There's a big split between the haves and have nots, particularly those who worked on the cleanup. Businesses are being told by banks to stop extending credit. Also backstabbing is going on, but before people were more congenial.

Other data collected from Cordova in 1992 do not support Beck's hypothesis that the anxiety community will evolve into a more active, politicized locality. This survey found that only 26 percent of our respondents had become more involved in community affairs since the oil spill. In contrast, over 40 percent indicated that they had become less active during the same time period. These findings point to patterns of social fragmentation, distrust, and isolation that are characteristic of corrosive communities.

While social and economic instability continue to plague Cordova, Exxon's legal strategy has perpetuated divisiveness and uncertainty.[66] Rather than enhanced community solidarity, a significant proportion of Cordova residents have experienced since the oil spill continuing social conflict, economic loss, deteriorated social relationships, increased social isolation, severe psychopathology, and loss of trust in self and others. A long-time Cordova resident summarized his corrosive situation as follows:

> I won't be the same, my family won't be the same, the community won't be the same. I don't go out on the Sound much any more. When I go, I don't see oil. (Unless you dig on the beaches) the scenery is just as nice as before, but is like someone turned off the sound. The [animals] are few, as are the birds. You cannot go two blocks in town without seeing some leftover from the spill. The papers, radio, and publications of any group talk about the oil spill, the environment, and our health. Every group has its own scientists, lawyers, and reports (none ever agree with anyone else). Mostly I'm just mixed up, I don't know who to believe or why. I don't trust my fellow man much any more and I don't know why. My life isn't as much fun and I don't know what to do about it.

CONCLUSIONS

Modern, high-consequence catastrophes are a critical element in Ulrich Beck's theoretical writings on risk society. We have attempted in this chapter to identify certain themes from Beck's oeuvre and to contrast his macro-level contentions with the micro-level formulations emerging from field studies of technological disasters. The conceptual *dis*similarity between the anxiety community and the corrosive community provides one avenue for examining the social responses to the *Exxon Valdez* oil spill in the light of Beck's predictions concerning an emergent risk society. As we noted above, Beck is rather ambivalent about the outcomes of the anxiety community. Political mobilization, or meaningful subpolitical action, is also associated with other structural changes contained in his wide-ranging risk society theory. In this chapter, however, we have focused solely on the issue of technological catastrophe and subsequent community response. Our analysis suggests that the contrasting concept of the corrosive community is more applicable to victims of the *Exxon Valdez* oil spill. The lay public's loss of trust in relevant institutions, prolonged economic dislocation, chronic patterns of psychopathology, and continuing community conflict has not created a social context conducive to political mobilization, community solidarity, or social movements.

We observe that when viewed as a macro-level theory of social change, Beck's writings may be temporally bound to the post-World War II period, geographically limited to northern Europe, and (as noted by Jeffrey Alexander) subject to cultural modification.[67] Our analysis of the aftermath of the *Exxon Valdez* oil spill reveals that some aspects of Beck's theory are simply not generalizable to localized hazards. Nonetheless, other insights from his work – such as the unbinding of science and politics – appear to be outcomes that correspond quite favorably with our findings from the *Exxon Valdez* case. However, local responses to competing scientific claims of ecological damage resulted in hostility to institutional claims and less participation in community organizations. For this localized catastrophe, we witnessed a pattern of internal conflict and social isolation rather than a mobilized consensus for subpolitical change.

Current social theorizing with respect to the environment provides an abundance of hypotheses that require detailed sociological analysis. In this chapter we have attempted to draw on certain themes from Beck's writings and to evaluate their applicability in terms of one localized disaster. This daunting objective invariably involved some 'theoretical slippage' to transform macro-level heuristics to plausible middle-range empirical outcomes. We acknowledge this limitation and urge others to pursue empirical inquiries into the viability of the ambitious work now being produced under the rubric of environmental social theory. Through these efforts we may be able to establish the macro–micro linkages between these discourses.

ACKNOWLEDGMENTS

This manuscript has benefited from the encouragement and suggestions of Maurie Cohen, David Gartman, and Mark Moberg. The recommendations of two anonymous reviewers have also improved the overall quality of this work. The technical assistance provided by Linda Burcham, Ginger Gossman, Jackie Ryan, and Pat Picou is also acknowledged. Appreciation is expressed to the College of Arts and Sciences, University of South Alabama and the Mississippi Agricultural and Forestry Experiment Station (Project No. MIS-4333) for partially supporting this research. Data used in this chapter were collected from funds provided by the National Science Foundation, Earthwatch Center for Field Studies, the Natural Hazards Resource and Applications Information Center, and the Prince William Sound Regional Citizens' Advisory Council.

NOTES

1. R. Heilbroner, *An Inquiry Into the Human Prospect* (New York: W. W. Norton, 1974); A. Giddens, *Modernity and Self-Identity: Self and Society in the Late Modern Age* (Cambridge: Polity Press, 1991); U. Beck, *Risk Society: Towards a New Modernity* (London: Sage, 1992); and U. Beck, *Ecological Politics in an Age of Risk* (Cambridge: Polity Press, 1995).
2. For example, see T. Parsons, *Essays in Sociological Theory: Pure and Applied* (Glencoe IL: Free Press, 1949); T. Parsons, *The Social System* (Glencoe IL: Free Press, 1951); and L. White, *The Science of Culture* (New York: Farrar Strauss, 1949).
3. For example, see Beck, *Risk Society* and *Ecological Politics*. Refer also to A. Giddens, *The Consequences of Modernity* (Cambridge: Polity Press, 1990); Giddens, *Modernity and Self-Identity*; and U. Beck, A. Giddens, and S. Lash, *Reflexive Modernization: Politics, Tradition and Aesthetics in the Modern Social Order* (Cambridge: Polity Press, 1994).
4. Giddens, *Modernity and Self-Identity*.
5. H. Vyner, *Invisible Trauma: The Psychosocial Effects of Invisible Environmental Contaminants* (Lexington, MA: D. C. Heath, 1988). See also Giddens, *Modernity and Self-Identity*; and Beck, *Risk Society*.
6. Beck, *Ecological Politics in an Age of Risk*.
7. J. S. Kroll-Smith and S. Couch, 'Symbols, Ecology and Contamination: Case Studies in the Ecological-Symbolic Approach to Disaster,' *Research in Social Science and Public Policy*, 5 (1993): 47–73; and K. Erikson, *A New Species of Trouble: Explorations in Disasters, Trauma, and Community* (New York: W. W. Norton, 1994).
8. See also S. Cable and C. Cable, *Environmental Problems, Grassroots Solutions: The Politics of Grassroots Environmental Conflict* (New York: St. Martin's Press, 1995).
9. See, among others, O. Duncan, 'From Social System to Ecosystem,' *Sociological Inquiry*, 31 (1961): 140–9; W. Catton and R. Dunlap, 'Environmental Sociology: A New Paradigm,' *The American Sociologist*, 13(1) (1978): 41–9; and A. Schnaiberg and K. Gould, *Environment and Society: The Enduring Conflict* (New York: St. Martin's Press, 1994).
10. Beck, *Risk Society*.
11. J. Hannigan, *Environmental Sociology: A Social Constructionist Perspective* (London: Routledge, 1995). See also U. Beck, 'World Risk Society as

Cosmopolitan Society? Ecological Questions in a Framework of Manufactured Uncertainties,' *Theory, Culture, and Society*, 13(4) (1996): 1–32.
12. Hannigan, *Environmental Sociology*.
13. For critiques of the constructivist position see: T. Benton, 'Biology and Social Theory in the Environmental Debate,' pp. 28–50 in M. Redclift and T. Benton, eds, *Social Theory in the Global Environment* (London: Routledge, 1994); M. Redclift and G. Woodgate, 'Sociology and the Environment,' pp. 51–65 in the same volume. The social constructivist position can be expanded in terms of being 'more real' or 'less real.' That is, social constructions embedded within and corresponding to decisions and policies of institutions may appear to be 'more real' to the lay public. See M. Hajer, *The Politics of Environmental Discourse: Ecological Modernization and the Policy Process* (Oxford: Oxford University Press, 1995).
14. B. Szerszynski, S. Lash, and B. Wynne, 'Introduction: Ecology, Realism, and the Social Sciences,' pp. 1–26 in S. Lash, B. Szerszynski, and B. Wynne, eds, *Risk, Environment and Modernity: Towards a New Ecology* (London: Sage, 1994).
15. Beck, 'World Risk Society as Cosmopolitan Society?'
16. See, in particular, Beck, *Ecological Politics*.
17. For example see K. Erikson, *Everything in its Path: Destruction of Community in the Buffalo Creek Flood* (New York: Simon & Schuster, 1976); Erikson, *A New Species of Trouble*; M. Edelstein, *Contaminated Communities: The Social and Psychological Impacts of Residential Toxic Exposure* (Boulder, CO: Westview Press, 1988); and S. Couch and J. S. Kroll-Smith, eds, *Communities at Risk: Collective Responses to Technological Hazards* (New York: Peter Lang, 1991).
18. M. Brown, *Laying Waste: The Poisoning of America by Toxic Chemicals* (New York: Washington Square Press, 1981); S. Couch and J. S. Kroll-Smith, 'The Chronic Technical Disaster: Toward a Social Scientific Perspective,' *Social Science Quarterly*, 66 (1985): 564–75; and D. Gill and J. S. Picou, 'Toxic Waste Disposal Sites as Technological Disasters,' pp. 81–98 in D. L. Peck, ed., *Psychological Effects of Hazardous Waste Disposal on Communities* (Springfield, IL: Charles C. Thomas, 1989).
19. Erikson, *A New Species of Trouble*. Refer also to A. Baum and I. Fleming, 'Implications of Psychological Research on Stress and Technological Accidents,' *American Psychologist*, 48(6) (1993): 665–72; J. S. Kroll-Smith and S. Couch, 'Technological Hazards: Social Responses as Traumatic Stressors,' pp. 79–91 in J. Wilson and B. Raphael, eds, *International Handbook of Traumatic Stress* (New York: Plenum Press, 1993); and M. Cohen, Economic Dimensions of Environmental and Technological Risk Events: Toward a Tenable Taxonomy,' *Industrial and Environmental Crisis Quarterly*, 9(4) (1996): 448–81.
20. A. Barton, *Communities in Disaster: A Sociological Analysis of Collective Stress Situations* (Garden City, NY: Doubleday, 1969) and G. Baker and D. Chapman, eds, *Man and Society in Disaster* (New York: Basic Books, 1962).
21. P. Shrivastava, *Bhopal, Anatomy of a Crisis* (Cambridge, MA: Ballinger, 1987); C. Perrow, *Normal Accidents: Living with High-Risk Technologies* (New York: Basic Books, 1984); and Beck, *Risk Society* and *Ecological Politics*.

22. Edelstein, *Contaminated Communities*; and Erikson, *A New Species of Trouble*.
23. T. Drabek, *Human System Responses to Disaster: An Inventory of Sociological Findings* (New York: Springer-Verlag, 1986).
24. Vyner, *Invisible Trauma*.
25. Kroll-Smith and Couch, 'Technological Hazards.'
26. W. Hallman and A. Wandersman, 'Attribution of Responsibility and Individual and Collective Coping with Environmental Threats,' *Journal of Social Issues*, 48(4) (1992): 101–18; and Erikson, *A New Species of Trouble*.
27. Drabek, *Human System Responses to Disaster*; E. Garrity and B. Flynn, 'Mental Health Consequences of Disasters,' pp. 101–21 in E. Noi, ed., *The Public Health Consequences of Disasters* (New York: Oxford University Press, 1997).
28. Kroll-Smith and Couch, 'Technological Hazards.'
29. This approach is fairly standard in the United States where it is the judicial system that is positioned to intervene in such situations. See J. S. Picou and D. Rosebrook, 'Technological Accident, Community Class-Action Litigation, and Scientific Damage Assessment: A Case Study of Court-Ordered Research,' *Sociological Spectrum*, 13(1) (1993): 117–38; and J. S. Picou, 'Compelled Disclosure of Scholarly Research: Some Comments on High Stakes Litigation', *Law and Contemporary Problems*, 59(2) (1996): 149–57.
30. W. Freudenburg and T. Jones, 'Attitudes and Stress in the Presence of Technological Risk: A Test of the Supreme Court Hypothesis,' *Social Forces*, 69(4) (1991): 1143–68. See also Beck, *Risk Society*.
31. Giddens, *The Consequences of Modernity*; Giddens, *Modernity and Self-Identity*; S. Lash and B. Wynne, 'Introduction,' pp. 1–8 in Beck, *Risk Society*.
32. Beck, *Risk Society*; D. Goldblatt, *Social Theory and the Environment* (Cambridge: Polity Press, 1996); and M. Cohen, 'Risk Society and Ecological Modernization: Alternative Visions for Post-Industrial Nations,' *Futures*, 29(2) (1997): 105–19.
33. Beck, *Risk Society*; and Erikson, *A New Species of Trouble*.
34. Beck, *Risk Society*.
35. Beck, *Ecological Politics*.
36. Beck, *Risk Society*.
37. Ibid.
38. E. Quarantelli, 'What is a Disaster? The Need for Clarification and Conceptualization in Research,' pp. 41–73 in B. Sowder, ed., *Disasters and Mental Health* (Washington, DC: US Department of Health and Human Services and National Institute of Mental Health, 1985); E. Quarantelli, 'Disasters and Catastrophes: Their Conditions In and Consequences For Social Development,' University of Delaware, Disaster Research Center, No. 281; and Garrity and Flynn, 'Mental Health Consequences of Disasters.'
39. Goldblatt, *Social Theory and the Environment*. For a contrasting view refer to the chapter in this volume by Michael Edelstein.
40. Beck, *Risk Society*.

41. Freudenburg and Jones, 'Attitudes and Stress in the Presence of Technological Risk.'
42. Note that this probability estimate does not necessarily mean a disastrous oil spill would occur only *after* the elapse of 227 years. Rather, a strict interpretation of this statement advises us that a catastrophic accident would take place once *within* this time span.
43. J. S. Picou and D. Gill, 'The *Exxon Valdez* Oil Spill and Chronic Psychological Stress,' pp. 879–93 in F. Rice, R. Spies, D. Wolfe and B. Wright, eds, *Proceedings of the* Exxon Valdez *Oil Spill Symposium* (American Fisheries Symposium 18, 1996); and D. Gill and J. S. Picou, 'The Day the Water Died: Cultural Impacts of the *Exxon Valdez* Oil Spill,' pp. 167–91 in J. S. Picou, D. Gill, and M. Cohen, eds, *The* Exxon Valdez *Disaster: Readings on a Modern Social Problem* (Dubuque, IA: Kendall-Hunt, 1997).
44. R. Spies, S. Rice, D. Wolfe, and B. Wright, 'The Effects of the *Exxon Valdez* Oil Spill on the Alaskan Coastal Environment' pp. 1–16 in Rice et al., *Proceedings*.
45. J. Fall and L. Field, 'Subsistence Uses of Fish and Wildlife Before and After the *Exxon Valdez* Oil Spill,' pp. 819–36 in Rice et al., *Proceedings*.
46. Picou et al., *The* Exxon Valdez *Disaster*.
47. R. Gramling and W. Freudenburg, 'The *Exxon Valdez* Oil Spill in the Context of U.S. Petroleum Politics,' pp. 71–91 in Picou et al., *The* Exxon Valdez *Disaster*.
48. L. Clarke, 'Supertanker Politics and Rhetorics of Risk: The Wreck of the *Exxon Valdez*,' pp. 55–70 in Picou et al., *The* Exxon Valdez *Disaster*.
49. W. Hirsch, 'Justice Delayed: Seven Years Later and No End in Sight,' pp. 271–307 in Picou et al., *The* Exxon Valdez *Disaster*.
50. E. Piper, *The* Exxon Valdez *Oil Spill: Final Report, State of Alaska Response* (Anchorage: Alaska Department of Environmental Conservation, 1993).
51. Details on the methodological procedures used to collect these data are available in previous publications. See J. S. Picou, D. Gill, C. Dyer, and E. Curry, 'Disruption and Stress in Alaskan Fishing Community: Initial and Continuing Impacts of the *Exxon Valdez* Oil Spill,' *Industrial Crisis Quarterly*, 6 (1992): 219–34; J. S. Picou and D. Gill, 'The *Exxon Valdez* Oil Spill and Chronic Psychological Stress'; D. Gill and J. S. Picou, 'The Day the Water Died: Cultural Impacts of the *Exxon Valdez* Oil Spill,' pp. 167–91 in Picou et al., *The* Exxon Valdez *Disaster*; and J. S. Picou and C. Arata, *Chronic Psychological Impacts of the* Exxon Valdez *Oil Spill: Resource Loss and Commercial Fishers*, Report to the Prince William Sound Regional Citizens' Advisory Council, March 1997.
52. R. Ott, *Sound Truth: Exxon's Manipulation of Science and the Significance of the* Exxon Valdez *Oil Spill* (Anchorage: Greenpeace, 1994); and Hirsch, 'Justice Delayed.'
53. Ott, *Sound Truth*.
54. J. Wiens, 'Oil, Seabirds, and Science: The Effects of the *Exxon Valdez* Oil Spill,' *Bioscience*, 46(8) (1996): 587–97.
55. Ott, *Sound Truth*.
56. Ibid.

57. All quotations, except those noted, were collected in the field. See J. S. Picou and D. Gill, *The* Exxon Valdez *Oil Spill Open-Ended Responses to Household Survey, 1989–1992* (Starkville, MS: Mississippi State University, Social Science Research Center, 1997).
58. R. Steiner, 'Probing an Oil-Stained Legacy,' pp. 111–20 in Picou et al., *The* Exxon Valdez *Disaster.*
59. Gill and Picou, 'The Day the Water Died.'
60. Ibid.
61. Picou and Arata, 'Chronic Psychological Impacts.'
62. M. Horowitz, *Stress Response Syndromes* (New York: Jason Aronson, 1976) and A. Seidner, A. Amick, D. Kilpatrick, 'Impact of Event Scale,' pp. 255–7 in M. Hersen and A. Bellack, eds, *Dictionary of Behavioral Assessment Techniques* (New York: Pergamon Press, 1988).
63. S. Cohen and G. Williamson, 'Stress and Infectious Disease in Humans,' *Psychological Bulletin*, 109 (1991): 5–24 and A. Baum, L. Cohen, and M. Hall, 'Control and Intrusive Memories as Possible Determinants of Chronic Stress', *Psychosomatic Medicine*, 55 (1993): 274–86.
64. Picou and Arata, 'Chronic Psychological Impacts.'
65. Beck, *Risk Society*; Freudenburg and Jones, 'Attitudes and Stress in the Presence of Technological Stress.'
66. M. France, 'Corporate Litigation: Playing Hardball Is One Thing . . .', *Business Week*, 1 July (1996): 32; and Hirsch, 'Justice Delayed.'
67. J. Alexander, 'Critical Reflections on Reflexive Modernization,' *Theory, Culture, and Society*, 13(4) (1996): 133–8.

Part V
Risk and Environmental Decision-Making

8 Discovering and Inventing Hazardous Environments: Sociological Knowledge and Publics at Risk

Stephen R. Couch, Steve Kroll-Smith, and Jeffrey D. Kindler

INTRODUCTION

Robert Merton and Alan Wolfe write about 'one of the least understood stages in the development of a science ... how [scientific] knowledge is consumed.'[1] Specifically, they are interested in how sociological knowledge 'becomes part of the culture and society that academic sociologists themselves study.'[2] The authors do an interesting job of tracing how certain sociological terms become part of the language of the larger culture, while other terms do not. They also consider the use of sociological research methods, especially survey research, in the larger society and the impact of sociology on social policy. Merton and Wolfe conclude: 'Our time seems particularly receptive to sociological ways of knowing' – for better and for worse.[3]

In contrast, Herbert Gans is not so optimistic regarding the social utility of sociology. In his interesting, though preliminary, tally of best-selling books by sociologists, he laments the absence of brisk public sales for most sociological texts, asserting 'that the discipline still has a long way to go before it makes a significant impression on the general public.'[4] On a still different note, Kroll-Smith and Jenkins observe the contemporary troubles sociology departments face in an era of shrinking budgets and conservative politics, but conversely point to the expanding role of sociological knowledge in criminal and tort court cases in the United States.[5]

In short, there is increasing discussion and some disagreement on the local, situated, practical utility of 'sociological ways of knowing,' or the intersection between communities and sociology. While there

173

is predictably a sociological voice or two asking the eternal question of relevance, what strikes us as interesting about this issue today is its affinity with much larger concerns about the relationships between experts, the keepers of instrumental rationality, and general publics. Also interesting, though not surprising, are the two different genres of discussion currently heard on this issue: the more theoretical voice of the European continent and the more empirical voice of Britain and the United States.[6]

This chapter explores a research field where the boundaries between sociological knowledge and lay knowledge appear to be particularly porous; indeed, where sociological knowledge frequently becomes autobiographical text for both individuals and communities. We will call this field the hazardous environment and argue that here sociological research often becomes local, situated knowledge and a resource for redescribing the self, communities, governments, and environments.[7] In the investigation of hazardous environments, in other words, sociologists are not simply discovering social and behavioral patterns, they are also, and perhaps more interestingly, inventing them.

While we have stated this idea as compelling and worthy of attention, we should also add that it is probably the case that sociologists do as much inventing as they do discovering in all substantive fields, not simply the hazardous environment. We will say more about this more general observation in the chapter's concluding discussion. What makes the hazardous environment interesting is the way in which sociological knowledge is self-consciously adopted by lay persons and communities as a kind of practical epistemology for rendering obscure and troubling matters intelligible.[8] However, and here is where the issue gets sticky, it is those same obscure and troubling matters that are being investigated by the sociologist. Sociological data itself, under such circumstances, becomes a part of the history of the community, a part of the sociological knowledge necessary to make analytical sense of the research site. It is thus both a discovery and, in so far as it becomes a prescription for local ways of behaving and thinking, an invention, a useful (or at least perceived as such) improvement that did not exist before the sociologist entered the community.

There is not a well-established tradition of inquiry into the ways sociological knowledge intersects with people and their communities at the level of the research act. There are the usual admonitions to avoid 'contaminating' the data by not becoming personally involved in the lives of the people we are investigating. There is also the occasional oppositional voice that encourages recognition of the mutual influence of the research act on both the investigator and the subject. 'Knowing and changing,' Gouldner reminds us, 'are distinguishable but not separate processes.'[9] Lastly, there is the specifically political 'participatory-action research' (PAR) developed by Latin American social scientists as an organizing tool to assist communities in their efforts to resist state and colonial authorities.[10] PAR, however, is pointedly not research, but sociology as a tool for political resistance. To be brief, as important as these perspectives are for sociology, they do not help us understand how or when sociological insights and conclusions may enter the mundane lives of people and organizations they are meant to describe, becoming a part of the way local worlds are constituted and thus a proper subject for sociological inquiry.

Our intention in this chapter is to take a step towards understanding when and how professional sociology is likely to be transformed into lay sociology. How, in other words, do lay persons appropriate professional sociological knowledge, and sometimes a sociologist or two, for pragmatic use to help resolve a local problem? To address the issue of when sociological data are likely to become local knowledge we will limit ourselves in this chapter to a brief description of the hazardous environment. We suspect this reciprocal hermeneutic, or the 'we interpret you as you interpret us' exchange, occurs more frequently than conventional methods books admit. Furthermore, we are certain that this dynamic interaction does occur in many research settings where physical and social environments are experienced as increasingly incoherent, if not downright dangerous. Next we set out in some detail two cases of sociological research in hazardous environments. Each example illustrates the transformation of professional sociology into lay sociology while also reminding us that this shift from discovery to invention does not occur uniformly, but is contingent on the specifics of the research site. Following the cases, we identify some of the characteristics of the kind of knowledge being produced in these local, situated environmental crises. A final note speculates on how this community-based, rational knowledge might offer a possible resolution to the perennial conflict between idealism and realism in sociology.

A PHENOMENOLOGY OF HAZARDOUS ENVIRONMENTS:
DISCOVERING (OR INVENTING?) A RESEARCH SITE

Nuclear contamination, hazardous and toxic waste streams, contaminated drinking water and more generally stratospheric ozone depletion, biospheric warming, and the loss of biodiversity are likely examples of what we mean by the term hazardous environments. Phenomenologically, a hazardous environment exists when people experience their physical environment in a condition far from the ordinary, as an essential puzzlement, full of troubling uncertainties and dangers.

The idea of a hazardous environment is not new. Mileti and his colleagues used the term 'extreme environment' as a title to their review of the social science literature on natural disasters.[11] Anthony F. C. Wallace introduced the concept of hazardous or 'extreme situations' into the literature in 1956 while studying human responses to a natural disaster. A hazardous situation occurs, according to Wallace, when socially understood coping strategies are rendered ineffective, while at the same time people experience a 'drastic increase in tensions, to the point of causing death or major personal and social readjustment.'[12] While we find this definition useful, it requires some extension to be applicable to the questions we take up here.

The *Random House College Dictionary* defines hazardous as a perilous condition, risky and dependent on chance. Something is considered predictable if it can be apprehended and responded to in a routine manner; that same thing might be experienced as hazardous if it eluded efforts at normalization. The idea of hazardous suggests the absence of a meaningful way of comprehending an event or circumstance that produces the (possibly) negative effect of rendering a situation incoherent. This idea is akin to that part of Wallace's definition of extreme or hazardous situations that focuses on the loss of effective coping strategies.

From this vantage point, a non-hazardous environment, on the one hand, may be said to exist when nature is embedded in a legitimate way of knowing that renders it innocuous and inoffensive. A non-hazardous environment is unlikely to be a cause of great concern; it is, rather, more likely to remain pre-reflective and a source of what Giddens calls 'ontological security.'[13] Non-hazardous environments are apprehended in an 'as if' manner. Indeed, most people, most of the time, act towards their physical environments 'as if' they are not dangerous; and they do so, in part, because people around them are also acting 'as if' the environment is safe.[14] 'As if' forms of consciousness are essential for the development of more complex social relationships.[15] They are prelinguistic, emotively apprehended contracts between participants that the world enjoys sufficient order to proceed with the tasks at hand.

Hazardous environments, on the other hand, are perceived as dangerous, in part because they elude either mundane or expert efforts to understand them. If non-hazardous environments are experienced in an 'as if' manner, hazardous environments are experienced in the more ambiguous manner of 'what if?' Although the absence of knowledge is important in defining hazardous environments, by itself it is not enough. Environments do not become hazardous simply because we do not have sufficient knowledge of them; at any point in time there are probably more things we do not know than know about nature.

What makes an environment hazardous is the joining of a diminishing fund of applicable knowledge with a drastic increase in tension between people and nature. More pointedly, hazardous environments are experienced as dangerous. The danger could be immediate and life-threatening or chronic and life-diminishing. A depreciated endowment of useful knowledge coupled with an inescapable sense of peril characterizes the hazardous environment. Thus, an environment may be said to be hazardous when it narrows the range of what people know about their physical world, while simultaneously intensifying their need to protect themselves by acting on that world with imperfect knowledge.

Finally, and not surprisingly, hazardous biophysical environments are likely to be at least partly responsible for personal and social disorganization as people are forced to suspend 'life as usual' and construct new understandings of themselves, their communities, governments, local industries, and so forth. If conventional discursive practices no longer make sense, then it is not surprising that people will be in search of alternative conversations that will shed some light on their predicaments. Recall Giddens' observation that 'To be a human agent is to know, virtually all the time, under some description, what one is engaged in and why.'[16] And before Giddens, Durkheim recognized our need to conceptualize as a distinguishing feature of our humanness, thus paving the way for his famous concept, anomie.[17] What neither Giddens nor Durkheim seriously consider, however, is the possible role of sociologists and sociological knowledge in the construction of mundane insights into human miseries.

Enter environmental sociologists, or at least those who have gone to the field to study human responses to breakdowns in human system–eco-system relationships.[18] Common to these field experiences is the lack of fit between formal research requirements and the peculiar demands of communities facing the uncertainty and fear of hazardous environments. Researching hazardous environments, we suggest, militates against a highly structured research design where expert sociologists remain outside the research setting except to administer standardized instruments to their research subjects. Instead, sociologists are drawn into the fray, pushed by the need for an in-depth understanding of complex and changing processes, and pulled by community residents who often perceive sociological knowledge as a resource to assist in making sense and responding to their crises. This is less the world of Merton and Wolfe, in which boundaries between sociologists and their subjects remain intact, and more the world of Beck, where boundaries between lay and expert blur, if not dissolve altogether.

In such situations, a reflexive process takes place in which sociologists and community residents study each other. Sociologists produce knowledge, which is communicated to community residents, who define their situation and act partly on the basis of that knowledge. This alters their situation, which is then studied by sociologists, who produce knowledge, which is communicated to community residents, and so forth. The process of knowledge creation and transmission is not unidirectional, but dialectical, involving constant interaction between expert and lay person and between expert and lay knowledge. From the point of view of traditional science, the process is messy, as sociologists become part of their own data, confounding the usual boundaries between themselves and their subjects.

The two cases to follow illustrate this process. Both involve communities that experienced a technological disaster; both involve situations in which consumers viewed sociological knowledge as critical to their ability to deal with their problems. In the first case two sociologists begin a study only to discover that they cannot gain access to certain critical data unless they agree to become part of the change process. In the second example a sociological study evolves into a relatively structured attempt to produce social change, in cooperation with community leaders and residents.

CASE ONE: THE CENTRALIA COAL MINE FIRE

In 1962, fire was discovered in a seam of coal just outside the borough of Centralia, Pennsylvania. A typical small coal-patch community nestled in the Appalachian Mountains in northcentral Pennsylvania, Centralia had seen its share of mine problems and disasters. But nothing would compare to the devastation caused by this underground fire.[19]

During the next two decades, over $5 million was spent to extinguish or control the blaze, but all to no avail. During that time, the fire crept closer and closer to the borough proper, causing increasing concern about the health and safety of Centralia's nearly one thousand residents. Then, in February 1981, a twelve-year-old boy fell into a hole that the fire had opened in his grandmother's backyard. He grabbed onto a tree root and was pulled from certain death by his cousin. This incident shot Centralia into the national news and galvanized residents to form the Concerned Citizens Against the Centralia Mine Fire, a grassroots group committed to securing effective government involvement to fight the fire or to move the community away from it.

In the fall of 1981, this chapter's first two authors evaluated Centralia as a possible research site. We were interested in how such an unusual environmental hazard would affect community life. We decided to begin a study by talking with various informants, attending borough meetings, and conducting a survey of adult Centralians, perhaps to be followed by additional research. In order to help us gain entry into the community, we asked to be put on the agenda at a meeting of the Borough Council. We expected to explain our study in about ten minutes and secure the council's formal 'permission' to work in the community. More importantly, we hoped council members would pass the word that sociologists from the university would be around, and that residents should talk with us if asked.

The meeting did not go as we had planned. Instead of a polite welcome, the council members aggressively questioned us on every aspect of our planned study for an hour and a half. They wanted to know our motivations, our methodology, what we planned to do with the results, and what we intended to do with all the money we would make from the book we would write. At the end of the meeting, the council president said he would inform us of the council's decision regarding our request for permission to do research in the borough. He never did.

Dismayed by our reception, we reassessed our strategy. We proceeded to talk informally with some Centralians, including the president of the Concerned Citizens. This person was encouraging, urging us to study the community and giving us full access to his meetings and records. His reaction to us could not have been more different from that of the Borough Council.

Eventually, it dawned on us that we were getting such different receptions because the community itself was divided. Our subsequent research discovered that there was an amazing level of social conflict within this small community, all revolving around the fire, its dangers, and what to do about it. The Concerned Citizens wanted the federal and state governments to take more action; anyone who would raise the level of awareness and publicity about the fire, including sociologists, was welcomed. In contrast, the Borough Council thought people were making too much of the fire, that it was not as dangerous as some contended. They feared that the government might move the community unnecessarily and against the will of most residents. Therefore, they opposed anyone coming into town who would raise issues and draw attention to the community.

In retrospect, we had stumbled across one of the most important conclusions we would reach in our study: this long-term technologically caused environmental disaster generated destructive social conflict that unraveled the social fabric of this small Appalachian community. During the three years we collected data in the town, at least seven separate grassroots groups formed, each with a different interpretation of the fire and with different solutions on how to combat it and the problems it created. A fire bombing, slashed tires, telephone threats, and frequent displays of hostility and viciousness at public meetings were indications that community social life had broken down. Residents violently disagreed about the scope and dangers of the fire and what to do about them. But they were in marked agreement about the extent to which Centralia as a community had broken apart, and about the stress they suffered because of the loss of social support.

While making this community a fascinating site for sociological study, the intense intra-community social conflict posed serious methodological and ethical challenges. We wanted to study the social dynamics, not of one faction or another, but of the entire community. How were we to gain entry and access to data from all sides in such a highly charged environment? More generally, how were we to develop a methodology that would capture this intensely fluid and changing community?[20]

As mentioned above, we conducted a survey of community adults. This gave us a snapshot of local demographics and opinions as of the summer of 1982. But we needed more in-depth and change-sensitive data. Therefore, in a reversal of the usual research strategies, we used the information gained from the survey to plan a participant-observation study. While Couch remained on the margins of the community, attending various public meetings and events, Kroll-Smith moved into a rented house in Centralia, living there for eight months and gaining in-depth insights into the workings of the community. During this time, Couch would debrief Kroll-Smith, trying to provide a more removed perspective on the data and watching for signs of over-identification with the community or any part of it by Kroll-Smith. Through this methodology, we hoped that we would gain the trust of all community factions and access to high-quality qualitative data from all factions in the community, while maintaining our objectivity.

The strategy was partially successful. We did gain detailed insights into community dynamics and culture, and into the conflicts between community factions. We also think we avoided over-identification with any particular group or faction. However, while we were able to gain at least minimal trust from most people, this varied greatly, depending on the group and the individual. Furthermore, we were unable to maintain the usual format for a sociological study wherein researchers gather data, analyze it, write their findings, and only then disseminate the results of their investigation.

The last two points are related. Centralia was so divided that our objectivity as researchers was continually being questioned by the town's residents. If Kroll-Smith was known to have interviewed a member of the Concerned Citizens, the wider community would view us to be allies of that group. If we were seen conversing with Borough Council members prior to a council meeting, we were seen as being in the Council's camp. Try as we might to assure all of our neutrality, we continually were, at some level, mistrusted.

This situation was exacerbated when certain segments of the community came to perceive us, and the sociological knowledge we were gaining, as useful resources. For example, in April 1982, a national relief agency awarded the Concerned Citizens a $30 000 grant. A new group, the Centralia Committee on Human Development

(CCHD), was formed by the Concerned Citizens to administer the funds. Viewing this as an important new player in the Centralia drama, we asked if Kroll-Smith could attend CCHD Board meetings. The CCHD replied that he could, but only if he agreed to act as a volunteer consultant to the Board.

Considering the Board's deliberations to be important data for us, we reluctantly consented to this arrangement. Ethically, we agreed with CCHD's stated goals, which were to heal the community. However, we paid a price for our decision. The Borough Council banned us from attending their closed workshop sessions. Eventually, we were able to gain the confidence of some Council members who acted as informants for us concerning the content of the workshop meetings. Nevertheless, gaining entry to one group did inhibit our access to another.

This bargain also allowed (or forced) us to discuss our interpretations of the Centralia situation while they were still in the formative stages. Thus, our ideas entered the community and became a part of the definition some people held of what was going on and, inferentially, how it could be resolved. For example, we came to see this mine fire as an example of a wider class of disasters, including chemical contamination and radiation poisoning. These disasters had characteristics that tended to split communities apart. We called them 'chronic technological disasters.'[21] This concept resonated with the experience of many Centralians and apparently helped them to understand something of what their community was going through. As it turned out, at least two years before the term made its way into the literature of our academic peers, it was part of the interpretive lexicon being used by miners, housewives, priests, and government officials to describe the Centralia situation.

Our involvement also influenced strategies to try to bring the community together. By the summer of 1983, most residents were staying home rather than subjecting themselves to the expressions of hostility that inevitably erupted at public meetings. Based on our knowledge that neighborhood was a very important level of social organization for Centralians, Kroll-Smith suggested to the CCHD board that they hold 'neighborhood-area meetings.' The objective of these sessions was to give people access to a convenient, non-threatening context within which to express their opinions and listen to the views of their neighbors. Meetings were held at several locations throughout the town and were led by skilled moderators from outside the community. Negative or personal comments were discouraged, while all opinions were written down on newsprint. Those remarks that elicited relatively general support were taken to Borough Hall and hung on the walls of the Council chamber, to be discussed at the council's next public meeting.

While the last community-wide public meeting drew twelve residents, about 320 people in total attended the neighborhood-area meetings. These sessions demonstrated to many participants that orderly, productive group discussions were possible in Centralia. Several residents said that their neighborhood-area meeting was the first time they had expressed an opinion regarding the fire and the future of their community without fearing reprisals. Many expressed hope that Centralians might be able to come together and to have some influence over their fate.

In fact, the longer-term practical outcomes of the neighborhood-area meetings were mixed. At the next Borough Council meeting, rather than dealing with the substantive issues contained on the newsprint that lined the council chamber, the Council summarily rejected the neighborhood-area meeting conclusions because the sessions had been sponsored by CCHD. Instead, the Council would conduct its own survey to find out what residents wanted. Following this action, the meeting degenerated into the usual non-productive and vociferous arguments between the council and residents.

However, the CCHD Board did take the newsprint results seriously. Those views included a strong sentiment that if the necessary funds could be found to relocate community residents, most would like to leave. Therefore, CCHD encouraged the formation of the Centralia Homeowners' Association (CHA), which successfully lobbied for federal relocation money. In the fall of 1983, Congress allocated $42 million to relocate those Centralia residents and businesses that wanted to move. Eventually, all but approximately fifty people decided to participate in the relocation program.

In the Centralia case, then, we researchers entered the community with plans to do a relatively conventional study of a community in crisis. We quickly discovered that this would be, if not entirely impossible, undesirable. Our methodology evolved in such a way that to gain access to the data we needed, we had to become part of the data ourselves. While not intending to do so at the outset, we sociologists, and the knowledge we possessed, became part of the story in Centralia. Obviously, this violated all sorts of scientific canons. But ironically, without active involvement in the community, our scientific findings would have been at least incomplete, if not misleading. It was only by stretching the canons of science that we were able to gain the information we needed to provide a valid interpretation of the Centralia story.

As for practical outcomes, we do not know if the Centralia situation would have ended differently had we not come to town. We do know that the sociological knowledge we gained, in interaction with community residents, helped some Centralians define their situation. We also had an impact through some structural suggestions we made, such as the neighborhood-area meetings. As for Centralians' interpretations of our impact, some thank us for helping them to understand what was going on, and some appreciate what they view as our assistance in organizing effectively for eventual relocation. However, some blame us for helping to destroy their community.

CASE TWO: CORDOVA AND THE *EXXON VALDEZ* OIL SPILL[22]

Early in the morning of 24 March 1989, the oil supertanker *Exxon Valdez* ran aground on Bligh Reef. The ship's cargo holds, opened by the razor sharp edges of the rocky outcropping, poured oil into the surrounding waters. Recognizing immediate trouble, the *Exxon Valdez*'s captain radioed the local Coast Guard station and announced: 'We've fetched up hard aground off Bligh Reef, and evidently we're leaking some oil.' Presaging the trouble to follow he continued, 'We're going to be here for a while.'[23]

The *Exxon Valdez* dumped approximately 11 million gallons of North Slope crude oil into the pristine waters of Prince William Sound, contaminating more than 1900 kilometers of Alaskan coastline. As fate would have it, the oil spill occurred at the beginning of the ecosystem's busiest time of regeneration, what ecologists call the bloom period. Spawning, birthing, and nesting, new life teemed both on the land and in the water. This spill was not only the largest single accidental discharge of oil in North American waters, it was also the most biologically damaging disaster in the continent's history.[24]

Sociologists Steve Picou and Duane Gill first visited Cordova, Alaska during the summer of 1989, shortly after the oil spill. Interested in how communities respond to disasters that do not immediately threaten human life or health, but substantially interfere with local economies, they wanted to study the effects of the accident on a small commercial fishing village. Not surprisingly, the *Exxon Valdez* oil spill seriously disrupted the fishing economies of southcentral Alaska's coastal settlements – indeed the disruption continues as we write. Picou and Gill set out to examine the human effects of ecological disruption on one local fishing community. In doing so, they coined the insightful term, 'renewable resource community,' or RRC.[25] An RRC is a 'population of individuals living within a bounded area whose primary cultural and economic existence is based on the harvest and utilization of renewable natural resources.'[26]

On their first visit to Cordova, they found a bustling beehive of activity. Exxon and the state and federal governments were engaged in a massive clean-up operation that was employing anyone willing to work. Money was pouring into the town almost as fast as the oil poured from the stricken tanker. Fishermen who owned boats leased or rented their vessels to Exxon crews at inflated prices. Local businesses were barely able to keep up with demand. Teenagers, housewives, and retired persons could find well-paid work if they wanted it. A frenzy gripped the town as people saw a way of making a quick dollar.[27] It is ironic that in their first visit to a natural resource community severely disrupted by an ecological disaster, Picou and Gill witnessed the collective effervescence of an economic boom.

Perhaps ironically, many Cordovans thought the two sociologists were in town to study the oil spill's ecological impacts. Professor Gill recalls an exchange he had with a resident in the early stages of the research: 'I introduced myself as a researcher studying the community impacts of the oil spill and did not represent Exxon or the government. The Cordovan replied, "Why aren't you out there cleaning that shit up?"'[28]

This was a reasonable question considering the focus of the media and the fact that the immense clean-up project directed almost exclusive attention to the oil spill's deleterious effects on the biosphere and the wildlife species inhabiting surrounding ecosystems. Bleak pictures of 'oiled' birds and otters haunted the covers of weekly news magazines while provoking the sympathies of almost anyone who watched the evening news.

Faced with the interesting fact that people were not focused on the socio-emotional effects of the oil spill, Picou and Gill took the opportunity to introduce themselves to Cordova's community leadership by pointing out that the accident was more than an ecological crisis. Consider, for example, Professor Gill's response to the above query regarding his research activities in Cordova: 'There are enough people out there already,' he explained, 'but no one is doing anything about the people living here. I am here to study what's happening to them.' The man who would have him cleaning up the oil replied, 'Well, come on in!' Prompted by the sociologists' concerns, several of Cordova's leading citizens began to consider the possibility that the oil spill could be a human as well as an ecological disaster. 'You mean there are social-psychological impacts?' they asked.

Despite the promising progress of their first attempts to persuade Cordova's residents of the importance of investigating the social and emotional effects of the oil spill, the sociologists remained for many people identified with the clean-up team. Approaching one resident for an interview, for example, Professor Gill was politely told that if he was in town because of the accident he should be washing rocks, not talking to people. This confusion aside, Picou and Gill were successful in gathering baseline data on the socio-emotional effects of the spill in so-called Time 1 (summer 1989).

Two years later they returned to Cordova to collect Time 3 data (Time 2 data were collected earlier by telephone and mail survey). By now the clean-up boom had ended, fishing was either severely restricted or the numbers of fish were down, and many Cordovans wondered how they would survive financially. While collecting their Time 3 data Picou and Gill presented their Time 1 report to the City Council, the local science center, and the Forest Service. Paradoxically, in spite of the economic boom in Time 1, respondents reported significant levels of social and psychological distress compared to a control community.

A core group of 15 to 20 local residents attended each of the presentations. Importantly, these community members were by and large town influentials – people other people listened to. Absorbing the specific language of stress and coping embedded in the broader language of the biospheric contamination of natural resource communities, this core group began to redescribe their predicament, using where appropriate the concepts of environmental sociology and social psychology. These individuals, for example, seized upon the abstract notion of a renewable resource community to make sense of the connection between the oil spill and community trauma. Redescribing their community as an RRC made some sense out of their immediate experiences. We can only assume that other residents listened to their redescriptions.

Anecdotal evidence for this assumption is found in an exchange Picou had with a local resident who was not part of the core group. Coinciding with their second visit to Cordova, attorneys were in town deposing people who intended to sue Exxon for damages inflicted by the accident. After his deposition, this particular man found Picou on the street and told him that among the questions posed by the attorney was one asking what knowledge did he have that he was stressed from the oil spill. His answer? 'Steve Picou's study told me so.' While we do not want to make too much of repartee in legal depositions, this instance does suggest how sociological knowledge can become personal capital as respondents define themselves in the words of the sociologist at a moment when a rhetoric of loss is called for.

There is more than anecdotal evidence, however, that sociology is informing the way Cordova's residents describe their predicament. Picou and Gill returned to Alaska in 1993 to present a paper at a symposium dedicated to the oil spill. Of the dozen or more academic papers presented, theirs was the only one that examined the social and psychological effects of the oil spill. Several Cordovans attended the conference and heard in the stylized and formal language of a scholarly meeting a detailed account of the longitudinal increases in personal and collective trauma following the accident. Moreover, the media, hungry for a new slant on the story, focused considerable coverage on the social-psychological data, in spite of the fact that it was under-represented in the symposium. A new language was emerging for making personal and collective sense of the *Exxon Valdez* oil spill.

A final phase of the research process would add appreciably to the role of sociology in redescribing the human experiences of the oil spill. In 1994, Professor Picou was asked to conduct a feasibility study to determine whether a mental health outreach program would be welcomed and effective in Cordova. By this time in the disaster process many residents were in a state of panic, shock, or focused denial on the devastating financial consequences of the oil spill. In the plain words of one clinical psychologist who visited the town with Picou, 'These people aren't connected.'

Determining the town was ready and willing to participate in a community outreach initiative, Picou was given permission to develop a community education program. In addition to creating peer listener groups in town, he prepared a guidebook entitled, *Community Stress Management for Technological Disasters: A Guidebook for Community Leaders and Mental Health Professionals.* Its table of contents reads like a sociological primer on technological disasters. The author writes:

> This Guidebook introduces the reader to social problems caused by technological disasters, provides information on their unique community impacts, [and] identifies community education strategies for mitigating these community impacts . . . [It] also reviews social science research which demonstrates that, over the last 30 years, the frequency and consequences of technological disasters have dramatically increased . . . This Guidebook provides information that identifies technological disasters as a modern social problem and responds to one of their primary negative impacts, i.e. long-term (1 to 10 years) social disruption and psychological distress.

Here sociological knowledge becomes an informing context for recognizing and adapting to a hazardous environment. To the degree the people of Cordova explained themselves and their miseries in the language of sociology, they became the people sociologists describe. If classic sociology turns subjects into objects by locating people inside a world that makes sense to sociologists, illustrated here is a quite different process, one in which the residents of Cordova merged with the sociologists, becoming the people Picou and Gill said they had become. In this context, the boundary between discovering and inventing, tenaciously defended in standard methods texts, becomes purposely blurred as citizen and sociologist change into people who can understand each other.

A final anecdote from Cordova illustrates nicely the way sociology becomes situated and mundane knowledge, defining the settings it seeks to analyze. On his last visit to the village Professor Picou addressed a citizens' workshop on the aftermath of the oil spill. In the course of his presentation he described the community as entering the recovery stage. Shortly after the workshop he is standing on a corner and overhears the following conversation between two people:

Person A: What's going on at the lodge?
Person B: Dr. Picou's back in town making a presentation.
A: Well, did he ride in on his white horse to tell us all about our problems?
B: He's talking about stages people go through after disaster.

A: Really. Well, what stage are we in?
B: Recovery.
A: Cool. That sounds good to me.[29]

In this brief exchange we glimpse, albeit briefly, how the insights and conclusions of sociology may enter the ordinary lives of people and organizations they are meant to describe, becoming a part of the way local worlds are constituted.

In studying the social-psychological impacts of ecological disruption on a renewable resource community, sociologists created a text about disaster. By itself this accomplishment is not particularly noteworthy. It becomes considerably more interesting, however, when local residents turned that text into a narrative to redescribe their personal and collective experiences, to refashion an explanation of a major oil spill that shifted attention from the ecological-biological definition of the problem to its social-psychological consequences. Momentarilly visibile in this act is the way sociology becomes part of the answer to the question, 'Who describes a disaster?'

LOCAL SCIENCE? A DISCUSSION

These two cases invite several conversations. We think two of the more interesting outcomes are epistemological and theoretical. First, hazardous environments appear to foster the development of a new variation of science, one whose claims to know are based in part on the situated, historical, and biographical features of discrete neighborhoods and communities. Second, from the vantage point of this alternative science, it is possible to see a resolution to the contested debates among sociologists who disagree over how or whether we can theorize the physical environment.

Most of modernity has been dominated by the ideal of rational scientific knowledge; social scientific knowledge, especially in the United States, was no exception. The legitimacy of this knowledge was based partly on keeping the subjects of research separate from the researchers, who controlled the investigatory process and were the experts in scientific rationality. Separating citizens from instrumental rationality ensured that modernity would succeed, as Alain Touraine writes, in separating the 'world of nature, which is governed by the laws discovered and used by rational thought, and the world of the Subject.'[30]

But nature and the Subject collided. A plethora of environmental disasters, including those discussed above, is changing the relationships of ordinary people to experts and expert knowledge. In many of these cases, the 'research subjects' – the 'objects of research' – are demanding to be active players in the research process, and are insisting that the research have practical value for them. Furthermore, they are not accepting at face value the validity of studies or the authority of experts, but are giving credence to their own experiences in understanding their world. In Ulrich Beck's colorful phrase, 'Gone forever is the power differential in which scientific experts drove laypeople into clearly delineated and continually shrinking areas, like Indians being pushed back into reservations.'[31] Or, more simply, the active Subject is back.

However, we are not seeing simply a rejection of rational, universal, scientific knowledge and a substitution of localized, experiential knowledge. The situation is more complex. Illustrated in this chapter's two cases is a confounding of expert and lay knowledge, with some of each type gaining legitimacy in the eyes of both laypersons and experts. Indeed, we may be witnessing the development of a new type of knowledge, one which relies both on objective knowledge and subjective experience. For want of a better term, we will provisionally call this new type of knowledge, 'local science.'

The modifier 'local' distinguishes this type of science from normal, universal science. If universal science is a form of knowledge applicable everywhere in all cases, local science is knowledge specific to a particular place (see also the chapter in this volume by Rolf Lidskog). Universal science, on one hand, can lay claim to global, generalizable knowledge because it specifically eschews history, biographical experiences, and the subtleties of tradition. By separating itself from the immediacy of community, universal science can (it claims) make statements about all individuals or communities, or at least those of specific types and classes. Local science, on the other hand, is far more restricted in its application. By joining principles of universal science with local histories, local science becomes a way of knowing limited to the specific experiences and needs of discrete communities. Local science could, of course, produce knowledge applicable to other cases or communities, but that is not its purpose. It is worth considering some other features that distinguish local from universal science.

Universal science is proven on the weight of accumulated evidence. Data are gathered through rigorous and systematic observation and experimentation, and accepted or rejected according to canons of scientific methodology. The research setting is meticulously controlled, causality is linear, and explanation is the goal. In contrast, local science starts outside of the rarefied atmosphere of the controlled research site. It is likely to consider almost any community experience or cultural norm as potentially important to its enterprise. In local science the problems of measurement are often eclipsed by the more fundamental problem of what, in fact, should be measured. Both universal and local science believe in Nietzsche's 'longest lie,' the peculiarly modern idea that outside statistics and observations await an obdurate world which, if we use the right methods, will reveal itself to us. The difference lies in what dimensions of that obdurate world are important to understand and measure. Importantly, local science is not tied to linear models of truth; truth is pragmatic. It is true, in short, if it works.

Moreover, universal science is studiously apolitical, or so it claims. By excluding community and biography, universal science assumes that its knowledge is value-free, unfettered by social and political values. Alternatively, local science is necessarily and self-consciously political. Produced to answer questions about what is dangerous to whom and who is responsible, local science is often in conflict with powerful corporate and governmental interests whose representatives, ironically, are apt to claim to know what is good for the community based on their versions of universal science.

In some respects, local science is a more honest version of the scientific enterprise than its counterpart and frequent adversary, universal science. After all, as historians of science tell us, it was never a choice between objective, value-free knowledge and subjective, value-laden knowledge. All knowledge is mediated, at the very least by the biases of investigators, the interests of corporate and government sponsors, and the conventions that constitute normal science at any given point in time. If local science is an openly political claim on rational knowledge, the legitimacy of universal science depends on successfully obscuring its situated, political, and paradigmatic biases.

Lastly, in the production of local science the structure of the relationship between expert and lay person changes. To produce universal science, the experts remain outside the process being studied to the greatest possible extent. Lay knowledge needs no 'experts' at all. Producing local science, however, is likely to be based in part on a dialectical interaction between experts and laypersons.

This could be expected to happen in varying degrees case by case. In the Cordova example, the interaction was quite structured and iterative, where research was conducted, analyzed, and disseminated to the community by experts, who then received feedback from the community and went on to study the changed community, and so forth. In Centralia, the interaction was less structured and more dialectical. But in both cases, the researchers and laypersons entered into a qualitatively different kind of relationship from that of the typical universal science model, one involving increased interaction and more active 'subjects.'

In fact, it is interesting to note how the validity of local science may be based on the often very personal relationships established between experts and laypersons in hazardous environments. From the laypersons' vantage point, some expert knowledge is needed to help them understand and deal with their problem. But how does one judge the validity of that knowledge when one is not an expert, and when experts and study results disagree? An important part of that evaluation resides in perceptions of the characteristics of the experts themselves. Is the expert trustworthy? Does the expert have hidden agendas? Does the expert understand and validate our lay knowledge and experiences? Is the expert willing to enter into dialogues and relationships with us to help us alleviate our problems? Ironically, lay legitimacy of parts of expert knowledge is produced not by the credibility of abstract systems, but by very personal criteria and relationships established with experts. This underlines Giddens' point about the crucial nature of the social relationships between local and universal systems.[32] The observation also suggests a possible resolution to the continuing debate among sociologists regarding the proper role of ideas and reality in theory and everyday life.

LOCAL SCIENCE AND THE REALITY–IDEALIST LAMENT

Anyone who pays even passing attention to sociology knows that it is a balkanized discipline. Most sociologists are experts rather than generalists. We prefer to be recognized for what we know about a discrete slice of social life: family, deviance, social movements, environments, and so forth. It might be argued that we are joined in conflict far more frequently than in consensus, and one conflict that consistently unites us is the debate over whether the world is an obdurate reality or a constellation of ideas. Consider this debate as it is applied to the environment.

The environment, as we know, is not mute. It cracks open, thunders, swells up, explodes, and often smells – to name just a few of its manifestations. But, and here is where it gets messy, it is inarticulate. The environment does not speak. Humans do. And it begets our conversations. At once organic and physical, and also invented in casual conversation, legal wrangling, and political controversies, it is not difficult to imagine how environments could be a theoretical enigma in social science.

The two cases presented here, and the third type of knowing discernible amid the collapse of the once well-defined distinction between sociological knowledge and lay knowledge, suggest that the idealist-realist lament may be too simple a rendering of the problem. Perhaps it is at those moments when people are defining their physical environments as hazardous that the complex interplay of the material and discursive properties of nature are more readily revealed. After all, it was not words that were buried at the Love Canal, and it is not language that is found in contaminated drinking water. Thus, environments that shift from 'as if' to 'what if' are momentary opportunities for sociologists to consider the interplay of the symbolic and physical properties of nature. But left here, the idealist–realist debate would continue with one side accusing the other of reifying nature. Suggested in this chapter, however, is another process, one in which the sociological texts of hazardous environments are transformed into local, situated ways of knowing, thus helping to create what they claim to analyze. Note, however, we are not claiming simply that sociological texts legislate local responses. Our argument is more complex. In the hazardous environment, abstract sociology and immediate, communal experiences merge to create – however fleetingly – a way of knowing that collapses ideal and real into a local science, a historical way of knowing that violates a few of the foundational assumptions of modernity's cult of instrumental rationality while not rejecting rationality altogether. In closing, it is when sociologists and lay persons are, at least momentarily, hard to distinguish that we glimpse the possibility of a third way of knowing environments and communities. But, when all is said and done, do we want to resolve one of the key conflicts that help to ensure our unity?

194   *Stephen R. Couch, Steve Kroll-Smith, and Jeffrey D. Kindler*

NOTES

1. R. Merton and A. Wolfe, 'The Cultural and Social Incorporation of Sociological Knowledge,' *American Sociologist*, 26(3) (1995): 13–37.
2. Ibid., p. 16.
3. Ibid., pp. 34–5.
4. H. Gans, 'Best-Sellers by Sociologists: An Exploratory Study,' *Contemporary Sociology*, 26(2) (1997): 131–5.
5. J. S. Kroll-Smith, 'Sociological Knowledge, Narratives, and the Courts,' pp. 1–18 in P. Jenkins and J. S. Kroll-Smith, eds, *Witnessing for Sociology: Sociologists in Court* (Westport, CT: Praeger, 1996).
6. U. Beck, *Risk Society: Towards a New Modernity* (London: Sage, 1992). See also A. Irwin, *Citizen Science: A Study of People, Expertise, and Sustainable Development* (London: Routledge, 1995) and S. Couch and J. S. Kroll-Smith, 'The Environmental Movement, Expert Knowledge, and Social Change,' *International Journal of Contemporary Sociology*, 34(2) (1997): 185–210.
7. On the 'extreme environment,' see also J. S. Kroll-Smith, S. Couch, and B. Marshall, 'Sociology, Hazardous Environments, and Social Change,' *Current Sociology*, 45(3) (1997): 161–78.
8. On the idea of a practical epistemology see C. Geertz, *Local Knowledge* (New York: Basic Books, 1983). Refer also to J. S. Kroll-Smith and H. Floyd, *Bodies In Protest* (New York: New York University Press, 1997), chapter 5.
9. A. Gouldner, *The Coming Crisis of Western Sociology* (New York: Basic Books, 1970), p. 497.
10. O. Fals-Borda and M. Rahman, *Action and Knowledge: Breaking the Monopoly with Participatory Action Research* (New York: Apex Press, 1991).
11. D. Mileti, T. Drabek, and J. Haas, *Human Systems in Extreme Environments* (Boulder, CO: Institute of Behavioral Science, University of Colorado, 1975).
12. A. Wallace, *Tornado in Worcester*, National Academy of Sciences/National Research Council Disaster Study #3 (Washington, DC: National Academy of Sciences, 1956), p. 7.
13. A. Giddens, *Social Theory and Modern Sociology* (Cambridge: Polity Press, 1987), pp. 35.
14. J. S. Kroll-Smith, 'Toxic Contamination and the Loss of Civility,' *Sociological Spectrum*, 15(4) (1995): 377–96.
15. Giddens, *Social Theory and Modern Sociology*; and Kroll-Smith and Floyd, *Bodies in Protest*.
16. Giddens, *Social Theory and Modern Sociology*, p. 5.
17. E. Durkheim, *Suicide* (New York: Free Press, 1951), p. 241.
18. M. Edelstein, *Contaminated Communities: The Social and Psychological Impacts of Residential Toxic Exposure* (Boulder, CO: Westview Press, 1988); K. Erikson, *A New Species of Trouble: Explorations in Disaster, Trauma, and Community* (New York: W. W. Norton, 1994); J. S. Kroll-Smith and S. Couch, *The Real Disaster Is Above Ground: A Mine Fire and Social Conflict* (Lexington: University Press of Kentucky, 1990);

W. Freudenburg, 'Contamination, Corrosion, and the Social Order: An Overview,' *Current Sociology* 45(3) (1997): 19–39; and J. S. Picou, D. Gill, and M. Cohen, eds, *The Exxon Valdez Disaster: Readings on a Modern Social Problem* (Dubuque, IA: Kendall-Hunt, 1997).

19. Kroll-Smith and Couch, *The Real Disaster is Above Ground.*
20. J. S. Kroll-Smith and S. Couch, 'Sociological Knowledge and the Public at Risk: A "Self-Study" of Sociology, Technological Hazards, and Moral Dilemmas,' *Sociological Practice Review,* 1(2) (1990): 120–7.
21. S. Couch and J. S. Kroll-Smith, 'The Chronic Technical Disaster: Toward a Social Scientific Perspective,' *Social Science Quarterly,* 66(3) (1985): 564–75.
22. This volume's chapter by Steven Picou and Duane Gill also discusses the case of the *Exxon Valdez* oil spill.
23. J. S. Picou, D. Gill, and M. Cohen, 'The *Exxon Valdez* Oil Spill as a Technological Disaster: Conceptualizing a Social Problem,' pp. 3–21 in Picou et al., *The* Exxon Valdez *Disaster.*
24. Ibid., p. 4.
25. J. S. Picou and D. Gill, 'Commercial Fishers and Stress: Psychological Impacts of the *Exxon Valdez* Oil Spill,' pp. 211–35 in Picou et al., *The* Exxon Valdez *Disaster.*
26. J. S. Picou, D. Gill, and M. Cohen, 'Technological Disasters and Social Policy: Lessons from the *Exxon Valdez* Oil Spill,' pp. 309–15 in Picou et al., *The* Exxon Valdez *Disaster.*
27. M. Cohen, 'Technological Disasters and Natural Resource Damage Assessment: An Evaluation of the *Exxon Valdez* Oil Spill,' *Land Economics,* 71(1) (1995): 65–82.
28. Quotations from Steve Picou and Duane Gill presented in the following passages are derived from interviews conducted by Steve Kroll-Smith during 1997.
29. S. Kroll-Smith and V. Gunter, 'Legislators, Interpreters, and Disasters: The Importance of How as Well as What is a Disaster,' pp. 160–76 in E. Quarantelli, ed., *Sociological Theories of Disaster* (London: Routledge, 1998).
30. A. Touraine, *Critique of Modernity* (Oxford: Blackwell, 1995), p. 57.
31. U. Beck, *Ecological Enlightenment: Essays on the Politics of the Risk Society* (Atlantic Highlands, NJ: Humanities Press, 1995), p. 52.
32. A. Giddens, *The Consequences of Modernity* (Cambridge: Polity Press, 1990), pp. 83–8.

9 Scientific Evidence or Lay People's Experience? On Risk and Trust with Regard to Modern Environmental Threats

Rolf Lidskog

PLANNING AND TECHNOLOGICAL DISASTERS

The town was a unique example of social engineering. With substantial resources and good planning, here were realized in a short time a great number of the ideals that had guided, for instance, the creation of the Swedish welfare state. The town was exceptionally well-planned – it was a showpiece with its housing, shops, sports centers, five schools, three swimming pools, pleasure park, 200-room hotel, and guest house for official visitors. Other facilities included a cultural center with a theater, a cinema, and a library. In the rest of the country people languished for long periods on the housing list, but in this town a family could almost immediately obtain a good apartment in one of the 18-storey blocks. There was plenty of food in the stores – in one of them a surprised visitor was able to count 14 different varieties of meat and sausage. There was even a greenhouse so that fresh tomatoes would always be available.

By investing in the community's physical and social infrastructure it was possible to attract the most qualified laborforce. Many young people went to live and work in the town as soon as they received their university degrees, the result being that the average age of the city's population was an incredibly low 26. The inhabitants had faith in the future, and their town seemed to them to be one of the most central places in the entire republic – just two and a half hours by car from the main city of the province, and just a day's journey from the capital and several popular holiday resorts. Furthermore, there were plenty of jobs, both for ordinary workers and for highly educated scientists and engineers.

Another advantage was the town's proximity to the countryside. The industrialization of the republic had been so rapid that a large proportion of the urban population had grown up in rural areas as the sons and daughters of farmers. Surrounding the town were expansive forested tracts of land with mushrooms and berries, lakes where one could either swim or fish – in short, there was a rich and unspoiled landscape. Especially in contrast to the way things were in a large number of other towns in the republic, there were no serious sources of pollution – the town's main industry did not use fossil fuels.

A distinct feature of the new town was the absence of social barriers. Here people came together from all corners of the large republic. There was work for everyone, and there was ample availability – on equal terms – of child care, schools, medical care, and leisure facilities. Apart from the four suites in the guest house, there was equality in the distribution of housing, and also equality of access to social and cultural activities. The managing director of the dominant company, for example, lived in a conventional apartment (rumored though it may have been that his bathroom was more exclusive).

The town bore witness to the feasibility of a community without barriers, planned so as to enable each and every member to have a good life. But there is a clear line of demarcation between the town and the world around, primarily to keep out the curious. This type of demarcation, however, is markedly different from most other types – for instance, the medieval fortified wall designed to protect townspeople against bandits, or the gated communities of today (with fences, security guards, and surveillance cameras) surrounding the homes of the wealthy to keep strangers out. No, the demarcation in the case of this town was designed to provide the opposite type of protection – the fences with their barbed wire were in place for the protection of outsiders by preventing them from entering the town. For the town has been put under quarantine and outsiders are warned off.

Today, twelve years after it was in full flourish, the town is far from a model of the good community without social or physical barriers. The human residents have moved away, and even though the main industry is still in operation it was never extended and its future is particularly uncertain. The workers now commute from places thirty and more miles away. What was a little more than a decade ago a town with an abundant cultural and social life, and a young population full of faith in the future, is now a ghost town closed off from the rest of the world. The name of the town is Pripyat, but it is better known for the name of its main industry – Chernobyl.[1]

ENVIRONMENTAL RISKS IN LATE MODERNITY

The Chernobyl episode raises some basic questions concerning the relation between knowledge, planning, and environmental risks. In particular, this chapter will confront the issue of whether the experience and knowledge of lay people has any relevance to the environmental risks of modern society. Not least in today's challenge to create an ecologically sustainable society, the role of the public is put in focus – should ordinary people be seen as simple knowledge receptors or as decisive knowledge creators?

Authorities ponder why lay people do not follow their recommendations for health and environmental protection. What makes members of the public ignore some hazards when there seems to be strong scientific evidence that the associated risks pose a real threat to their health and immediate environment? For example, why do people living in the northern part of Sweden continue to eat mushrooms, freshwater fish, and meat from reindeer and roedeer, despite official warnings that these natural foodstuffs, since the Chernobyl disaster, contain radioactive cesium in an amount that is far above the permitted level for food?

However, from another perspective the opposite question can be raised, namely why do lay people seem to have such trust in experts and their recommendations? For example, why are the residents of Oskarshamn (on the southeast coast of Sweden and home to a nuclear-power plant and its interim storage facility for high-level radioactive waste) so convinced that nuclear power, and even deep disposal of the spent nuclear fuel, can be handled in such a way that these activities will not constitute any threat to the local population and surrounding environment?[2]

The case of Chernobyl discussed above illustrates public *ignorance of science*, where citizens seem not to have any confidence in experts' recommendations. The latter case describing the situation in Oskarshamn exemplifies *public adoration of science*, where people appear to trust science and expert systems without any reservations.

This chapter discusses both of these oppositional public dispositions toward science, looking in particular at the complex relationship between scientific knowledge and lay understandings with respect to environmental risks.

The following section describes an environmental discourse in which the environmental risks of modernity are characterized by their remoteness from lay perspectives and knowledge. Science has therefore become the necessary institution to create knowledge of modern risks. However, this discourse maintains that even if ordinary people may not have anything substantive to contribute to the processes of knowledge production, they should be included in the proposed solution. This contention falls from the claim that there is a strong requirement that all actors in society should take responsibility in the movement toward ecological sustainability. The chapter then moves to a discussion of planning theory and the traditional model of rational-scientific planning. I contrast this approach, which goes hand in hand with contemporary environmental discourse, with the communicative model of planning. Counterposed in such a way we seem to face a situation in which we have to choose between the ecologically proper and the democratically sound action. I then introduce a perspective designed to transcend the dichotomy between rational-scientific and communicative planning models in which communication constitutes a means to elaborate better knowledge of environmental problems. The chapter then suggests that we currently confront a situation of plural rationalities. As the case of Pripyat shows, not only lay people, but also experts, failed in their judgment of risks. This error occurred because all risk conceptions – those of experts, as well as those of ordinary people – are situated in a social context. By way of conclusion, the chapter observes that we face a competitive situation where different actors struggle to be seen as legitimate providers of knowledge on environmental risks. To listen to all actors is a way to enrich the process of knowledge production and hopefully create a better awareness.

RISKS IN LATE MODERNITY: BEYOND HUMAN PERCEPTION AND CONTROL?

Increasingly, the more bounded risks of premodern society have been replaced by the unbounded risks of modern society, a clear example of this being the Chernobyl disaster. Spatial boundaries collapsed in the case of Chernobyl and the radioactive fallout affected regions far away. Also temporal demarcations gave way as children born after the disaster developed cancer attributable to the accident. We recall the questions posed by Ulrich Beck: When does a nuclear accident stop? When should we stop counting its effects? What Kai Erikson describes as 'a new species of trouble' is here not limited to people living in localities in which novel kinds of technological disasters occur.[3] Instead, we see that this type of local accident can have national, regional, and even global consequences. The Chernobyl catastrophe is for Beck the kind of trouble that is a central characteristic of the risk society toward which we are moving. In this new society, risks are fundamentally research-dependent and transcend the classical borders of the industrial society – class (social divisions), space (national territories), and time (existing generations).[4] In the cases Erikson describes we can glimpse what Beck thinks humanity's everyday life will look like if the development toward the risk society is not stopped. This is not the place to discuss to what extent Beck's dramatic view of society's evolution appears reliable (i.e. his judgment regarding the magnitude of the new environmental risks), but instead this chapter takes as its point of departure what Beck and Erikson – as well as other social scientists – seem to agree upon, namely the new character of the risks that contemporary society faces.

Both human action and technological systems create a host of unforeseen consequences. Concurrently with technological advance, the untoward effects extend further and further in space and time. This applies not only to technological disasters such as that at Chernobyl, but also to present-day 'creeping' and diffuse environmental dilemmas, for example acidification and climate change.[5]

Environmental problems are not new for humankind. They have been with us for a long time, and perhaps have been a permanent companion for humanity's whole existence. However, earlier environmental threats were local, scattered, and in many cases relatively simple to manage because they were quite easily defined spatially and temporally.[6] This situation has changed and one of the features of today's environmental problems is that they are increasingly diffuse (difficult to delimit in space and time) and hard to grasp conceptually. They are, in many respects, invisible to the layperson's perception and beyond his or her range of normal experience. In certain cases, contemporary threats are of such a 'delayed-action'

type as to involve possible consequences only for future generations. This development, from problems that are visible and manifest
to prognosticated problems, is largely due to the fact that today's
risks are technological and not natural.[7] Also, the character of nature
itself has been changed, because human action has far-reaching
influences on the environment, and thus social scientists have come
to speak about a 'socially created environment.'[8] Thus a new characteristic of environmental problems has emerged: an increasing
remoteness from the perception and experience of the individual.

These novel environmental risks are, at least in the short run,
hard for lay people to conceive of because it is difficult to perceive
any direct effects from the perspective of everyday life. Of course,
when risks are transformed into catastrophes – such as in the case
of Chernobyl – they often become readily detectable and know-
able for lay people, not least because they are intimately affected
themselves. In such situations, ordinary people may formulate 'popular epidemiologies' or 'lay epidemiologies' through the use of their
own experience and local knowledge.[9]

Obviously, this new kind of environmental risk does not totally
replace the old ones. Many traditional local environmental concerns – such as noise and poor water quality – exist parallel to the
new concerns. However, what many commentators today see as global
environmental problems, and are items on the agenda of international politics, are in many cases of this invisible variety, being
projections with very few apparent empirical consequences at this
stage.

As mentioned above, a widespread view among scholars, as well
as politicians and lay people, is that science is crucial for discovering and conveying information about modern risks, that it is mainly
through research that we obtain knowledge of complex environmental and technological hazards. Accordingly, science has come
to represent a sort of extension of the ordinary perception of politicians and the general public. This increasing dependence on the
scientific has given science a new role with respect to environmental policy and to the identification of environment-friendly actions.
Paramount is the voice of science in advising how to avoid environmental risks. This development forms the basis for the statement
that science is the principal social institution trusted as being competent to make knowledge claims about environmental risks. Today,
science often defines the scale of the problems, the ground for
conflicts, and the scope of solutions in environmental policy-making.[10]

Thus, we currently face a situation in which science and the mass media produce and distribute an increasingly vivid picture of a world threatened by environmental destruction. At the same time, these threats are becoming more remote from our perceptual apparatus and acquiring form as abstract prognoses that are beyond lay people's own knowledge and experience. Accordingly, in late modernity we are living in a paradoxical situation where lay people become increasingly conscious about different environmental risks while simultaneously many of these threats are further removed from – in many cases beyond – individual perception and control. The danger of today involves a symbolic meaning of the unfamiliar and the unknown.[11]

This new situation provides an important, but in many cases forgotten, element of explanations concerning public reactions to certain kinds of environmental risks, such as bovine spongiform encephalopathy (BSE), genetically modified food, or the siting of hazardous facilities. Concerning the latter, for example, this kind of public decision represents for local people a predicament that is the reverse of the one sketched above. It means here that environmental risks that up to this point have been diffuse and spread, specifically in the form of products characteristic of advanced industrial societies, are now becoming concentrated in particular places. From the local perspective a siting can be seen as a development from a diffuse threat to a risk that is concentrated and 'materialized,' and in this sense perceptible. As I have shown elsewhere, the establishment of a plant for the management of hazardous waste becomes, in many cases, a social representation of the risks, insecurities, and complexities of modern society, and is thus to be seen as a spatial concentration of risk.[12]

The interpretation elaborated above may foster a view of lay people's reactions as deeply irrational and selfish, as simple so-called 'Not-in-My-Backyard,' or NIMBY, phenomena (see also the chapter by Michael Edelstein in this volume). Following from this evaluation, the layperson is seen as not able to provide useful knowledge concerning environmental risks, and it is only for political and democratic reasons the authorities and/or other responsible parties have to devote attention to lay (and other non-experts') concerns.[13] The fundamental question is whether the experience and knowledge of lay people have any relevance when facing the kind of risks that are seen as characterizing modern society. If they are incomprehensible to non-experts, only made visible and understandable to them through researchers' assessments and scenarios, then lay people will have nothing to add to the process of knowledge production concerning these risks. Furthermore, because these risks involve conjectures – probabilities of events that may be realized in the future – there exists no personal experience of them, which also is seen as a reason why lay people's risk judgments are not invalid. Before turning its attention to the question of whether lay people have anything to add to knowledge production regarding environmental risks, the next section will introduce some themes from planning theory to see how this field conceptualizes the tension between citizen participation and expert knowledge.

PLANNING, DEMOCRACY, AND SUSTAINABLE DEVELOPMENT

During the last two decades the global environment has developed into the third major issue in world politics, comparable only to international security and the international economy. So far, the most comprehensive strategy for global action on sustainable development is Agenda 21 endorsed by the 178 government delegations that attended the Río Summit in 1992.[14] Agenda 21's 40 chapters cover almost everything about the planet and how humans interact with it. If it is realized it may be a way to avoid Beck's scenario of a coming risk society.[15]

The post-Río agenda does not only parcel out major roles to science and governmental bodies as part of its effort to allocate responsibility for attaining sustainable development. Most well-known here is probably the part of Agenda 21 where nine major 'stakeholders' or 'partners' are explicitly mentioned, namely women, children and youth, indigenous people, non-governmental organizations, local authorities, labor unions, business and industry, scientists and technologists, and farmers. One reason for this encompassing strategy is that political action requires legitimacy from groups and organizations, which is of decisive importance given the great changes required in habits and lifestyles across society. Citizens' values and knowledge constitute a political reality that decision-makers need to consider.

In Sweden, for example, this inclusion of public interests is visible through the increasing use of economic instruments (environmental taxes and fees) and social instruments (e.g. voluntary recovery of paper, glass bottles, batteries, and aluminum cans) in environmental policy. By using the mechanisms of the market, and by informing and educating citizens, the government tries to favor necessary changes in the production system, as well as in citizens' lifestyles and consumption patterns.[16] Consumer power and (ecologically) enlightened citizens have during the 1990s become central pillars in the strategy for making Sweden more ecologically sustainable.

However, to a large degree public participation is restricted to being an important *means* to reach this goal – citizens are viewed as critical actors in the implementation phase of environmental policies, but not in the steps leading to their formulation. The overall goals themselves are typically determined by scientists and governmental authorities. According to this perspective, there is a need for citizen engagement, but in a way that is guided by expert advice. This view of citizen engagement is also salient in Alan Irwin's study of the relationship between science and the public.[17] In his case studies, Irwin finds that a 'scientific-centered' outlook was in operation where citizens' resistance and ignorance regarding the statements of expert bodies were interpreted as obstacles to rational and constructive debate.

From this standpoint – that environmental risks are fundamentally research-dependent – traditional scientific-rational planning (which planning theorists refer to as synoptic planning) is the most relevant answer in today's quest to move modern societies toward greater environmental sustainability. However, as we will see below, there may be relevant alternatives to this planning model.

In his contribution to communicative planning theory, the Norwegian scholar Tore Sager describes the tension between synoptic and incremental planning.[18] After Charles Lindblom presented his popular theory of 'muddling through,' the debate between synoptic and incremental planning came to occupy a central position in planning theory.[19] *Synoptic planning* is usually defined in a way that presupposes perfect information. However, few advocates would agree with the description of perfect knowledge, and therefore Sager revises the synoptic planning model to at least assume that all other actors have inferior knowledge compared to the planners/experts. The synoptic approach does not exclude communication, but it is a one-way process of information exchange. Its purpose is to inform the lay public, not to see ordinary people as providers of useful knowledge or as legitimate actors with the right to influence the planning process. Synoptic planning is based on an instrumental rationality, where the dissemination of knowledge is a part of the planners' strategy to persuade others to support their proposal, that seems to fit with the present environmental discourse and its emphasis on the role of the expert.

As discussed earlier, parallel to the development of a discourse of the knowledge-dependency of modern environmental risks, there has been an appeal to increase public participation – but also the engagement of non-governmental organizations (environmental groups, as well as business firms) – in environmental policy-making and planning. In planning theory, there have been efforts since the early 1970s to transcend the instrumental rationality on which traditional (synoptic) planning has been based. More than 25 years ago, John Friedmann presented a planning theory – transactive planning – explicitly based on communication.[20] A more recent contribution along these lines comes from John Forester who puts forward the notion that planning should contribute to emancipation by arranging for dialogical practice throughout the decision-making process.[21] Today the elaboration of a communicative-planning paradigm is continuing, an effort advanced in the shadow of Habermas's early quest for an emancipatory political process and in his later discussion of communicative rationality.[22]

Disjointed incrementalism is most often seen as the alternative to synoptic planning. However, this planning approach only implies limits on the instrumental type of rationality without being based on an alternative form of unbounded non-instrumental rationality. By describing an incremental process that is a purer expression of Habermas's communicative rationality, Sager makes the contrast between synoptic and incremental planning more deep-rooted. In this elaboration, the difference is based on divergent kinds of rationality. While synoptic planning is based on a strategic (instrumental) rationality, *dialogical incrementalism* is grounded in a communicative rationality. In this latter type of planning experts are only one among many voices, without precedence over others. The presupposition of dialogical incrementalism is that no particular agency or interest has a monopoly on the production of knowledge and analysis concerning a proposed plan or policy.

In the synoptic process planners have nearly unlimited calculative capacity and in the dialogical incremental process they (but also other actors as well) have nearly unlimited communicative capacity (see also the chapter by Klaus Eder in this volume). Therefore, synoptic and incremental planning can be viewed as theoretical opposites with regard to information, knowledge, and communication. To use Habermas's terms, synoptic planning involves a strategic rationality, whereas dialogical incrementalism involves a communicative rationality. Obviously, one single form of planning has rarely been entirely adhered to in practice. However, through this ideal-type formulation Sager creates fixed reference points for discussing cognitive and communicative aspects of planning.

Yet even if there exist powerful democratic reasons for advocating the planning ideal of dialogical incrementalism, we have to be skeptical about whether the result of this kind of process really is consistent with policy-making and planning for sustainability. Does not development toward sustainability imply that experts' knowledge of the environmental situation must be guiding, whatever the opinions of different citizen groups (and other non-scientific interests)? Not least modernity's environmental challenge – where its threats are increasingly diffuse and difficult to delimit in space and time – seems to raise questions about the relevance of the communicative ideal put forward by these planning theorists.

In his investigation of the adequacy of different normative planning theories for meeting the demand for sustainable development, another Norwegian planning researcher Peter Næss supports this contention.[23] In systematically evaluating the benefits and limitations of dominant planning models in relation to the goal of sustainable development, he argues that while synoptic planning (at least potentially) is well suited to ensuring effective management of natural resources and the environment, incremental planning has a number of inherent properties that are problematic in relation to long-term stewardship. Where synoptic planning tries to elucidate all possible options for action, incremental planning chooses alternatives in a way that deviates little from today's largely *ad hoc* practices and analyses.[24] Thus, Næss concludes that incrementalism creates no opportunity to consider the future effects and aggregated, long-term consequences of small steps.

Thus, there seems to be good justification for limiting citizen influence on environmental policy-making, leaving such complex matters to experts with their specialized knowledge and recondite calculations. From this point of view it can be stated that information about lay people's attitudes and behaviors does not add any substantial knowledge to environmental planning. The reason experts and other authorities need to become informed about lay perspectives is instead because ordinary people are part of a political reality that must be taken into consideration. Politics for ecological sustainability needs, at least in the long run, some kind of public legitimacy in a democratic state. The alternative, at worst, might be the creation of an eco-fascist regime dictating what should be correct behavior in the pursuit of sustainability.[25]

Does this assessment mean that more democratic decision-making will result in less sufficient environmental policies? Is it the case that present-day environmental challenges demand radical policy-making that does not have the time to take the roundabout path through the arrangement of democratic procedures? Is it more rather than less science and synoptic planning that constitutes the solution to our environmental predicaments?[26] In this sense there seems to be a tension between democracy and sustainability, between participation and survival, and between lay people's view and the experts.

However, we can express doubt about Næss's statement that synoptic planning is best suited for dealing with the long-term use of natural resources, as well as for addressing environmental problems on an aggregated level. As described in the introduction to this chapter, the creation of the Chernobyl plant and the town of Pripyat constitutes an exceptional example of synoptic planning, where both the community and its major industry were created on the basis of science and expert knowledge. Does not the Chernobyl disaster show that even synoptic planning is fraught with a high degree of uncertainty when it comes to the possibility of foreseeing future consequences?

However, we can respond to this objection by noting that the failure of synoptic planning concerns only those kinds of technological risks posed by a nuclear reactor and not other types of planning (e.g. planning for ecological sustainability). Under such circumstances, we can continue to judge the synoptic planning of the town of Pripyat to have been successful, and thus this conceptual approach might still be well-suited for the work of moving society toward ecological sustainability. Furthermore, the case of Chernobyl is not a good example of synoptic planning. Even if the plan itself was a product of comprehensive planning by specialist experts, restricted economic resources and technological competence, together with the lack of time, meant that the nuclear-power plant was not built in accordance with official plans. Not least, the facility was constructed in conjunction with similar installations at Ignalina and Kursk and this constrained the availability of both building materials and money. Following from that, it was faults in the implementation of the plan, rather than the plan itself, that caused the Chernobyl disaster. This means more, rather then less, synoptic planning is the cure that will prevent further technological catastrophes like that of Chernobyl.

However, this argument misses one decisive factor. All plans are carried out in a social context, which means that when the schemes are being implemented they need to be interpreted and modified in accordance with local specific circumstances. This caveat imposes no hindrance to the realization of the plan, and is indeed in many cases a way to make the plan better – in the implementation process actors not involved in the formulation of the original design brief may have the opportunity to provide their specific knowledge that in many cases is of considerable relevance, and the plan may be accordingly revised. Also, as Giddens has emphasized, a feature of today is that expert systems – social as well as technological – are interconnected.[27] This means that the controlled world of the laboratory differs to a large degree from the world of everyday practice.[28] As Ravetz and Funtowicz explain in discussing post-normal science, the more 'scientific' knowledge is, the more constricted is the area of its application in relation to the real problems facing humanity.[29]

COMMUNICATION, KNOWLEDGE, AND ENVIRONMENTAL RISKS

The dichotomy between expert and lay understandings of risks is based on a certain view of knowledge, where specialist knowledge (including planners) is superior to that of other actors. This view has been contested both in the planning theory literature and in general social theory. In planning theory, there seems to be a retreat from synoptic planning, and instead the argumentative aspects of planning are stressed where all organizations are seen as containing important social, political, and cognitive elements.[30] Concerning social theory, Ulrich Beck and Anthony Giddens have been criticized for their cognitive-centered view and their detractors have instead advanced the need for alternative kinds of knowledge distinct from expert knowledge.[31] The point I am making here is that how we judge the relevance of citizens' knowledge of environmental risks is in the long run of decisive importance for the possibility of achieving any measure of ecological sustainability.

Beyond Strategic Rationalism and Dialogical Incrementalism?

Ulrich Beck argues that science and technology in our society try to deconstruct the (valid) risk consciousness of lay people by creating a false trust based on a belief that it is through technological means possible to control all the threats that advanced societies produce. He names this 'a symbolic detoxification policy.'[32] With the end of true–false positivism, natural science no longer has an exclusive right to judge what should be seen as risky or safe. Instead, experiments – not least real-life experiments (different kinds of technological hazards that are purposefully introduced into society) – have thus become fundamentally ambiguous and open to interpretation. The experience of the public breaks away from controlled scientific experience and the two engage in a competitive struggle over the meaning of the results.[33] The contemporary situation can be characterized as one of plural rationalities and diverse forms of knowledge.

This situation causes Beck to state that what he names 'scientific rationality' (i.e. experimental logic, mathematical probabilities, and laboratory tests) should not have precedence over lay people's social rationality.[34] Accordingly, 'people must say farewell to the notion that administrations and experts always know exactly, or at least better, what is right and good for everyone.'[35] Development toward a good (i.e. less risky) society is, according to Beck, carried through by means of a new relation between social and scientific rationality, a new perspective on knowledge. At the same time, he still pins his hopes on (a renewed) science. This optimism can be interpreted as meaning that he still maintains a cognitive-centered position where science still remains key when discussing knowledge production and political action.[36] The opportunity to emancipate social practice from science occurs *through* science. It seems to be a form of scientization of the protest against science, involving a plea for an alternative science.[37]

Similarly, Giddens' discussion of trust with regard to expert systems and access points seems to emphasize the cognitive aspect of human agency. Lay people's trust in expertise – which is maintained or built up at so-called 'access points' – creates islands of certainty in a world characterized by rapid change, insecurity, and unpredictability.[38] He provides no alternative to the experts when discussing the establishment and reproduction of human beings' ontological security.[39] For both Beck and Giddens the traditional dependency

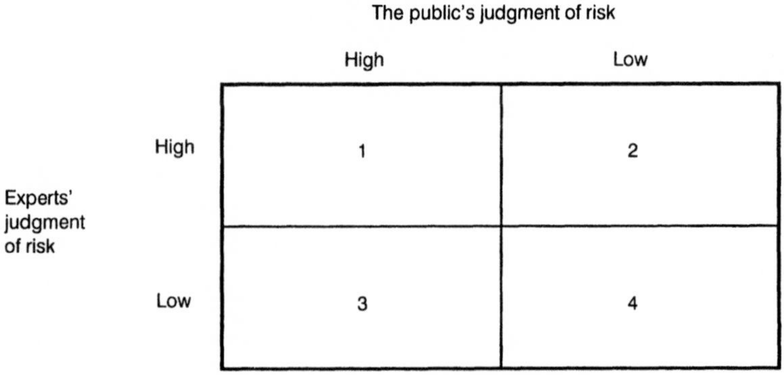

Rolf Lidskog

The public's judgment of risk

Figure 9.1 Experts' and lay people's judgment of risk

on science seems to be only replaced with a new form of such dependency. Thus, the two theorists can be interpreted as still sharing modernist assumptions concerning the decisive role of science in society. Before elaborating a proposal for an openness to diverse understanding and knowledge regarding environmental problems, I will first say something about lay people's and experts' roles in the discovery of environmental risks.

When determining whether a phenomenon should be seen as posing a risk or not, four different alternatives are possible between the judgments of experts and of citizens (see Figure 9.1).

In the upper left-hand quadrant (labeled 1) we have hazards that scientists as well as lay people agree constitute risks, for example nuclear radiation and certain chemical materials (e.g. prohibited pesticides). The upper right-hand quadrant (labeled 2) concerns threatening agents or activities that experts unanimously judge as risky, but where lay people by and large do not attribute any risk (e.g. household radon). The lower left-hand quadrant (labeled 3) encompasses those hazards that experts do not perceive as constituting any risk, but lay people do (e.g. siting conflicts where the experts judge the facility to be safe, while the local population sees it as an acute threat to their health and well-being). Lastly, the lower right-hand quadrant (labeled 4) consists of phenomena that neither scientists nor the lay public see as constituting any risk – but in time perhaps a change of judgment will occur (e.g. chemical products and substances that today are seen as unproblematic).

Environmental risks may be discovered in various ways, and Figure 9.2 describes two processes of how knowledge of potential hazards

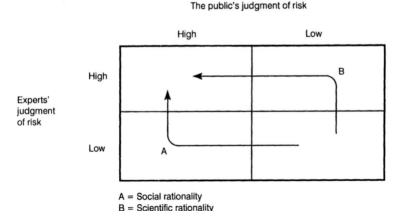

Figure 9.2 is shown with the axes and labels:

The public's judgment of risk

High   Low

Experts' judgment of risk — High, Low

High — B

Low — A

A = Social rationality
B = Scientific rationality

Figure 9.2   The social definition of environmental risk

is acquired. The fundamental difference between these two methods concerns the ways in which we discover new environmental risks, namely whether it is through lay people's experience and knowledge or through scientists' tests and observations.

Using Beck's terminology, *scientific rationality* means here that a substance, material, or activity – that originally is not seen as constituting any risk – is discovered by science as implying a certain threat to health and/or the environment. In time, more and more scientific evidence supports this initial assessment and through research communication this view is spread among the public. An example of this process is provided by chlorofluorocarbons (CFCs) which were discovered by chemists in 1931 and became an important part of industrial production and commercial products (e.g. electronic circuits, refrigerating systems, insulating materials). Medical scientists welcomed the use of the substance because they did not judge it be toxic or carcinogenic. It was with Molina and Rowland's article in *Nature* in 1974 that a debate commenced concerning the effects of CFCs on the ozone molecule.[40] Science has been the key actor in this process, and its views regarding the effects of CFCs on stratospheric ozone have been disseminated to the public.

Social rationality means that environmental dangers are first discovered by lay people without any formal scientific training. As popular knowledge accumulates science reaches a threshold at which point it needs to take a stand with regard to these claims. Frequently lay claims cause science to investigate whether this non-systematic knowledge may be (scientifically) valid or not. In some cases – as in the present controversy regarding the health effects of low-frequency electromagnetic fields – the scientific community has not found enough empirical evidence to support lay knowledge claims. In other cases, lay people and non-scientists judge a hazard to be harmful to health or the environment a long time before science and the authorities have turned their attention to these problems and a process toward juridical regulation has started.

Of course, the categories of scientists and lay people are in most cases not homogeneous. In many cases there exist intense arguments inside the scientific community – for example concerning whether technological systems are able to dissolve the risks connected to nuclear energy – where no expert closure is achieved.[41] Furthermore, as sociologists of scientific knowledge remind us, modern science is not an undifferentiated and consensual activity, but is instead a collection of various practices taking place in different social institutions. Therefore it is more correct, as Irwin argues, to think about *sciences* rather than a singular science.[42] Consequently, we need to view not only social rationality, but also scientific rationality, as being shaped by historical and social factors, meaning that expert judgment inevitably involves contextualized knowledge.

Similarly, lay people do not constitute an unvarying category – as mentioned above in the brief discussion of the competing perspectives involved in siting conflicts – but have different interests, values, knowledges, and experiences. The structures of contemporary society imply a multiplicity of lifestyles and value systems, all of which exist more or less side by side and are embraced by individuals and groups with different levels of readiness to act in concert.[43]

Furthermore, in many cases the processes of both scientific and social rationality are not as obvious as Figure 9.2 suggests. In many instances, the two processes are intertwined in the discovery of a certain hazard. In the case of risks associated with nuclear energy (in particular those involving the spent nuclear fuel), scientists, politicians, and grassroots activists in Sweden took part in a process that during the 1970s led to a relatively broad distribution of risk consciousness concerning this technology. Discovery of the health effects of certain herbicides is another example of this dialectical process. Phenoxyacetic acid, for example, was introduced as a herbicide in Sweden in the early 1950s. The producers of this herbicide declared that the substance posed no threat to human health, and that workers spreading the chemical did not need to wear any protective equipment. In the 1960s, researchers found that phenoxyacetic acid contained the dioxine TCDD. By the early 1970s, a few ecotoxicologists began warning that phenoxyacetic acid could cause cancer. The relatives of some forestry workers who had developed pancreatic cancer insisted that it was caused by the herbicide. Despite these incipient warnings, the Swedish Environmental Protection Agency declared that phenoxyacetic acid did not constitute any risk to the health of people working with the chemical. However, in 1992 its use was forbidden in Swedish forestry, and in 1997 the World Health Organization declared that the dioxine TCDD is carcinogenic for human beings.

Thus, the point here is not to foster a dichotomy between experts and lay people – as depicted above, 'science' and 'the public' are anything but homogeneous categories – but instead to draw attention to the fact that lay people's experiences and insights are regularly included in the knowledge production of environmental risks.

Scientific Knowledge and Everyday Life

Most people – researchers as well as lay people – would agree that scientific and social rationality grasp the process of how environmental (and other) risks are *discovered*. Some environmental problems do relate more closely to life experience than others. This forms the basis for the development of lay epidemiologies where health effects are associated with certain kinds of technological artifacts. Affected persons can causally link changes in health, foul-tasting water, and so forth to the use of a specific herbicide or a proximate landfill. Lay evaluations may then encourage researchers to focus attention on the hazard, but some commentators would claim that only science can develop knowledge on this matter. In other words, lay experiences on their own are insufficient and we need expert knowledge to replace lay epidemiologies with scientific ones. This sort of verification is required because there exists a multitude of examples where lay epidemiologies have been incorrect and where lay people over- (and under-)estimated risks.

This standpoint is true in the sense that social networks support particular forms of risk consciousness, as illustrated by the case of 'hazardous oases.'[44] Over time, a 'subjective immunity' often develops, meaning that a hazard becomes integrated into the everyday knowledge of the people living in proximity to it and they do not reflect upon its risks or indeed upon its very existence.[45] The source of threat becomes a natural part of the lifescape and people integrate coping strategies into their everyday activities to reduce its obtrusiveness. Among risk researchers there is a unanimity of opinion that people reckon they can cope with familiar situations and underestimate risks assumed to be under their control.

In situations where there is little chance of change, a gradual habituation to certain risks occurs and the hazard is subsumed into collective consciousness. An example of this process can be found in the adaptive strategies of the population in northern Sweden with regard to the consequences of the Chernobyl disaster. According to recent research, hunters and fishers in the most severely affected areas are exposed to at least as great an amount of cesium as Sami husbanding reindeer.

According to a widely circulated account, a couple living in this region stopped picking mushrooms and berries following the accident in 1986. Instead of eating the rabbits, they hung the animals' carcasses on the barn wall. The rabbits were not even fed to the dogs because of the high level of radioactivity they contained. Despite the fact that the couple knows that the amount of cesium is still above the permitted limit, they have once more begun to eat locally harvested food and wild meat. They reaffirm their decision to live in this rural setting because such a lifestyle affords the opportunity to farm and make use of accessible forest products. When asked by a journalist why they eat contaminated food despite the authorities' recommendations, the couple remarked, 'You lower your sights. You've got to, to be able to live ... Nowadays we pretend the Chernobyl disaster never occurred.'[46]

This sort of denial seems to be a general phenomenon among people living in the vicinity. An indication of this dismissal of the significance of the hazard is the decreasing number of people that check their personal cesium levels, despite the fact that the tests are free.

However, the processes that create subjective immunity and familiarity do not only influence lay judgments; they are also relevant when discussing researchers' perceptions and evaluations of risks. In many cases, lay people question science and its foundations of rationality, seeing it as a cultural form of knowledge with no privileged access to truth. Through the process of reflexivity, science has ceased to be considered more legitimate than other social activities, each of which involves different forms of judgment.[47] Science is no longer viewed as having a necessarily civilizing, progressive, and emancipatory role in revealing the fundamental qualities of society. As Wynne writes,

[A] general reason for possible divergence between expert and public knowledges about risks is that expert knowledge embodies social assumptions and models framing its objectivist language, and that lay people have legitimate claim to debate those assumptions.[48]

In certain cases, lay people may have more essential knowledge than the scientists, for example farmers are in close contact with their own geographical area. Contextually generated knowledge on specific conditions may be more relevant for the local population than the universal, abstract, and 'context-free' statements of science. An apposite narrative, illustrating the clash between two forms of knowledge – one grounded in science's search for cross-situational generality and one in lay people's case-specific understanding of local conditions – can be found in a Swedish novel. The County Administrative Board in northern Sweden has sent out a question- naire concerning the quality of the fresh water. An elderly man reacts and writes the following letter to the authority:

There's water that's as cold and dense as the rock – you can't drink it. And there's water that is so thin and weak there's no point in drinking it. And there's water that trembles when you drink it, and gives you the shivers. And there's water that's bitter and tastes like sweat. And there's water that's sort of dead – the water spiders sink straight down into it as if it was air. Oh yes, there are as many sorts of water as there are sorts of sand on the shore. So that bit of paper we've been sent, where we're supposed to write what the water's like – it's hopeless. There's no way the water can be put into a few lines. If, like me, you've lived for 70 years, you've learned enough about water for the Board to drown in.[49]

Earlier in this chapter I argued that lay people are important in the identification of environmental risks and that we should see them as producers of knowledge concerning hazards. However, in the (experts') writing of the history of the discovery of environ- mental problems non-institutional forms of experience and knowledge are easily deleted because they emanate from outside the expert system.[50] Lay people have access to 'data' regarding environmental risks in society, though they may derive their observations on the basis of different kinds of rational considerations. We can highlight this process by turning again to the interview with the couple living in northern Sweden. The husband describes how his hunting party exercises great care with elks that contain up to 2500 Bq/kg (the permitted level is 1500 units). He explains the members' reasoning: 'There are seventeen of us to share the meat, and we all receive some with a high cesium content and some with a low, to spread the risk.'

Similar coping strategies characterize the Sami people husbanding reindeer. The Chernobyl disaster contributed to increasing costs and declining prices, leading in turn to dramatic growth in herd size and earlier slaughter (before the reindeer have gone from grazing green feed to the lichen containing cesium). Slaughter prices dropped by 46 percent from 1986 to 1991, while the overall price index went up dramatically during the same period. Under such circumstances, there is great likelihood that the larger herds will lead to overgrazing of pasture and an ecological breakdown.[51] The problem is that the Swedish authorities do not seem to have taken the specific knowledge of the reindeer herders – about mountain ecology and the conditions of Sami culture – into consideration when developing management strategies to address overgrazing.[52] As stated above, scientific knowledge is not neutral, but involves particular cultural norms and epistemological assumptions.

To emphasize the cognitive and cultural aspects of both scientific and lay knowledge implies that risks are viewed through cultural filters. This filtering process operates both directly through our five senses and indirectly through extensions to our perceptual apparatus in the form of stories, news reports, statistics, and research. These filters are essential and unavoidable. They serve as automatic pilots that function largely without our awareness – we do not see that our interpretations are influenced by culture. Thus a cultural perspective on risks unmasks a world of plural rationalities, it discerns order and pattern in risk-taking behavior and the beliefs that underpin it. As Beck states, what is at stake in the risk conflicts of today is not so much risk avoidance, as the definition of risk in this new situation of growing competition between overlapping discourses of risk.[53]

TOWARD A COMMUNICATIVE APPROACH TO RISKS

Irwin describes how the prevailing approach to public policy-making remains firmly embedded in a modernistic perspective.[54] Accordingly, science constructs the definition of risk issues, and all other concerns, including alternative forms of understanding and different value structures, become peripheral. The prevailing approaches to policy-making have characteristically been based on a set of assumptions that place science at the core. The public is seated ringside, but certainly not at the center of the environmental action, and any problems in the relationship between science and citizens are interpreted as the consequence of either public ignorance or public irrationality.

As this chapter emphasizes, we need to leave this perspective behind. Science should no longer be seen as the only producer of legitimate knowledge. Instead, we must highlight the reflexive character of science, meaning that its skepticism is extended to the inherent foundations and external consequences of science itself. This demystification opens up new possibilities for questioning science and its commitment to rationality – no scientific statement is 'true' in the old sense any longer (i.e. unquestionable, eternal truth). With the loss of its indisputable claim to truth, science now has to struggle to gain legitimacy. People today have more flexibility to ignore scientific statements on risks. This new public autonomy *vis-à-vis* science is thereby not necessarily based on a disavowal of scientific knowledge, but is instead justified from a perspective that sees lay knowledge as more relevant than that provided by experts.

Because expert knowledge is not necessarily superior to other forms of knowledge, the latter forms – for example local knowledge gained through personal experience – can be relevant. Thus, the right of lay people to be heard and to influence decision-making processes is based not only on democratic values, but also on the fact that such participation can enrich the process of knowledge production. However, and most importantly, we must not totally reject scientific knowledge by over-privileging public knowledge. To replace an uncritical trust in one form of knowledge with uncritical trust in another kind means that the dichotomy between lay and expert is still in operation. Instead, we must transcend the tension between synoptic planning and dialogical incrementalism, between the knowledge of the expert and the knowledge of lay people.

When we realize that objective knowledge does not exist we create a communicative space into which the participants have the opportunity to step. This means that actors need to be aware that none of their perspectives, knowledge, and experience is superior to those of others. Each consciousness – irrespective of to whom it belongs – always demands critical correctives.[55] No one has access to objective knowledge and definitive truth, instead all are called upon to communicate. It is through communication that we create knowledge, and through such processes social rationality and scientific rationality have to meet. As Healey, in discussing communicative planning theory, observes:

> A communicative approach to knowledge production – knowledge of conditions, of cause and effect, moral values and aesthetic world – maintains that knowledge is not preformulated but is specifically created anew in our communication ... We cannot, therefore, predefine a set of tasks which planning must address, since these must be specifically discovered, learnt about and understood through inter-communicative processes.[56]

This means that we can redefine the dichotomy between (scientific) knowledge and (participatory) democracy. From this perspective a dialogue among lay people, politicians, and scientists does not constitute a hindrance for decisions guided by knowledge. Rather, it is through this sort of dialogue that we gain knowledge of environmental risks. Assimilation of diverse perspectives obviously will not occur in isolation, but in an open and conflict-filled communication where different views and interpretations can confront one another and be set in relation to one another. Wider societal diffusion of this approach may lead to a system of governance involving multiple and democratic systems of negotiation among various actors at different levels. This is something that contemporary political theorists are seeking.[57] Furthermore, emphasizing that science itself rests upon social assumptions will not only make science itself more reflexive. Such a turn may have a similar effect on policies for sustainable development, making visible their underlying assumptions concerning the natural, as well as the social world.[58]

However, there is no guarantee that public debate will lead to consensus, even if it does generate improved understanding and policy legitimation. The primary reason for including the public in deliberations is that such participation will hopefully lead to greater awareness. In this process, we need to recall Ravetz and Funtowicz's key observation. We should not view the 'high systems uncertainties' we face today as a negative attribute. Rather, this sort of openness can be a positive quality of our experience of the real world, one that makes life rich and stimulating, perhaps sometimes even leading us on from mere knowledge toward wisdom.[59]

ACKNOWLEDGMENTS

This chapter is based on research from a project on environmental conflicts sponsored by the Swedish Nuclear Inspectorate and the Swedish Council for Building Research, as well as a program of work on international policy-making underwritten by the Swedish Council for Planning and Coordination of Research. I wish to thank Maurie Cohen and two anonymous reviewers for valuable comments on an earlier version of this chapter. I also thank Malcolm Forbes for generous help with the language.

NOTES

1. For a discussion of the siting of the nuclear-power plant to supply Kiev with electricity, the choice of reactor technology, and the decision to build both the facility and the town of Pripyat, refer to P. Read, *Ablaze: The Story of Chernobyl* (London: Mandarin, 1993). For the ecological consequences of the Chernobyl disaster, see, for example, V. Savchenko, ed., *The Ecology of the Chernobyl Catastrophe: Scientific Outlines of an International Programme of Collaborative Research* (Carnforth: Parthenon Publishing Group, 1995); and V. Davydchuk, 'Ecosystem Remediation in Radioactively Polluted Areas: The Chernobyl Experience,' *Ecological Engineering*, 8(4) (1997): 325–36.
2. In addition to hosting its current range of nuclear facilities the Swedish government is presently considering Oskarshamn for its suitability to serve as a site for deep disposal of radioactive waste. See P. Hedberg and G. Sundqvist, 'Oskarshamn – unikt i Sverige?' pp. 69–122 in R. Lidskog, *Kommunerna och kärnavfallet: Svensk kärnavfallspolitik på 1990-talet* (*The Communes and the Spent Nuclear Fuel: Swedish Policy for Radioactive Waste Management in the 1990s*) (Stockholm: Carlsson Bokförlag, 1998).
3. K. Erikson, *A New Species of Trouble: Explorations in Disaster, Trauma, and Community* (New York: W. W. Norton, 1994).
4. U. Beck, *Risk Society: Towards a New Modernity* (London: Sage, 1992) and U. Beck, 'The Anthropological Clock: Chernobyl and the Contours of the Risk Society,' *Berkeley Journal of Sociology*, 32 (1987): 153–65.
5. We have, as Kai Erikson states, both chronic conditions and acute

220   *Rolf Lidskog*

events, as well as combinations of them. See Erikson, *A New Species of Trouble*, pp. 21.

6. S. Sörlin, 'Problem Continents and Island Experiences: Environment and Science in the Past and in the Present', pp. 14–29 in A. Nordgren, ed., *Science, Ethics, Sustainability: The Responsibility of Science in Attaining Sustainable Development* (Uppsala: Acta Universitatis Upsaliensis, 1997).

7. S. Cutter, *Living with Risk: The Geography of Technological Hazards* (London: Edward Arnold, 1993).

8. U. Beck, *Risk Society*; P. Dickens, 'Society and Nature,' *Developments in Sociology*, 9 (1993): 121–66; and B. McKibben, *The End of Nature* (New York: Anchor Books, 1989).

9. P. Brown, 'Popular Epidemiology: Community Response to Toxic Waste-Induced Disease in Woburn, Massachusetts and Other Sites,' *Science, Technology, and Human Values*, 12(1) (1987): 76–85; P. Brown, 'Popular Epidemiology Revisited,' *Current Sociology*, 45(3) (1997): 137–56; and A. Irwin, *Citizen Science: A Study of People, Expertise, and Sustainable Development* (London: Routledge, 1995).

10. D. Jamieson, 'The Epistemology of Climate Change: Some Morals for Managers,' *Society and Natural Resources*, 4(4) (1991): 319–29.

11. I should stress that not only individuals, but also organizations (even nation-states) have difficulty understanding and managing these kinds of risks. Despite this situation, organizations – for example governmental bodies and private companies – constantly need to respond rapidly to risk events reported and distributed around the world through the development of information technology.

12. R. Lidskog, *Radioactive and Hazardous Waste Management in Sweden: Movements, Politics, and Science* (Uppsala: Acta Universitatis Upsaliensis, 1994) and R. Lidskog, 'From Conflict to Communication? Public Participation and Critical Communication as a Solution to Siting Conflicts,' *Planning Practice and Research*, 12(3) (1997): 239–49.

13. Cf. the American nuclear-waste researcher Luther Carter who advocates that radioactive-waste siting should be characterized by an 'uncompromising concern for technical soundness and public safety,' which for him means that no local or non-scientific opposition should be allowed to affect siting plans. The British researcher Stan Openshaw articulates a similar perspective, stating that authorities should employ scientific argument to declare any opposition invalid. See L. Carter, *Nuclear Imperatives and Public Trust: Dealing with Radioactive Waste* (Washington, DC: Johns Hopkins University Press, 1987), p. 5; S. Openshaw, 'Making Nuclear Power More Publicly Acceptable,' *Nuclear Energy*, 27(2) (1988): 131–6; and S. Openshaw, S. Carver, and J. Fernie, *Britain's Nuclear Waste: Safety and Siting* (London: Belhaven Press, 1989).

14. G. Porter and J. Brown, *Global Environmental Politics*, 2nd edn (Boulder, CO: Westview Press, 1996), p. 1; I. Elander and R. Lidskog, 'The Rio Declaration and Subsequent Global Initiatives,' forthcoming in N. Low, B. Gleeson, I. Elander, and R. Lidskog, eds, *Consuming Cities: The Urban Environment in the Global Economy after the Rio Declaration* (London: Routledge, 1999).

15. The concepts sustainable development and risk have mostly referred to different parts of the complex of environmental problems. Scholars have applied the term sustainable development to the utilization of natural resources without compromising the ability of future generations to meet their own needs. They have tended to connect risk to human-made threats generated by the design faults of technological systems. However, I would argue that these two categories are now beginning to merge and to overlap. Global climate change concerns, for example, on both the input side (utilization of fossil energy) and the output side (release of carbon dioxide and the environmental risks associated with it) are expressions of this convergence. Furthermore, the contemporary utilization of resources takes place through the massive use of technology, and expert systems are created to manage natural resources. Also, an important part in the strategy for ecological sustainability is the avoidance of environmental risks by replacing hazardous activities with more sustainable ones.

16. According to its national Agenda 21 report, Sweden now has more environmental taxes and charges than almost any other country in the world. The government has constructed these economic tools with the explicit aim of making environmental impact a price factor. Some of these instruments are reactive, as in the case of the polluter-pays principle which does not become operative until after the occurrence of environmental harm. Other instruments are preventive as in the cases of environmental fees and taxes (gasoline, oil, energy use, nitrogen oxide, and carbon dioxide). Besides having a steering capacity, these policy interventions have become important sources of public revenue and the Treasury estimates that the proceeds of environment and energy-related taxes will account for 3.7 percent of Swedish gross domestic product in 1998. See *From Environmental Protection to Sustainable Development: National Report on the Implementation of Agenda 21* (Stockholm: Ministry of the Environment, 1997) and I. Elander, R. Lidskog, and M. Johansson, 'Environmental Policies and Urban Planning in Sweden: Goals, Strategies, and Instruments,' *European Spatial Research and Policy*, 4(2) (1997): 5–35.

17. Irwin, *Citizen Science*, pp. 17–30.

18. T. Sager, *Communicative Planning Theory* (Aldershot: Avebury, 1994).

19. C. Lindblom, 'The Science of "Muddling Through,"' *Public Administration Review*, 19(2) (1959): 79–88.

20. J. Friedmann, *Retracking America: A Theory of Transactive Planning* (New York: Doubleday, 1973).

21. J. Forester, *Planning in the Face of Power* (Berkeley: University of California Press, 1989).

22. J. Habermas, *Knowledge and Human Interest* (Boston, MA: Beacon Press, 1971) and J. Habermas, *The Theory of Communicative Action, Volume 1: Reason and the Rationalization of Society* (Boston, MA: Beacon Press, 1984).

23. P. Næss, 'Normative Planning Theory and Sustainable Development,' *Scandinavian Housing and Planning Research*, 11(3) (1994): 145–67.

24. See, for example, Lindblom, 'The Science of "Muddling Through."'

Lindblom argues in this classic article that action alternatives should only be small steps in relation to the present situation. Planners can then gain experience quickly and use this knowledge to evaluate the next step.

25. Hardin argued that Western nations could not, or indeed should not, become 'lifeboats' to save all developing countries from famine. Instead, only those nations with vigorous population-reduction policies should be given aid. Critics of Hardin described the proposition as an example of ecofascism or scientific racism. See G. Hardin, 'Living on a Lifeboat,' *Bioscience*, 24(10) (1974): 561–8. For a description of the background to this controversy refer to D. Pepper, *Modern Environmentalism: An Introduction* (London: Routledge, 1996).

26. For further discussion on this point see M. Cohen, 'Science and the Environment: Assessing Cultural Capacity for Ecological Modernization,' *Public Understanding of Science*, 7(2) (1998): 149–67.

27. A. Giddens, *Consequences of Modernity* (Cambridge: Polity Press, 1990).

28. The following anecdote illustrates the differences between the planning of public authorities and the planning of citizens in the post-Chernobyl situation. A mother, later evacuated from the zone, related that her family tried to avoid buying cheap food because she thought that the expensive sausage was made from meat of good quality. Local authorities later informed her that it was precisely the costly sausage that contained contaminated meat. The reason behind this paradox was that since the expensive sausage was so costly, government authorities presumed people would not buy as much of it and thereby consume less. See S. Aleksijevitj, *Bön för Tjernobyl* (*Prayer for Chernobyl*) (Stockholm: Ordfront, 1997), pp. 190.

29. J. Ravetz and S. Funtowicz, 'Commentary,' *Journal of Risk Research*, 1(1) (1998): 45–8.

30. See, for example, J. Friedmann, *Planning in the Public Domain: From Knowledge to Action* (Princeton, NJ: Princeton University Press, 1987); P. Healey, 'Planning Through Debate: The Communicative Turn in Planning Theory,' *Town Planning Review*, 63(2) (1992): 143–62; and F. Fischer and J. Forester, eds, *The Argumentative Turn in Policy Analysis and Planning* (Durham, NC: Duke University Press, 1993).

31. See, for example, Irwin, *Citizen Science*; S. Lash, 'Reflexivity and its Double: Structure, Aesthetics, Community,' pp. 110–73 in U. Beck, A. Giddens, and S. Lash, *Reflexive Modernization: Politics, Traditions, and Aesthetics in Modern Social Order* (Cambridge: Polity Press, 1994); S. Lash and J. Urry, *Economies of Signs and Space* (London: Sage, 1994); and B. Wynne, 'May the Sheep Safely Graze? A Reflexive View of the Expert–Lay Knowledge Divide,' pp. 44–83 in S. Lash, B. Szerszynski, and B. Wynne, eds, *Risk, Environment, and Modernity: Towards a New Ecology* (London: Sage, 1996).

32. U. Beck, *Ecological Politics in an Age of Risk* (Cambridge: Polity Press, 1995), p. 8 and U. Beck, 'From Industrial Society to Risk Society: Questions of Survival, Social Structure, and Ecological Enlightenment,' *Theory, Culture, and Society*, 9(1) (1992): 97–123.

33. Beck, *Ecological Politics*, p. 124. See also A. Blowers, 'Environmental

Scientific Evidence or Lay People's Experience? 223

Policy: The Quest for Sustainable Development,' *Urban Studies*, 30(4/5) (1993): 775–96.

34. Beck does not elaborate on the characteristics of social rationality, only contrasting them with scientific rationality. Implicitly, however, he seems to mean knowledge based on lay people's experiences, perception, and reflections – that is knowledge emanating from everyday life. See, for example, Beck, *Ecological Politics*, p. 184 and Beck, *Risk Society*, pp. 58–9. In these instances Beck seems to equate science and scientific rationality with 'scientism' (cf. Irwin, *Citizen Science*, p. 109 and Lash and Wynne, 'Introduction,' p. 108 in Beck, *Risk Society*).

35. U. Beck, 'The Reinvention of Politics: Towards a Theory of Reflexive Modernization', pp. 1–55 in Beck et al., *Reflexive Modernization*, especially p. 29. Cf. also A. Giddens, 'Risk, Trust, Reflexivity,' pp. 184–97 in the same volume, particularly pp. 185–6.

36. See, for example, Lash and Urry, *Economies of Signs and Space* and R. Lidskog, 'In Science We Trust? On the Relation between Scientific Knowledge, Risk Consciousness, and Public Trust,' *Acta Sociologica*, 39(1) (1996): 31–56.

37. Beck, *Risk Society*, chapter 7 and Beck, 'From Industrial Society to Risk Society,' p. 119.

38. A. Giddens, *Modernity and Self-Identity: Self and Society in the Late Modern Age* (Cambridge: Polity Press, 1991), p. 18.

39. As Lash has observed, while ethnomethodology asks the question, 'How do we routinely achieve meaning,' Giddens, in effect, poses the question, 'How do we consciously achieve ontological security.' Furthermore, ethnomethodology wants to dispute expert systems by looking behind them at routine activities. In contrast, Giddens argues that people cope with such insecurity only, or at least best, through the use of expert systems. Giddens thus appears to see expert systems as instruments that help us to achieve security, while Beck views them as obstacles to the achievement of such security. See Lash, 'Reflexivity and its Double,' p. 117.

40. M. Molina and S. Rowland, 'Stratospheric Sink for Chlorofluoromethanes: Chlorine Atom Catalyses Destruction of Ozone,' *Nature*, 249 (1974): 810–12.

41. See, for example, T. Brante, S. Fuller, and W. Lynch, eds, *Controversial Science: From Content to Contention* (Albany: State University of New York Press, 1993); B. Campbell, 'Uncertainty as Symbolic Action in Disputes among Experts,' *Social Studies of Science*, 15(3) (1985): 429–53; and E. McMullin, 'Scientific Controversy and its Termination,' pp. 49–91 in T. Engelhardt and A. Caplan, eds, *Scientific Controversies: Case Studies in the Resolution and Closure of Disputes in Science and Technology* (Cambridge: Cambridge University Press, 1987).

42. Irwin, *Citizen Science*, p. 51.

43. R. Burkhart, 'Consensus-Oriented Public Relations as a Solution to the Landfill Conflict,' *Waste Management and Research*, 12(3) (1994): 223–32 and P. Macnaghten and J. Urry, 'Towards a Sociology of Nature,' *Sociology*, 29(2) (1995): 203–20.

44. The idea is analogous to the notion of 'nuclear oases,' i.e. geographic

places where nuclear installations or wastes already exist and where a disposal facility is welcomed. An example of this phenomenon is Sellafield in Britain, an installation that provides 11 000 jobs in an area offering few alternative sources of employment. Another instance is Hanford in the United States where local enthusiasm for a radioactive-waste repository is overwhelmed by hostility throughout the rest of Washington State and is particularly concentrated in the larger cities of Seattle and Spokane (over 200 miles away). See, for example, A. Blowers, D. Lowry, and B. Solomon, *The International Politics of Nuclear Waste* (New York: St. Martin's Press, 1991), pp. xviii, 326.

45. M. Douglas, *Risk Acceptability According to the Social Sciences* (London: Routledge & Kegan Paul, 1986).
46. Quoted in C. Johansson, 'Det tysta landet', *Tur and Retur*, 2 (1994): 9–13, 36. Radioactive cesium has a half-life of 30 years. In the affected municipality of Gävle the highest amount of cesium in an elk (5780 bBq/kg. meat) was found in 1993, seven years after the accident. Swedish authorities found in that year 77 percent of the roedeer tested had cesium levels above the permitted standard.
47. M. Douglas, *Risk and Blame: Essays in Cultural Theory* (London: Routledge, 1992) and Macnaghten and Urry, 'Towards a Sociology of Nature.'
48. Wynne, 'May the Sheep Safely Graze,' pp. 59.
49. T. Lindgren, *Merhabs skönhet. (The Beauty of Merhab)* (Stockholm: MånPocket, 1985), p. 143.
50. Wynne, 'May the Sheep Safely Graze,' p. 59.
51. Swedish Governmental Official Report, *Hållbar utveckling i landets fjällområden (Sustainable Development in the Swedish Mountain Area)* (Stockholm: Allmänna förlaget, 1995).
52. S. Antilla and E. Torp, 'Environmental Adjustment and Private Economic Strategies in Reindeer Pastoralism: Combining Game Theory with Participatory Action Research,' *Acta Borealia*, 13(2) (1996): 91–108.
53. U. Beck, 'Risk Society and the Provident State,' pp. 27–43 in Lash et al., *Risk, Environment, and Modernity*, especially p. 36.
54. Irwin, *Citizen Science*, p. 62.
55. Cf. P. Ricoeur, *De l'Interprétation: Essai sur Freud* (Paris: Seuil, 1965).
56. Healey, 'Planning Through Debate,' p. 153. See also M. Sotarauta, 'Escaping the Strategic Policy-making Traps by Soft Strategies: Redirecting Focus,' *Nordisk Samhällsgeografisk Tidskrift*, 24 (1997): 48–62.
57. D. Archibugi and D. Held, eds, *Cosmopolitan Democracy: An Agenda for a New World Order* (Cambridge: Polity Press, 1995); J. Cohen and J. Rogers, eds, *Associations and Democracy* (London: Verso, 1995); D. Held, *Democracy and the Global Order* (Cambridge: Polity Press, 1995); and D. Zolo, *Cosmopolis: The Prospect of a World Government* (Cambridge: Polity Press, 1996).
58. Macnaghten and Urry, 'Towards a Sociology of Nature,' p. 210 and R. Lidskog, 'Society, Space, and Environment: Towards a Sociological Reconceptualization of Nature,' *Scandinavian Journal for Housing and Planning Research*, 15(1) (1998): 19–35.
59. Ravetz and Funtowicz, 'Commentary,' p. 47.

10 Taming Risks through Dialogues: the Rationality and Functionality of Discursive Institutions in Risk Society
Klaus Eder

DISCOURSE: A FUZZY CONCEPT

'Discourse,' in the sense of communicative and argumentative inter-action, has become a concept central to the understanding of modern society and its culture. This notion is now also gaining importance in the field of environmental studies. In this context, the term refers to the problem of how to communicate rationally about risks in modern society. Discourse is seen as a solution to environmental problems, as an institutional form especially well-suited to what Ulrich Beck refers to as 'risk society.' Discourse thus appears not only as a rational, but also as a functional, device for addressing the collective risks generated by modern societies.

These emerging political narratives regarding risk contain three problems. First, what does discourse mean exactly? Second, what does it mean to claim that discourse is rational? Third, what does it mean to say that discourse is functional? Let me start with the first problem in this triad.

In formulating a definition of the concept it is initially useful to note that discourse requires a specific spatial setting. This approach is topical, especially given our mythical heritage. Let us take for example the legend of King Arthur and his famous round table. What King Arthur tried to do in assembling his knights in such a way was an institutional approach for realizing discourse. Around a circular table everyone is equal. No individual assumes a privileged role in this kind of setting because there is no favored position. A round table is the most equalizing device imaginable. This is discourse – institutionalized dialogue.

This is the narrative explication of discourse. For someone trained in a social-philosophical culture shaped by the communication theory of Jürgen Habermas, the non-narrative or analytical answer is somewhat different. According to this convention, discourse refers to our capacity to coordinate our actions through communicative action. Discourse is a mechanism for transforming dissent into consent. Obviously, discourse has to do with communication and the force of the better argument in a dialogical situation. For someone schooled in the French tradition of Michel Foucault, discourse would mean something else again, namely a mechanism that controls on an elementary level what we think and do. Discourse, from this point of view, is the most compelling form of power, invisible in its operation.

These distinctions allow us to clarify the concept of discourse. Discourse refers first to a social relationship, where at least two people communicate with each other, using the elements that human speech offers to shape interaction through language. One way to distinguish this definition is to refer to discourse as dialogue, to emphasize its process-oriented nature. Second, discourse includes the outputs created in this communicative interaction, to the universe of meaning produced and reproduced through communication. This notion of a discursive universe would grasp this second definition and it would do justice to the way in which Foucault uses the term. Discourse thus has a double but related meaning. It is the social process through which participants generate a universe and it is the outcome of such a process – the meaningful universe as a social fact imposed upon us.

The second question raised above concerns the purported capacity of discourse to communicate rationally about risks and to generate a shared understanding for dealing with them. Such comprehension can be achieved by communication that involves either persuasion or acceptance of better arguments. In an ideal world the generation of a consensus through discursive argumentation would be preferable. In this sense, I could already answer the question posed. It is rational to use discourses, for they would allow us to build an ideal world – a paradise on earth. However, since the Fall we can think of paradise only counterfactually. This is exactly the solution Habermas proposes for the rationality of discursive forms of communication, namely that they are counterfactually rational.

It remains for us to address the third question that I raised above – is it functional to engage in discourse to communicate about risks in modern societies? This is a very challenging question, and it is here where the sociologist enters. The unavoidable answer is that it depends. More specifically, it depends on context. In some instances it might be utterly counterproductive to engage in discursive processes to communicate about risks – for instance when a nuclear power station is melting down. In other situations it might be very functional to use discourse to communicate about risks. It is determining the appropriate circumstances for the rationality of discourse that is my topic in this chapter.

Let me at this stage summarize my initial argument. It is always rational to engage in discourse, but it depends on context whether it is also functional to seek a rational consensus about risks in modern societies.

DISCOURSE IN THE MODERN CONTEXT

What are the general contextual conditions in which discourse makes sense? The initial all-embracing parameter is 'modernity'. Discursive structures were less a part of the republican than the democratic political thought that accompanied and legitimated modern political institutions.[1] The parliament and the contemporary judiciary, with its adversarial system ('dialogues between attorney and defendant with the judge as the mediator of this discourse,' to use a normative qualification and self-understanding of this institution), belong to the worlds of discourse that emerged with modern societies. Robert Wuthnow even describes the major cultural innovations in European modernity as outcomes of communities of discourse.[2] He sees modern science, the Reformation, and the socialist movement as being bound to a specific way of organizing discourses. Discourse then is a constitutive part of modernity and this link explains the particular resonance of the way in which Habermas tried to explicate its presuppositions, namely as a society in which the validity claims built into any kind of discourse (validity claims related to pure reason, to practical reason, and to aesthetic reason) have been decoupled from each other and thus could unfold the potential inherent in each of them.[3]

There is also an empirical element to this theory. In his early publications Habermas pointed to the phenomenon of associations, political clubs, reading societies, and so forth since the late-eighteenth century as the source of what the philosophers of the time described as *Öffentlichkeit* – a public space where critique and enlightenment could be practiced and where opposition to the traditional state could be fomented.[4] Through participation in these social forms participants developed rudimentary discursive structures and it is in these contexts that we have to locate the sources of modernity. Association is contrasted with and opposed to the corporation in nineteenth-century political thinking and analysis. It is what distinguishes the modern present from the premodern past. The creation of associations can be viewed as the inner motor of the evolution of modernity. These fundamental forms of association are characterized by voluntariness, equality of membership, free debate, and dialogue.

Influenced by the intellectual interpretations of the eastern European revolutions of the late 1980s, *Öffentlichkeit* has been more recently relabeled as 'civil society.' This is the association writ large, in which collective participation and dialogue generate the basic legitimacy of political decisions. Discourse has become the central institutional device to distinguish a modern from a pseudo-modern society. This argument, for instance, has been important in several eastern European countries to mark the distance between the socialist past and the new democratic era.

Today, there are further contextual conditions in which discourses are practicable. This situation has to do with a mushrooming of institutions claiming dialogue as their mode of functioning. Discourses seem to invade the contemporary world, in places where one might never have imagined them to exist. Round tables, for example, have become a prominent symbol of political mobilization in the period of German reunification. This particular institutional approach was reinvented by citizen groups that were thinking about how to create collectively – through rational discourse about political differences – the new Germany.

Discourse was not, however, restricted to debates regarding reunification. This phenomenon also became paramount in the context of attempts to find political solutions to environmental problems. Discourse is enacted in dialogical procedures such as political forums and public discussions about environmental risks involving both non-governmental organizations (NGOs) and industry.[5] Even the European Commission has begun to establish discourses under the label of 'dialogues' such as the 'Social Dialogue between Social Partners,' a consensus-seeking institution for organizing industrial relations with the aim of tackling controversial social policy issues.[6] Various sponsoring organizations stage dialogues between different nation-states, cultures, or ethnic groups designed to generate understanding.[7] Clearly dialogues abound – a circumstance that should not be reduced to the particularity of German political culture. While discourse might have found especially fertile soil in Germany, this mechanism appears to be a general feature of organizing social relationships in modern societies. Societies have evolved such practices not only to confront increasingly complex managerial issues, but also to satisfy constraints that require them to solve dilemmas democratically. Discourse provides an approach for defusing tensions that could lead to protests. The term 'risk society' focuses this problem. Such societies develop by producing unintended consequences and fail to find legitimate ways of politically resolving the resulting complexity.

The evolution of modern political institutions reacts to the increasing complexity of contemporary societies. The effects can be analyzed in three dimensions. The first outcome is the extension of horizontally organized systems of negotiation among collective actors, that replaces classic hierarchical forms of political decision-making. Horizontal coordination thus becomes an alternative to more customary vertical coordination. The second upshot is an implication of the first; more specifically, discourse is the mode of relationship that presupposes horizontal systems of negotiation. While in the vertical case you need to command, in the latter case you have to talk – often endlessly. Discourse becomes functional precisely when strategic action leads to bottlenecks – assuming no one wants the system to fail. The third element is reflexivity. Institutions are reflexive when they produce spaces in which goals of political decision-making are defined outside the realm of normal procedures. To enable decision-making to move forward the procedural environment becomes the object of social reflection.[8] Goals are no longer seen as part of an established value system or an ontological order; rather they become part of a social process within which goals are defined and redefined. Society becomes, as Niklas Luhmann has argued, self-referential. Values that orient decision-making are used to engage in their definition through dialogical procedures that address such values. It is this self-referentiality that makes discourse an ultramodern institution.

To conclude then my second argument, dialogue is a feature of modernity that increases in importance – dialogues abound today. It is this abundance that makes it rational for social actors to engage in discourse.

THE DOUBLE FUNCTION OF INSTITUTIONALIZING DISCOURSES

To say that it is functional to engage in discourse in complex societies is more of an empirically grounded hypothesis than a theoretically based argument. This observation, however, begs a question, namely why should actors engage in discourse at all? The Habermasian argument has been because of the force of the better argument. Habermas himself has relativized this claim by assuming that we refer in discourses to counterfactual situations, to idealized instances of human interaction. The task is to think further, while avoiding lapsing into debate about what should be the case. Let me pose a supplementary question that might lead us through the jungle of social reality and focus the discussion. What is a good theoretical explanation for discourse being functional in modern, complex societies?

The argument for a social function, leaving aside the long methodological and epistemological debates on the limits of functionalism, is basic to explaining why discourses are institutionalized at all. The theoretical contention is that in a functionally differentiated society the contingency of action increases. The greater the number of possibilities for action, the more interdependent is the choice for action. When complexity expands, the risks associated with a particular action increase as well for there are so many alternative ways to act. To the extent that choices can no longer be socially structured by attributing them to, for example, institutions such as class, state, religion, and science the risks revert to individuals.

This is one meaning of risk society. It is not the environment *per se* that turns modern society into risk society, but rather the structure of modern societies themselves and their mode of creating complexity through functional differentiation (see also the chapter in this volume by William Freudenburg). The environment then becomes a vehicle to help focus the problem of risk-taking and this has led to its emergence as the central metaphor for describing risk society. In other words, it is not Chernobyl or genetic technology, but functional differentiation that forms the basis for describing modern society as risk society.

Because traditional institutions fail to provide solutions to risks, they have to be dealt with on the individual level. The institutions of modern society seem to be unable to respond to novel threats in a way that encourages trust. People perceive risks as things that target them personally, and this contradicts the way in which they are normally incorporated into modern society. In most cases, the state treats individuals as partial persons who care about their health and then go to the hospital, who care about education and then send their children to university, who care about meaning and then go either to church or to the psychiatrist, who care about their income and then negotiate individually or collectively about their labor contract. These activities no longer work to reduce the insecurities and uncertainties of action that modern societies produce. To narrow the contingency of action, therefore, we need to build new institutions. These observations bring me to my central thesis. The institutionalization of dialogue is a mode of making meaningful the selection of actions, given the profound contingencies operating in contemporary societies. Discourses allow us to control the risks that we encounter, given extant uncertainties. But this finding leads me to ask how can the formal establishment of discourses help to reduce the contingency of action and thus allow for the reproduction of modern societies that pay for their complexity with high risks?

To answer such a question a theory of the institutionalization of discourses has to be made explicit. Discourses gain permanence when they serve two functions: a *regulatory* function of avoiding non-decisions on complex issues and an *expressive* function of providing an image of making decisions in an acceptable way.

These dual functions are in fact a first step toward explaining the institutionalization of discursively organized procedures. The initial observation is that they are part of the transformation of corporatist arrangements that have accompanied the rise (and fall) of the welfare state. It is with the decline of the welfare state and the ascendancy of common good problems such as the environment that new institutional forms of politics emerge. In contrast to the corporatist model, the discursive model is based on the idea of dialogical forms of consensus building. Such procedures will become increasingly important as more traditionally regulated institutions fail and difficulties providing common goods require us to take into account a number of different voices to produce acceptable political decisions.

As I have noted above, political institutions have a double function. They fulfill the instrumental function of regulation and they achieve the symbolic function of integration. Institutions are means of producing collectively accepted decisions and symbolic devices of sense-making for those concerned with such decisions. For an institutional analysis of the social functions of discourse this awareness of a double function will be crucial because institutions are dependent on fulfilling both responsibilities simultaneously. The open questions then are how are these functions linked? Which comes first? What happens when functions are partially met? Is there a homology of both dimensions? Can they eventually substitute for each other? Does their relationship vary historically?

An interesting argument concerning the functionality of discourses for regulation has been proposed by Seyla Benhabib and others.[9] The argument contends that since the complexity of issues is so great, no one is capable of calculating the future consequences of a decision. Therefore, the probability of finding one correct solution is low. Expert advice does not help, because experts usually disagree. Nonetheless, we still need to make decisions. What is better suited to this requirement than a procedure that binds people to their commitments as they emerge during collective debate, given that any regulatory device designed to identify the best decision is doomed to fail? Talking is thus an implication of complexity and it has the function of politically regulating social processes.

The expressive function is linked to the self-understanding and the self-presentation of decision-making bodies to those constituents who are concerned with their outcomes. This expressive function has undergone a deep structural change in the course of the last few decades. The opportunity for the public to observe decision-making bodies has increased enormously. Every morning one reads about the activities of such entities in the newspapers and every evening one watches them on television. Decision-makers are ubiquitous, which means they have to present themselves to the public as if they were acting in the latter's interest. They have to engage in image and identity politics (as do industrial and pressure-group actors). The greater the opportunities for the public to observe decision-makers, the more they are forced to show a coherent and convincing face. To stage discourses is a way to fulfill this expressive function. Since discursive procedures carry an impression of 'goodness,' actors can use this property to satisfy this second function of institutionalized discourses.

In this chapter I have so far managed to avoid the naive normative question of whether discursive procedures are really discursive. Rather, I have argued that discursive institutions can be analyzed from a functionalist perspective that requires us to do nothing more than identify the conditions under which the institutionalization of discursive forms of conflict resolution are at a premium. I claimed the existence of two such conditions. First, the predominance of discourse derives from the prevalence of highly complex issues for which there is no clear solution. Second, discourse thrives in a social environment that does not allow for authoritarian solutions, but requires instead democratic forms for handling common good issues. Environmental risk is particularly demanding on these two counts. The need to address these issues is even seen as a rationale for demanding more democratic forms of conflict resolution and paradoxically the application of discursive approaches of problem resolution compounds further their complexity.

RISK DISCOURSES: CASES OF DISCURSIVE INSTITUTIONALIZATION

To give some flesh to these observations I would like to elaborate upon several empirical cases of the discursive handling of conflicts concerning environmental risks. In these examples discourse plays an important role within horizontally organized systems of negotiation between collective actors with diverging and contradictory interests. The cases have emerged in Germany over the course of the last two decades and share a rather stable and clear organizational structure.[10]

We can divide these examples into four types:

1. Expert dialogues institutionalized as *Enquete-Kommissionen*;
2. Political dialogues institutionalized as *Energiekonsensgespräche* (dialogues to promote consensus on energy policy);
3. Inter-organizational dialogues between environmental groups and the German chemical industry (so-called 'Hoechst' dialogues);
4. Mediation procedures that use third parties to resolve problems such as the siting of large and ecologically costly construction projects (e.g. airports, waste incinerators).[11]

For a sociological analysis the following discussion will concentrate on the first and fourth dialogue-types in this classificatory scheme, namely expert dialogues and mediation procedures. The other two dialogue-types will occupy less of our attention and will be referred to only for purposes of contrast.

These cases reveal a great deal about the organizational form of dialogues on risks. They provide data on both the symbolic context (the use of the metaphor of discourse by different actors participating in discursive procedures and the discursive strategies of different actors) and the actor context (the increase in the number and type of actors in these organizational forms and the role of the public as observer).

The *Enquête-Kommissionen* consist of political actors, experts, and NGO representatives. The organization does not decide on issues, but rather provides a forum to debate competing interpretations and solutions to risk issues such as genetic technology or climate change. The participants define an agenda for action, open policy windows, and enable society to broaden the options upon which to draw in making decisions – or at least for avoiding non-decisions. The actor constellation is typical for post-corporatist arrangements. More pointedly, this means the public is present in these organizations and this composition modifies the degree of secrecy vs. publicness involved in setting an agenda for policy-making.[12] Actors' understandings of their roles are defined by the initial set-up. In particular, actors have to be open to the arguments of the other participants and all have to engage in open debate. The public thus plays an important role in these organizations, specifically because the bodies are extremely dependent on public reaction. *Enquête-Kommissionen* even draw their legitimacy by impressing the public, and public support is the main power resource available to such organizations.

Mediation procedures differ quite markedly from *Enquête-Kommissionen*. This second class of deliberative institutions must produce decisions and act mainly in the non-public realm. The wider public in most cases is not even very interested in the proceedings.[13] Nonetheless, the collective action of the actors participating in mediation is dependent upon shared meanings that are presented as a way of handling conflicts discursively with the help of a 'reasonable man' who presides as facilitator.[14] It is this engagement that gives legitimacy to decisions (if there is one), both for the internal public (those who have lost in terms of interests defended) and for the external public.

It is important to recognize that these two categories should be viewed not only as symbolic, but also as 'material' organizational devices for resolving issues involving environmental risk. Accordingly, a sociological analysis must examine their real functioning and organizational rationality. Such an analysis looks at access to institutionalized discourse, motivation, and efficiency and effectiveness of discourse.

The entrance ticket into *Enquête-Kommissionen* is competence, with the paradoxical effect of hardening differing scientific certainties while nonetheless binding participants into an ongoing discursive process. The requirement of competence entails a bias in favor of those who can more easily mobilize expertise. Partial compensation for this selectivity is a specific characteristic of risk issues, namely that they are defined by uncertainty concerning their probability and effects. In any expert assumption dealing with risk strong, non-technical presumptions are unavoidable.[15] The lack of technical certitude can, however, be offset by an ability to employ rhetorical resources. Participants need to be able to afford the time necessary to engage in debates and have the ability to articulate well-argued worldviews and philosophies. Both preconditions for successful engagement privilege interests that are normally marginalized in such contexts, most prominently social movement organizations. Power positions in such discursive environments are difficult to monopolize. To be convincing, participants need to minimize their instrumental commitments (expectations for personal gain) in favor of normative motivations. In other words, they need to evidence a belief in the rational force of argumentative dialogue and behave in a way that supersedes parochial interests. The result of such organizational activity is definitional work, agenda setting, and the articulation of good metaphorical devices for influencing eventual political decisions. Since there is no decision-making power, the influence of these organizations is in preventing non-decisions.

Again, the cases of mediation differ systematically from expert dialogues. Access is open to all individuals and institutions with a stake in a pending decision. However, those who participate have to invest time to learn about alternatives, costs that normally go beyond the capacity of ordinary citizens. Thus, people specializing in particular issues tend to be individuals who enter such procedures with the aim of defending themselves against bureaucratic rationality and industrial interests. Participants' motivation is first of all strategic and often arises from a 'not-in-my-backyard' stance.

These cases constitute specific types of discourses for solving social conflicts and for resolving real material problems. Interestingly, they have developed more or less outside of established political institutions and have been based either on some general procedural law imposed by the political-legal system or on voluntary rules negotiated among the participants. With respect to the discursive mode of functioning, the expert dialogues are closest to the model and mediation procedures the most removed. Whereas in the first case the problem of defining a common good is paramount, in the latter case the dilemma is how to distribute the costs of preserving the environment. In expert dialogues the strategic game of defending interests is minimized while in mediation the objective of protecting one's personal stake is central. The two ideal-types define the endpoints of a continuum of discursivity with inter-organizational dialogues and political dialogues situated between these two poles. These latter two alternatives combine strategic interests and concern for common goods, a combination that makes them highly volatile institutional forms.

Therefore, all four cases combine to a different degree distributive and common good questions related to some notion of the good life, to ideas of collective values, and even to identities. The environment is thus both a problem linked to redistributing the costs of using natural resources and a form of debating the adequacy of the modern relationship of human beings to nature. Environmental politics is a politics of redistribution and a politics of identity, and it is this combination that makes it relevant and interesting.

We can construct from the preceding discussion a theoretical model that gives us analytical tools for describing and understanding the empirical cases. To do so I will propose two ideal-type discursive institutions.

TWO IDEAL TYPES OF DISCURSIVE INSTITUTIONS

In the practices discussed above I identified two regulatory models of discursive procedures. The first model can be found mainly in the literature on mediation, especially environmental mediation. There the mediation of *interests* is the dominant theme. Nonnegotiable claims have to be transformed into negotiable positions to break deadlocks. The discursive procedure helps to identify interests, to do away with zero-sum games, and to promote principled discussions. On the basis of a shared definition of the central issue participants seek and discuss possible solutions. The guidelines that emerge from this process bind actors to the extent that they have contributed to their invention. Such procedures try to encourage win-win options in which all participants gain.

Critics have attacked this model of discursive procedures because of its narrow focus on individual interests. Environmental risks, it is said, are far beyond the horizon of such a limited scope since they involve problems of collective action. Solutions to these questions require the social, temporal, and spatial distribution of risks and their consequences, most particularly perhaps the costs of risk minimization. These situations are no longer limited to the distribution of goods, but involve definitions of a new relationship between human beings and nature, a new value system, and a new definition of the good life for a community. Discursive procedures that only look at the individual interests of participants will therefore not be able to take into account the specific quality of risk in contemporary societies.[16]

Such critiques make clear that, given a lack of societal consensus and shared values regarding technology and nature, there is a strong need for legitimation. The attractiveness of discursive procedures rests on their capacity to promote social integration in a society where few other bonds exist. The plausibility of a unifying function depends on the participants inside such procedures, as well as those individuals who observe the activities as members of the public. Both participants and the wider public must believe discourses are better. They have to be convinced that genuine debate occurs, an exchange of all possible positions on an issue takes place, and everyone has a chance to express their position. In other words, interests must be submitted to the test of intersubjective validation. A model of discursive debate not tied to the constraints of decision-making is seen as a means to clarify the ultimate purposes of the issues being considered. Thus, the model is based not on a distributive logic, but on a reasoning that defines common goods. Participants enter into discourse not to solve distributive problems, but to address the issue of how to generate common goods in the first place.

There is a structural dilemma built into discursive institutions whether they treat common goods or distributive problems, namely that they try to maximize deliberation and participation simultaneously.[17] The democratic idea that underlies the principle of participation is equality of access to deliberative procedures. However, the greater the number of people who participate, the more unrealistic deliberation becomes. To realize this objective one has to restrict the number of individuals who can talk. One solution to this problem is representation – and this is the classical solution employed in modern political institutions such as the parliament.

Neo-corporatism uses a different strategy that assembles the most powerful and consequential actors (industry representatives, trade unionists, politicians) to represent the different interests of society. Post-corporatist arrangements, such as the discursive institutions dealt with here, are different in one respect. They add a fourth actor in the form of public interest groups and social movement organizations. Civil society – represented by NGOs – enters the deliberative space, but this form of representation differs from the classic idea of 'one person, one vote.' NGOs represent competing interests in civil society in terms of issues and their affiliated publics. However, this dependence makes them highly vulnerable to their specific issue-publics. In particular, NGOs must make sure their constituents continue to give support.[18] Many such organizations have had to suffer the painful experience (as have representatives of mid-sized industries) that this dependence is problematic.

The dilemma can be summarized as follows. In traditional political institutions formal representation (one person, one vote) wins over deliberation. These institutions maximize individual participation, but this generates unintended consequences. Election rituals of aggregating votes resemble the logic of a lottery and such procedures raise questions for institutional legitimacy. Moreover, governance is compromised because of the inherent ungovernability of many of the problems that contemporary societies face. The lesson to be learned from the analysis of discursive institutions is that deliberation wins over participation and frequently goes beyond unanimity. Deliberation helps to overcome the gridlock of collective action by communicating interests in a way that forces participants to reflect on their interests and values and to look for new combinations in which the maximum number of people receive some benefit.

The theoretical proposition then is that as modern societies are forced to face issues of preserving common goods that give distributive questions a secondary role, the more deliberation will dominate participation. When individual interests are touched by distributive decisions, everyone should have the right to participate in decisions that may affect them. When common goods are at issue universal participation is less a problem and the need to avoid freeriding moves to the fore. However, every common goods problem eventually becomes a distributive problem as soon as its preservation costs have to be allocated.

The conclusions that follow from our empirical observations are that in all these cases distributive problems had to be combined with common-goods problems. In all these instances, dilemmas characteristic of traditional modernity and dilemmas characteristic of reflexive modernity (to use Beck's somewhat metaphorical language) were inextricably linked. The cases also raise a question. What procedures should one follow to resolve the conflicts tied to them? What happens is that after the end of confrontational politics in environmental matters actors involved in this arena start to engage in institutionalized collective action that moves in two directions. On the one hand, actors become oriented toward resolving complex matters such as the formulation of energy policies or the control of genetic technology. On the other hand, they begin to use discourse as a mode for organizing institutions of collective action. Actors – industrial actors as well as political and social movement actors – obviously find it rational to engage in discourse. This is the empirical observation. How should we make sense of this observation theoretically? I will turn to this question in the following section.

EXPLAINING THE RISE OF DISCURSIVE INSTITUTIONS IN RISK SOCIETY

So far the discussion in this chapter has been on the phenomenological level. Before approaching the explanatory problem of why discursive institutions have emerged in modern risk societies the threads of the argument I have presented so far need to be pulled together. My starting point was that discourses are part of the rationality that modern societies claim for themselves. I proceeded to argue that the emergence of discursive institutions responds to a functional need in modern societies, namely to provide collective decisions in a world where clear and technically convincing answers are no longer possible. Moreover, the complexity of contemporary issues requires the involvement of as many perspectives as possible, both for reasons of efficiency and legitimation. We must keep both rationality and functionality in mind to answer the question of why discursive institutions have become so widespread in the environmental field where risky decisions are standard.

Our description of the functionality of discourses for regulating or taming risks in complex societies already provides some elements for an explanation of why discourses are good for modern societies.

However, we still lack a conceptual framework for making sense of the various pieces. The theoretical answer requires elaboration of why it is good for societies to engage in discursive modes of decision-making.

The theoretical framework that provides an answer is the *neo-institutionalist* approach. Neo-institutionalism claims that institutions are more than simply outcome-oriented devices (an idea dominant since Plato and Aristotle). Institutions also define a life form. They consist not only of rules, routines, organizational structures, strategies, and communication technologies that help to realize a goal such as regulation or control – institutions also embody symbols and meaning that define what is good for all. These attributes are not only arguments, but comprise classifications, representations, scripts, and schemata. The 'new institutionalism' provides a way of linking both dimensions. Why is such an institutional theory relevant for the cases I have in mind? I suggest that it has to do with the need both to create institutions for collective action that protect common goods and to cultivate a sense of collectivity in a world in which the customary bonds of community such as class culture and ethnic culture are in decline.

The first point is rather self-evident. Common goods require the involvement and the binding of a plurality of actors, including those concerned with the use or misuse of such responses. This grouping often encompasses whole populations regardless of class, age, gender, and so forth. Common goods also present problems that provoke increasing public attention and media coverage, and this implies that the actors in the field of environmental politics are in a situation of permanent public observation.[19]

The second point is less obvious. The contention that contemporary society dissolves traditional cultures implies the need for a substitute.[20] Focusing this argument on the special case of political institutions, it could be asserted that we can no longer rely upon the symbolic grounds that the European nation-state has claimed as justification for its existence, namely a collective identity defined as the nation. Political institutions have to reconstruct their symbolic basis. The nation, as we experience it today, is deconstructed and reconstructed while contemporary discourses make its symbolic foundation even more fluid. The substitute not have to be another kind of national symbolic marker and it need not be situated on the same level and spatial ground as the national community. From regional administrations to the European Union to transnational cultures are ranged possible alternatives. The implication is that a collectively shared symbolic denominator, one that underlies the production and reproduction of political institutions, is required.

Now what can serve as a substitute for the lost paradise of community? It is 'discourse,' a concept empty of substance, a procedural device for creating communal bonds. The realization of discourse in the form of a readiness to justify and problematize descriptive, normative, and evaluative judgments implies no restrictions on time, access, or participation. Such guidelines give rise in turn to a threefold reflexivity consisting of a reflexive relation to procedural principles, a reflexive relation of the participants in the procedure to their interests and motives, and a reflexive relation with respect to their bounded rationality. Who would not like to live in such a world? It is a powerful device, ideal for legitimating an institutional design that can claim these characteristics for itself. Furthermore, it is a mechanism that does not commit to a pre-existing symbolic community. In this sense, it is truly modernistic because it leaves behind all of the traditional bonds invoked in current communitarian thinking.

This is a reason why cooperative agreements using dialogues are effective for creating institutions that help to reduce the contingency of action in a risky world. We can thus explicate why the staging of discourses is good for legitimating such institutions in a detraditionalized world. The neo-institutionalist position puts these two arguments together by claiming that discursive institutions do not have to be discursive in the emphatic sense and that they will never be so. On the contrary – and this is the disillusioning aspect of neo-institutionalist theorizing – discourse is a device for legitimating horizontal forms of cooperation and non-hierarchical forms of institution-building. It is the seductive nature of this device that makes non-vertical forms of political institutions work.

Thus, my explanation of the institutional change in the environmental field is very simple. Using the cultural means at its disposal, every society develops methods to respond to the complexity of life. Those adaptations that turn out to be useful for actors will survive. For modern environmental actors it has been advantageous to select discourse as the symbolic form to justify their organizational practices. A neo-institutional explanation of the emergence of discursive institutions of collective action for common goods seems – at least for the time being – the most convincing.

TAMING RISKS THROUGH DISCOURSE AND THE RISK OF DISCOURSE

My argument has been that 'new' discursive institutions compensate for the deficits of traditional political institutions by limiting the contingency of action in a risky world. In addition, they provide new symbolic forms through which institutions can gain legitimacy in a detraditionalized world. Contrasted to the pessimistic scenario of a risk society devoid of organizational and symbolic power to find solutions to the threats it produces, we can view discursive institutions as a counter-process.

Discourse may even reduce risk, but its primary function is to redistribute responsibility by binding societal members into accountable relationships. Against the notion of organized irresponsibility that has pervaded much recent social science argumentation the (obviously unintended) function of redistributing responsibility through discourse provides a better fit with the empirical evidence. Independently of whether these discourses really reduce risk, they have a symbolic institutional effect – withdrawal from a context of collective responsibility is a costly endeavor.[21]

This is not to contend that discourses are the magic key. Their instability, national particularity, and problematic internal functioning suggest fruitful grounds for rebuttal.[22] There is, however, an even stronger argument that raises concerns about the institutionalization of discourses for risk management in modern societies, namely that these are hazards of engaging in a volatile type of institutional design. Discourses can generate unstable and self-legitimating secondary forms of community building that are in a sense exposed. They are just a regulative idea with no tradition, solidarity, or force. Attempts designed to give some clothes to the naked idea – constitutional patriotism, civil religion, and new collective identities – remain vague. What is common to these ideas of community is that we have to create and give them symbolic representation to make them more readily recognizable.

The risk of discourse is that it invites compensatory community. This institutional form encourages highly particularist collectivities to replace communal understandings of risk with implicit and tacit understandings. The result of discourse would then be previously antagonistic communities each advancing idiosyncratic risk definitions and proposing their own mitigation measures. The risk society would become a society of competing fundamentalisms based on inferred interpretations of nature.[23]

No risk without a chance. The counter-proposition is that the collectivity emerging in discursive institutions, reduced to its essential substance, consists of nothing more than the commonality of the participants in discourse. This does not mean that these communities of discourse behave according to some ideal (even if counterfactual) discursive rule. What proponents do when they define themselves as environmentalists, ethnic communities, constitutional patriots, and so forth is to use discourse as an option for representing the collective. However, this is merely an interpretation to be used in discursive contexts. Discursive institutions allow for playing with community because this notion is deemed desirable as long as it helps to promote a common good that coincides with organizational goals.

In such an institutional context action for the common good can even be motivated rationally.[24] For in such instances, it is rational to be discursive. It is rational to engage with discursive institutions because they minimize unintended consequences involving, for example, technology gaps within industry. Moreover, it is rational to engage with these institutions because they help industry and social movement organizations avoid dangerous breaches in credibility. This in turn explains the rise of an industry dedicated to the management, production, and staging of discourse.

There is a social consequence even to this rational choice. Participation in such discourses binds actors to procedural rules. These constraints force them to enter a discourse to respect the interests of others and to engage in time-consuming processes of conflict resolution and consent mobilization. As such, discursive procedures enable actors to act strategically in a legitimate way. However, this form of discipline also limits possibilities of strategic action because actors' conduct must remain compatible with their self-presentation as credible participants in discursive relationships. In other words, symbolic reference puts limits on action. The first constraint is that the public watches and judges performance according to the legitimating image presented to it. When one uses discourse one must be careful not to cheat the public or to undermine its expectations. The second limitation is that the other in an institutionalized relationship judges behavior in terms of its compatibility with the mutually determined rules. To prevent becoming the 'bad guy' one must stick to the principles of engagement. Exit becomes a very costly option indeed.

CONCLUSIONS FOR DEMOCRATIC THEORY

Is discourse a rational and functional device for solving the problem of ecological rationality in modern society? The usual response is that discourse produces noise, impedes decision-making, and is *passé*. The answer that comes out of the preceding discussion is counter-intuitive. Discourse is rational and functional precisely when decisions on complex matters must be made. I have developed this seemingly paradoxical argument using a series of case studies on discursive forms of dealing with environmental risks.

The theoretical arguments that stem from such a conclusion can be summarized in terms of the following four points.

First, the institutionalization of discourses depends upon the way in which instrumental and symbolic functions are linked. Traditional theory separates these two functions as competing rationalities. Accordingly, the symbolic elements of legitimacy are played off as more rational than means–ends relationships. Both rationalities are, within a neo-institutionalist perspective, simply two sides of the same coin.

Second, discursive institutions are particularly suited to social complexity. Because decisions in modern societies are always risky – as indicated by contradictory, expert-based evidence and by uncertainty regarding the consequences of decision – the only way out is not to produce 'correct' answers but to generate decisions for which everybody takes responsibility. This argument turns on its head the old contentions that discourses are too time-consuming, feasible only for small communities, workable only in societies that economize on time, and decoupled from the contingencies of concrete interaction systems.

Third, the neo-institutional emphasis on the reciprocal dependence of instrumental and symbolic functions in decision-making provides the basis for a genuinely sociological theory of discursive institution building – a theory reduced neither to the narrow horizon of efficient action nor to the ideological horizon of participatory action. Such an approach renders obsolete the utopia of self-legitimating communicative action and the overly optimistic prospect of the collective good emerging from interest-based individual action pursued through the market.

Fourth, discursive procedures are nascent social institutions that should – beyond their ideological representations and often against the moral intentions and interpretations of both their critics and defenders – be considered seriously as a candidate for reducing the environmental risks to which increasingly complex societies are susceptible.

In speculative conclusion, one could argue that a new approach for democratic decision-making is emerging that is different from the one that has shaped the history of political institutions over the past two centuries. The history of modern institution building has been conditioned by the idea that officials who regularly make poor decisions should be peacefully replaced by kicking them out of office. This is the electoral device based on the principle of majority rule. However, fostered by issues such as the environment, this democratic mechanism now shows some signs of fatigue. Discursive institutions might be a new way not only of taming risks, but also of holding accountable both the state and civil society. A Leviathan attacked and beleaguered by opposition movements is not the only option for risk society. The alternative is to create institutions for discursive decision-making that can become serious options for transforming the political landscape of the old nation-state and for hastening the arrival of the new society coming into view on a transnational and global level.

NOTES

1. Republicans were more interested in the national community of citizens as a basis for democracy than democrats who were looking for an abstract community of 'debating citizens.' The split between republicans and democrats ('radicals') in the nineteenth century is reproduced today in political theory in the debate between communitarians and universalists.
2. R. Wuthnow, *Communities of Discourse: Ideology and Social Structure in the Reformation, Enlightenment, and European Socialism* (Cambridge, MA: Harvard University Press, 1990).
3. See J. Habermas, *The Theory of Communicative Action: Lifeworld and System. A Critique of Functionalist Reason, Volume II* (Boston, MA: Beacon Press, 1987). The normative aspect has been taken up again in 'Facticity and Validity' (German edition 1992).
4. See J. Habermas, *The Structural Transformation of the Public Sphere: An Inquiry into a Category of Bourgeois Society* (Cambridge, MA: MIT

Press, 1989), originally published in 1962 in German. Refer also to his comment on his own work in the English edition and the discussion in C. Calhoun, ed., *Habermas and the Public Sphere* (Cambridge, MA: MIT Press, 1992).

5. An example is the campaign started in the mid-1990s by the German chemical industry on 'Chemical industry in dialogue' (*Chemie im Dialog*). To understand the context of this discourse it is important to know that in German the word *Chemie* can mean chemical industry, chemical substances, or chemical science, thus offering a polysemantic field for dialogues. An analysis is given in S. Barthe, M. Dreyer, and K. Eder, *Reflexive Institutionen? Eine Untersuchung zur Herausbildung eines neuen Typus institutioneller Regelungen im Umweltbereich*, DFG-Abschlußbericht, Projektnummer 25/7 (München: Münchner Projektgruppe für Sozialforschung, 1997), pp. 139–212; and K.-W. Brand, K. Eder, and A. Poferl, *Ökologische Kommunikation in Deutschland* (Opladen: Westdeutscher Verlag, 1997).

6. In Germany something similar has been tried in this field in the form of the *Pakt für die Arbeit* (The Pact for the Workers), a kind of institutionalized dialogue between capital and labor, involving industrial associations, trade unions, and government. It, however, failed.

7. The idea of discourse has even entered foreign policy-making. The 'critical dialogue' with Iran (ended in 1987 in the course of pragmatic normalization of diplomatic relations between the German foreign ministry and the Iranian government) has helped to legitimize a special relationship between the two governments.

8. Luhmann's notion of 'autopoietic systems' can be usefully applied here. In order to close an open social system, it has to be closed semantically through limiting the range of available options. To do this limiting by inventing procedures that create semantic closures is the highest form of social reflexivity imaginable. See N. Luhmann, *Social Systems* (Palo Alto, CA: Stanford University Press, 1995).

9. S. Benhabib, *Democracy and Difference: Contesting the Boundaries of the Political* (Princeton, NJ: Princeton University Press, 1996).

10. I have studied the cases cited here in the context of a larger empirical research project. For further details see Barthe, Dreyer, and Eder, *Reflexive Institutionen?* All the cases included in this initiative were German which produces a certain national bias, though parallel developments can be found on the European level, namely in France and Britain. Comparative research, however, is still to be done.

11. Mediation procedures are certainly not a German speciality. Nonetheless, they have been less successful in Germany which perhaps points to a feature of German society. Alternatively, *Enquête-Kommissionen*, a German creation, has worked quite well. Inter-organizational dialogues and consensus talks are still very much contingent upon personal investment and strategic power games where charisma is important. There is no discursive case, but they all refer to the regulative idea that through rational argumentation involving a certain number of actors (ideally all actors) a problem can be brought closer to a rational solution.

12. Corporatism is defined as the secret informal coordination of con-

sequential collective actors, mainly political parties, trade unions, and industry. All of these participants have an interest in keeping the proceedings within existing organizational confines.

13. This has been confirmed by an extensive analysis of media coverage of mediation procedures in Germany. See Barthe, Dreyer, and Eder, *Reflexive Institutionen?*

14. This is the *locus classicus* of mediation research. Refer to L. Nader, ed., *Law in Culture and Society* (Chicago: Aldine, 1972).

15. This is the argument of B. Wynne, 'Risk and Social Learning: Reification to Engagement,' pp. 275–97 in S. Krimsky and D. Golding, eds, *Social Theories of Risk* (Westport, CT: Praeger, 1992); and B. Wynne, 'Uncertainty and Environmental Learning: Reconceiving Science and Policy in the Preventive Paradigm,' *Global Environmental Change*, 2(2) (1992): 111–27. Wynne argues that the thematization of social standards is inevitable in debates about risk issues. Scientific evidence alone does not suffice because as soon as the data are made public it is no longer possible to hide the underlying social assumptions.

16. See U. Beck, *Risk Society: Towards a New Modernity* (London: Sage, 1992).

17. K. Eder, 'Die Dynamik demokratischer Institutionenbildung: Strukturelle Voraussetzungen deliberativer Demokratie in fortgeschrittenen Industriegesell-schaften,' *Kölner Zeitschrift für Soziologie und Sozialpsychologie*, 35 (1995): 327–45.

18. This support for NGOs can be measured in terms of organizational membership, the free time members spend working on campaigns and funding activities, positive talk in public about organizational activities, or a 'good record' in public opinion.

19. Actors might try to hide undesirable information, but this becomes riskier the more public attention remains high and as long as the media report immediately. The case of the incidents at Hoechst, a German multinational chemical company, is an ideal case here.

20. This argument has been widely put forward in the debate on the individualization of life courses and its consequences on class cultures in modern societies. See A. Weymann, ed., *Handlungsspielräume: Untersuchungen zur Individualisierung und Institutionalisierung von Lebensläufen in der Moderne* (Stuttgart: Enke, 1989); and H.-G. Brose and B. Hildenbrand, eds, *Vom Ende des Individuums zur Individualität ohne Ende* (Opladen: Leske und Budrich, 1988) on individualization as a central parameter of structural change in modern society. Refer also to U. Beck, *Risk Society* and K. Eder, *The New Politics of Class: Social Movements and Cultural Dynamics in Advanced Societies* (London: Sage, 1993) on the consequences of individualization for politics and collective action.

21. This is especially true for NGOs that engage in discursive procedures only to find they could only leave these institutional arrangements with high costs to their legitimacy. Reacting to the demands of their constituency (which often was in disagreement with what had been debated in dialogical contexts) caused them to lose face in the eyes of the public. The same holds true for political and industrial actors.

22. The question of whether the emphasis on discourse is a German pre-occupation is a good one. The answer is that there may exist a particular cultural resonance for dialogues in Germany that influences the degree and speed with which discursive procedures have become institutionalized. That complexity requires discourse is, however, a claim for a structural property that exceeds claims of cultural particularities.
23. Vegetarian movements, health movements, and communal movements are cases to be studied in such contexts. See K. Eder, *The Social Construction of Nature: A Sociology of Ecological Enlightenment* (London: Sage, 1996). See also J. Gusfield, 'Nature's Body and the Metaphors of Food,' pp. 75–103 in M. Lamont and M. Fournier, eds, *Cultivating Differences: Symbolic Boundaries and the Making of Inequality* (Chicago: Chicago University Press, 1992).
24. Such action does not require normative motivation which is a much less stable human motivation.

Part VI
Conclusion

11 A Historical Perspective on Risk
David Lowenthal

We are fast learning that we all live in the same risky world. To understand and cope with environmental problems, we need to surmount differences deeply embedded in particular histories, languages, and modes of thought. This is very much evident in the strikingly different perceptions and approaches of the American scholars who have contributed to this volume in comparison to the authors from continental Europe.

Dwelling on these differences should not, however, cause us to lose sight of fruitful historical likenesses. There are certainly considerable differences between European meta-theory treatments, perhaps best exemplified in this volume by Klaus Eder's chapter, and the empirical approaches to risk issues presented by Michael Edelstein and the other American contributors. The formulation of a more integrated perspective might require us to recall and build upon long-standing German empirical traditions in environmental science. Developing out of Johann Herder's synthesizing delineations of national cultures, that tradition gained strength through the Humboldt brothers' descriptions and analyses of diverse natural and cultural realities. In pioneering empirical surveys of environmental use and misuse, German geographers like Carl Ritter and Eduard Hahn traced interrelations among man, other species, and terrain. From the mid-nineteenth century until the 1930s, the studies of German foresters, both at home and at the French forestry school at Nancy, provided the intellectual and experimental underpinning of silviculture – understanding how trees grew, were used, and needed to be replenished not simply for harvesting, but for the sake of the environment as a whole. This rich empirical tradition is too often forgotten by theoretical analysts today.

Perhaps the main reason to better understand how we are both alike and different is our growing recognition of the transnational nature of environmental hazards. We are all in it together, not only with regard to obviously global matters like climate change and ozone depletion, but in local 'not-in-my-backyard' issues with which we are all concerned. In dealing with both global and local risks we work within similar and interrelated socio-economic and environmental systems. Whatever our differences in mindset and modes of coping, we more and more realize we must learn from one another.

Learning must also expand to embrace a wide variety of expert knowledge within each national culture. Discussions of risk often focus on the clashing perspectives of lawyers and economists, but each of us is in some measure both lawyer and economist – not to mention ecologist, sociologist, and environmentalist. Inheriting all these traditional stances, we each encounter the inescapability of economic needs, litigious needs, social needs, and spiritual needs. In expressing these diverse requirements – whether individually or collectively – we often convey self-contradictory environmental views, as well as views that conflict with our environmental actions. To cope with environmental and technological risk, it is as crucial to become familiar with our own internal discords as it is to understand cultural and national differences.

As a historian, I take my point of departure from Richard Cobb, recalling a visit from Vlado Dedijer who was about to write an official life of Tito. 'Professor Cobb, I want to know what is your method, what is your methodology? How do you go about doing history?' 'Well,' says Cobb, 'You go and read a lot of books and then you read some more and then you write. And then you realize you have not read enough, so you read some more and then you come back and write again. That's what you do.' 'Oh,' says Dedijer, 'Is that all there is to it?' 'Oh, yes,' says Cobb. 'You'll find that's what the best historians do.'[1] Cobb's total rejection of theoretical insight may seem absurd, but I do share the suspicion common among historians that imperial social science may lack clothes.

The contributions to this volume have a tendency to abandon the nitty-gritty of risk for the heights of general theory. This causes me to wonder whether the issue of risk is deliberately eschewed. After all, several authors advise that risk avoidance is common among victims and non-victims alike. More to the point, the topic of risk has become all-embracing, involving every realm of life. An American colleague whose concern was perceptions of nuclear risk once asked me to introduce him to somebody who set odds on extreme events. I made an appointment at the headquarters of Ladbroke's betting agency. Beyond rows and rows of computers sat Ron Pollard, a small, balding guru with pencils behind each ear, today's and yesterday's newspapers littering his desk. He was busy assessing risk. Each time a caller rang to place a bet he recalculated to ensure Ladbroke's came out ahead. Expectant mothers phoned in to insure against twins at odds of 33–1. Ron took odds on almost anything – the new Archbishop of Canterbury, the winner of the next Booker fiction prize. But he took no bets on nuclear accidents or other life-threatening events; some crafty lunatic might blow up the Firth of Forth Bridge if odds were set high against it. Nor did he take bets on highly improbable long-shots against which Ladbroke's could not cover itself.

Not all environmental management requires risk analysis, but it increasingly is seen to involve risk. Beyond the level of meta-theory, this volume throws light on differences between past and present perceptions of and reactions to environmental risk. One such salient change seems to be the increasing invisibility of serious hazards. In the past, threats of material shortages, deforestation, and soil exhaustion were apparent to ordinary observers with the unaided eye. In the present, risks like global warming and ozone-layer depletion and lethal nuclear residues are not just invisible but detectable only with highly sophisticated technology. Moreover, such threats often make themselves felt only after long delay, while their consequences may endure for millennia or longer. It is famously said that most of Chernobyl's victims are not yet even born.[2] Coping with such hazards appears far more difficult than anything our gloomiest predecessors had to face.

Moreover, we now recognize that environmental impacts have unintended consequences whose multiple and irreversibly cascading outcomes may never be known. From a natural ecology of supposed stasis and stability we have moved to an awareness that some changes may never be containable, and that there is no way we can revert to a *status quo ante*. The consequence is a high level of general unease, first among analysts, and then among the public to whom uncertainties are transmitted. This makes the angst of our time perhaps uniquely traumatic, although no epoch has lacked apocalyptic Jeremiahs.[3] A comparative view of past and present types and levels of anxiety would be most instructive.

For instance, between 1810 and 1840 the northeastern part of the United States suffered a series of unheralded natural disasters. There were seemingly aberrant weather patterns with frosts and snows in July and spring floods that washed out mills in every river valley. No one knew what was going on or to what to attribute it. Was it an angry god? Was it malevolent British vengeance? People could not see, even when it was pointed out, the now obvious link with deforestation and agricultural settlement. Similar blindness afflicted pioneering American farmers at least until the 1930s. When ecology-minded foresters began warning of the consequences of such impacts and calling for environmental reform, few entrepreneurs or politicians paid heed, and those who did supposed the cure would be cheap and simple. Some observers were as alarmed as today's environmentalists, but just as the impacts they feared were different, so were the reasons for their fear and the reforms they proposed.

Another big shift in apprehension regarding risk is growing public disillusionment with government and industry in general, and science and technology in particular. To be sure, science has never seemed wholly miraculous or problem-free, but today more than ever scientists seem to have feet of clay. Mistrust of science and government agencies reliant on scientific data is widespread. Other misgivings abound. Big science is enormously more expensive, not only in actual costs, but as a proportion of national and global incomes – inevitably so, given research into ever less accessible extremes of size, temperature, and remoteness. Moreover, science's negative consequences now loom larger on the immediate horizon than its positive conquests. Furthermore, many technological miracles are nowadays largely discounted in advance.

Relatedly, the damage now attributed to unintended and unforeseen environmental impact is no longer confined to purely physical realms of life – soil, water, flora, and fauna. Many of the chapters in this volume stress damage not just to biological, but to social, ecology – the fraying of human communities by pathologies of risk, victimization, disillusionment with expertise and authority. What is being eroded is not simply land and physical resources, but social and individual spirit. That families and communities can be broken perhaps beyond recovery is a relatively new and profoundly significant component of our awareness of risk and loss.

Hence we are newly concerned that community voices be heard, that local expertise be harkened to, and this is the message of the chapters comprising Part V of this book. Despite their important message, to my mind these authors fail to pay sufficient attention to certain other defects of science – notably the hubris that enables scientists to ignore or repress awareness of how scientific faith itself departs from rationality, bends in accordance with authority, and accepts its own values on faith. One of these failings is the fallacy of quantification – the notion that mere numerical expression suggests that we have certain knowledge, that we are in control, and that we can deal instrumentally with aspects of change that are in fact quite unpredictable. Fritz Schumacher once contended that statisticians need to develop a qualitative understanding of matters concerning values not usefully amenable to quantification. They retorted, 'You claim there are things we can't measure, but it's not true. We say, if you can't measure it, measure it anyway.' Obsessive quantifiers, most pointedly perhaps the proponents of the rational actor paradigm described in the chapter by Ortwin Renn and his colleagues, are apt to deploy highly precise measurements so as to simplify the complexity of environmental unknowns, and thereby reduce their fearfulness.

Let me conclude this final, summarizing chapter with a half dozen points that I feel provide grounds for fruitful examination and have only been touched on briefly, if at all, in this volume.

- *Community.* We are not sufficiently aware of communities as social organisms – entities whose essential functions endure beyond individual life spans. Their persistence reflects voluntary compacts inherited and ever renegotiated among the living, the dead, and the unborn. Faith in communities that transcends individual experience is, as Durkheim put it, a universal and necessary religion, a faith crafted by uniquely human agencies of memory and prospect.[4] Communities thus resemble other durable societal institutions, and their endurance and often presumed immortality involve a calculus of risk much more complex and far-reaching than that normally deployed on behalf of individuals.

- *Choice.* Several chapters in this volume emphasize that we face ever expanding arenas of choice as consumers, as residents, and as citizens; indeed, we have no choice but to choose. Freedom of choice is commonly held to be a virtue, but it is a virtue with limits. While choice may seem desirable as an abstract goal, it also imposes huge burdens on individuals and communities. Modernity may require making so many decisions as to overload us beyond our ability to cope. Physiological and social mechanisms are inadequate to handle with the number and magnitude of choices we are forced to make. Experts tell us, 'We are just the technicians. We can tell you what the facts are. You have to

decide.' Who can make all these choices? Who can assay the
statistical probabilities and uncertainties embedded in abstruse
technical data? Who can rationally decide whether or not to in-
quire into genetic information that may predict our own and our
children's likelihood of some ailment, treatable or not, at the
likely cost of some fearsome insurance claim? There are choices
many think it better not to have to make, futures we may not
want to confront. Their sheer number is already daunting, even
unmanageable. 'Give me a martini,' says the exhausted man to
the bartender. 'Gin or vodka?' 'Gin.' 'On the rocks or straight
up?' 'On the rocks.' 'Twist or olive?' 'Oh, hell, make it a Scotch.'

- *Resources.* Resources are not a physically determined given. Environmental goals vary with time and with culture. Fossil fuels,
now an essential resource, were not seen as such at all until the
mid-nineteenth century. The same holds true for clear air and
clean water. The absence of pollution was not conceived in such
terms. Commentators occasionally remark that history is a resource. As the anthropologist Arjun Appadurai writes with regard
to India, the past is a scarce resource.[5] But other cultures regard
the past as something of which they have far too much. Resources,
like risk, can be properly assessed only in their particular cultural
and temporal contexts.

- *Nature.* That nature is likewise a cultural construct, socially defined, requires further examination than it has received in this
book. To the query 'Is a dead fish a social fact or a natural fact?'
the social constructivist typically answers 'I don't care.' Bewil-
derment on this point within wider intellectual circles is deserved,
because the two cannot be understood separately. Nature is everywhere part of culture, culture embedded in nature. Neither exists
without the other. The two realms are disaggregated in Western
converse for the sake of a spurious simplicity and in the interest
of a supposed morality. But they are segregated only in our minds,
never on the ground. Only by recognizing their essential unity
can we come to terms with environmental risk.

- *Urgency and catastrophe.* Apprehension of disaster dominates the
rhetoric of environmental management as a whole. 'A Special
Moment in History' is what Bill McKibben tells us we occupy.
He asserts, 'The fate of the planet will be determined in the
next few decades, through our technological, lifestyle, and population choices.'[6] Though this sounds unarguable, it is groundless
nonsense. No generation determines planetary fate. However, no

one can be galvanized to do anything about it, perhaps even be bothered to read McKibben's book, unless told the moment is now.

Urgency and apprehension of impending catastrophe drives other causes too. For instance, in the realm of cultural heritage nothing gets done without a crisis. Can we avoid the bind of being reactive all the time instead of proactive? Should we aim to do so? The short answer is yes, if only to promote modes of awareness that do not presuppose environmental risks are ever finally laid to rest. The reasons warrant a conference in their own right.

• *Armageddon, new and old.* We forget at our peril a long history of fears, not only of risk but of wrecking the world. 'Do I dare disturb the universe?' To Emily Dickinson's global angst T. S. Eliot gently riposted, 'Do I dare to eat a peach?' Yet apocalyptic mindsets may be found not only in neurasthenic poets and tribal indigenes. Rather, they resurface episodically, and from millennium to millennium, in mainstream Western society. Apocalypse fuels the fundamentalism that coexists with modern environmentalist concern. These potentially self-fulfilling prophecies themselves exacerbate old and create new species of environmental risk.

NOTES

1. Adapted from R. Cobb, *A Sense of Place* (London: Duckworth, 1975), pp. 47–8. Dedijer's, *The Road to Sarajevo* (New York: Simon & Schuster, 1966) was, Cobb exulted, 'an excellent and very readable book unencumber[ed by] methodology.'
2. U. Beck, 'Risk Society and the Provident State,' pp. 27–43 in S. Lash, B. Szerszynski, and B. Wynne, eds, *Risk, Environment, and Modernity: Towards a New Ecology* (London: Sage, 1996).
3. For these issues, see my 'Awareness of Human Impacts: Changing Attitudes and Emphases,' pp. 121–35 in B. Turner, ed., *The Earth as Transformed by Human Action* (New York: Cambridge University Press, 1990).
4. E. Durkheim, *The Elementary Forms of Religious Life*, trans. K. Fields (New York: Free Press, 1995, originally published 1912), pp. 213–14, 351–2, 372, 379.
5. A. Appadurai, 'The Past as a Scarce Resource,' *Man*, 16 (1981): 201–19.
6. B. McKibben, *The End of Nature* (New York: Anchor Books, 1990).

Index

Printed in the United States
203142BV00004B/1-3/A